CHRISTIAN THEOLOGY
AFTER THE SHOAH

CHRISTIAN THEOLOGY
AFTER THE SHOAH

By
James F. Moore

Studies in the Shoah

Volume VII

University Press of America
Lanham • New York • London

Copyright © 1993 by
University Press of America®, Inc.
4720 Boston Way
Lanham, Maryland 20706

3 Henrietta Street
London WC2E 8LU England

Excerpts from the New Revised Standard Version of the Bible,
copyright 1989 by the Division of Christian Education of the National
Council of the Churches of Christ in the USA are used by permission.

Library of Congress Cataloging-in-Publication Data

Moore, James F.
Christian theology after the Shoah : a re-interpretation of the Passion
narratives / James F. Moore.
p.   cm. — (Studies in the Shoah ; v. 7)
Includes bibliographical references and index.
1. Holocaust (Christian theology)   2. Passion narratives (Gospels)
3. Theology—20th century.   I. Title.   II. Series.
BT93.M66   1993   231.7'6—dc20   93–2806 CIP

ISBN 0–8191–9074–8 (alk. paper)

The paper used in this publication meets the minimum requirements of
American National Standard for Information Sciences—Permanence
of Paper for Printed Library Materials, ANSI Z39.48–1984.

TABLE OF CONTENTS

PREFACE

This book has developed over several years through stages of thinking each of which adds a dimension to the direction of the book. The intention of the book is to provide an outline for doing Christian theology after the Shoah. This means that this theology must be Christian and must respond to the challenges that the Shoah presents to Christians and their theology. I first approached this topic by looking at various responses to the Shoah by leading Christian thinkers. That paper presented first at the American Academy of Religion in Anaheim, California, and subsequently published, traced a spectrum of views among those who aim to take the Shoah seriously as a Christian concern. That study led me to two important discoveries. First, theologies, no matter how sensitive they might be to the issues at hand, continue to lend themselves to distortion. What is needed may not be the development of one theology but rather a process by which theologies can be modified and scrutinized regularly. Later, I came to identify this process as a kind of Christian midrash.

But what is that? Midrash is both an interpretive method and a discreet body of literature that is exclusively Jewish in character. I can neither produce something Christian that matches these ancient and authoritative texts of Judaism nor would a Christian copy satisfy the aim of this book. Still, the character of Midrash that corresponds with Jewish theology and interpretation of Torah when identified as a process comes closest to defining the sort of method I contend is necessary for post-Shoah Christian theology. In the early pages of this book, I offer an extended description of the midrashic process that will be used in the latter portions of the book.

My second discovery in that early paper was that Christian theological language has become subject to radical ambiguity after the Shoah. This insight, gained from David Tracy, has an immediately negative impact on Christian theologizing. Normal Christian speaking when placed into the context of the Shoah is seen in a radically negative light (the simple notion of forgiveness, for example, becomes impossible to define given the variety of possibilities that forgiveness can take on in the Shoah). But, I also learned from Tracy that ambiguity can have a positive impact on theology, releasing theologians to re-vise their theologies and open up the possibilities of Christian theological thinking.

A second paper delivered at Oxford in 1988 became the opportunity for me to explore the implications of a theology released by this positive impact of ambiguity. This paper operated with two basic presumptions. First, I presumed that the heart of Christian teaching—theologies of the cross and resurrection—would be the best test for seeing new possibilities for Christian theology. Second, I presumed that these teachings also formed the basis of much of Christian anti-Judaism and, thus, provided the best test for the negative critique especially arising from the Shoah. I again discovered that the process of looking at these theologies, done here by looking at the texts of the passion narrative from Christian scriptures, is as vital as the product. I was led to see that this process could be identified as a Christian midrash. I, also, discovered that Christian scriptures provided a fascinating starting point for reflection because the texts of scripture were filled with ambiguities, ironies, and paradoxes that could lead to radically different developments in Christian teaching depending on which line of thought or trajectory of an ambiguity were taken. The sources for Christian theology are filled with productive ambiguity perhaps because they were written with that ambiguity intended.

My task had, thus, been set. I needed to follow this process (a Christian midrash) through a full reading of the passion narratives so as to judge what the various trajectories of meaning are. Still more primary than this task though are the beginning criteria for judgment. I continue where I began, a theology that takes seriously the challenges of the Shoah. The theology must be a post-Shoah Christian theology. The early pages of this book attempt to sketch what that means for the doing of theology. Also, this theology learns from the earlier papers that any Christian thinking as with any religious thinking after the Shoah cannot be done in isolation. Nothing should be said that cannot be said in the presence of the burning children (as Irving Greenberg has taught us). For Christians, that means that all Christian theology must now be done presuming the context of Jewish-Christian dialogue. Finally, the record of Christian antisemitism that is often connected to Christian teaching becomes an ongoing hermeneutic of suspicion. Thus, any Christian theology must be so constructed so that it does not in any way reproduce the "teaching of contempt," to use Jules Isaac's phrase. These are the basic presumptions of this book.

Still, maintaining this mixture of presumptions and accomplishing these tasks in a single book is bound to be daunting, especially in a book designed to maximize the effect of ambiguity. The reading of scripture in this book is exegesis but it is not modern exegesis in a strict sense. I do not attempt to apply redaction criticism to the texts, a tactic that others have used effectively. I also use form and source criticism only sparingly. The method employed in this book is rather a midrashic process, a process that has the nature of leaving questions and interpretation possibilities open for exploration. The aim is to provide material for theologies. Even so, there is a critical voice that ultimately suggests readings of Christian thought that are not acceptable anymore. This voice will be heard more throughout the chapters as critical turning points for interpretation arise.

There is also a creative dialogue voice in this book. The book is not an exercise in dialogue, but the conclusions rendered often suggest directions for dialogue. The book is directed primarily toward Christian scholars of the Shoah but these same Christian thinkers do presume, as I do, that what we have to say can and will provide points of interchange between us and our Jewish partners in dialogue. In this way, I hope that our many Jewish friends who have also been so very supportive of my work can be invited to participate in this process of shaping a post-Shoah Christian theology. At points in the book that are especially ripe for such dialogue, this voice will be made clearer.

There is also a midrashic voice in this book. Yes, the book is, itself, a midrash, in the sense of a midrashic process. Still, there are points along the way that lead to new insights about the stories of the Christian scriptures and extend those scriptures in new directions. These are discrete midrash that must be given, quite explicitly, a separate voice. The shift to these brief sections of the book is so dramatic (from academic discourse to the form of story) that a specific indicator showing the shift is needed. Surely such an indicator is not ordinarily necessary, but since these discrete midrash are housed within a text of both an academic and dialogical purpose, I will note the turn to discrete midrash more emphatically than might seem needed.

Emil Fackenheim wrote some years ago that Hitler's *Weltanschauung* was like a dramatic script which Hitler devised to orchestrate a real play. The appeal to this imagery seems bizarre at first. Elie Wiesel once said that he could not write a play about the Shoah because it would not really be about the Shoah. Fiction simply fails before reality in this case. At any rate, we ought not believe that fiction truly tells the story of the Shoah. Perhaps that is Fackenheim's point as well. He does not suggest that drama can lead us to understand Hitler's creation (can the imagery help us understand the "why?" question that Fackenheim believes is so elusive?)

He argues just that the metaphor can help us see how bizarre the reality is—a worldview played out as if scripted by a director who gave the essence to the plot.

That we must conclude that the Shoah is bizarre reality that escapes even fiction leads us to wonder about the spate of recent films, books, plays that nevertheless intend to lead us into the world of evil. I am still amazed by the fascination with evil that remains a theme for the artist and a craving for the viewer. Can we believe that we are beyond the idolization of evil that made Hitler's drama possible? Surely we must continue to say that reality belies fiction. It is one thing to be confronted with evil even in the stark forms possible with modern technology and quite another to participate in the play, or should we say in Hitler's play?

This book is not a play or story of the Shoah. Whatever I can say would add little substance to what is said far more adequately by the survivors and the diarists who did not survive. This book is, however, a story (or fragments of a story) of how Christians must talk about themselves and their faith and their lives after the Shoah. We can hope that reality again will outstrip the story. Only the next generations will show.

I am indebted to so many people for the ideas, support, criticism and assistance otherwise that helped give birth to this book. Good friends—Zev Garber, Richard Libowitz, Alan Berger, Bob Everett—who have listened to me and given me the chance to share my ideas have played an important role beyond what they realize. A number of groups of people have been supportive along the way giving me the feeling that I had something to contribute and working to give me the opportunity to do that—Gideon Shimoni, Burton Ruby and the Burton Ruby Foundation, Peter Knobel, the good people at Sinai Temple in Michigan City, Indiana, and at Emanuel Congregation in Chicago, Paul Mendel and the people at the Council of Christians and Jews in London. Other friends have inspired my thinking and continue to give new insight to me even if our views might differ from time to time—John Pawlikowski and Jacobus Schoneveld. My colleagues at Valparaiso University in my department and among administrators have supported my work through patience, encouragement and financial assistance. Surely, my family has been more than willing to give of themselves so that I can attend just one more conference or spend months away writing. My gratitude to them, my children Dana and Michael and my wife Elaine, is felt more than any other.

Still, I must reserve my closing words for someone who is more than merely a friend, as important as that is. Without Joe Edelheit I would not have begun teaching a course on the Shoah let alone known how I might do that. He has been my close associate in thought and purpose from the very beginning of my work in Jewish-Christian dialogue. Without his energy and his willingness to be there as a confidante from the outset, this book would not have been written. In a very real way, his voice is the partner in dialogue that is explicitly missing in this book but is implicitly felt throughout. It is to this friendship and our common hope that I dedicate this book.

INTRODUCTION:
A NEW CHRISTIAN MIDRASH

The Burning Bush

The ancient symbol of the burning bush which in the book of Exodus is identified with God's presence before Moses is one fascinating example of the biblical preoccupation with fire as a religious symbol. This example is unique in that the fire engulfs the entire bush but does not consume it. Thus, the symbol contains a striking contradiction that if maintained remains a puzzling paradox. It is this paradox that ultimately clouds any attempt to give meaning to the symbol other than the mere presence of God. Fire, of course, is often used as a symbol of God's presence (the pillar of fire, fire on the mountain, tongues of fire) but only in this instance is the extraordinary paradox maintained.

Perhaps we are taught by this symbol of the impenetrable essence of God that remains hidden from us and our attempts to make sense of the divine. If that is so, and it probably is, then the whole religious history of the people of Israel and indeed of the Christian people is one of following a mystery which eludes every attempt to become comfortable in knowledge and sure of one's destiny. There is a lesson in that for our generation as well, perhaps especially for our generation.

There is another message that is conveyed by the symbol as well. That message is that the fire which destroys human flesh does not consume God. This is an awe-full message that means for Moses and for us that the very presence of God is fearful and dangerous. No one enters into the presence of God, indeed even relationship with God without risk. And we are confused because God's presence includes both revelation and destruction at least in potential. How can we dare to enter into that presence?

But our generation has learned a further lesson. The fire that would not consume the bush is not the fire of our generation. In our time has been lit a fire that not only threatens to destroy human flesh and spirit but the spirit of God as well. And this is a mystery to us that is shrouded in unbelief and shock. We have never known before a force so evil that it can consume the presence of God and diminish its awe-ful power for us. This fire has been aptly called Shoah, the destruction of European Jewry.[1]

The New Revelation of Fire

Wiesel's views of the Shoah are portrayed in images, often through stories that capture reality through people. Indeed, stories are the medium through which revelation of God's presence has been handed from generation to generation for four millennia of the Jewish people. These stories are also part of the tradition of Christian reflection of God's acts and promises. Thus, the image of fire means nothing let alone the presence of God apart from the story of this (these) people. The context and story line bears the revelation and not merely the image. Thus, an image can be unfolded in different ways through the telling of stories.

The story of the Shoah is different. There is a text that we can all read but the story does not bear the revelation of the presence of God. Indeed, the story bears only emptiness of meaning. Even in its most positive aspects, the story remains pure negativity.[2] The story tells nothing to enhance us or to explain for us. The story is a story of destruction, of negation, of a struggle to survive that should not have been necessary but is now forever necessary.

That means that the story is a new revelation not of God's presence but of God's negation, of radical evil.[3] It is no wonder that Wiesel argues that the story cannot be told, indeed should not be told.[4] Radical evil is that which no one can fully explain or even describe since the negation reaches the roots of all human experience and beyond. This evil is that which threatens to destroy God and the whole story of God's people. We surely did not need this story to understand either humanity or the divine. We already could know of the infinite possibilities and the radical finitude of the human. And we already know of fullness of the divine in history in both its clarity and mystery. This new story imposes itself on all of that and shakes us to our foundations. It is as Arthur Cohen has said a tremendum, a caesura in history, a breaking of the story.[5] It is the story that cannot be but was.

I have witnessed the agony of those who try to tell about their experience. How many times will they say, "And, of course, you will not believe this"? But we do believe the story because we know it is true. It is real, more believable than hope, and goodness, and even God. But we should not believe the story. The almost commonplace, you will not believe this, is an aside that means more. It is a plea to our sanity that the story isn't, can't be true, ought not be true. But the story is told not as fiction but as reality, inescapable reality, inexpressible reality. No wonder that the full depths of the story will never be told since to continue the story, to embellish the story is impossible. We do not know the words nor have the strength to keep telling the story. But we must keep telling even if we know that telling the story is not telling this story. We must do so because this is a new revelation. Now we know and cannot forget. We know what humans can be brought to do. We know how much God will allow or that God cannot stop or will not stop or does not care to stop. And this is a mystery beyond us with no words to describe. So we must keep telling because we have no choice but to stand beside God in the face of radical evil. There is no choice here and there was no choice for so many others.

We must do so also because it is the story, our story, that is threatened. We are now challenged to see if we can tell our story still without breaking, without admitting that it is a farce.[6] The 4000 year old story of truth, of God's presence, now is threatened. It seems like fiction now. What was truly unbelievable has become reality and what ought to be believed turns into fiction. If we do not try to tell the story, then we must confess only negation. All positive meaning will be lost. We will have denied the Spirit of God and abandoned our world to the story of Shoah and fire will mean only death and darkness: The kingdom of the night.

A Christian Theology After Auschwitz

This book is one effort to reconstruct a Christian theology, in short the Christian story, in the face of the kingdom of the night. The image of fire is not the only image that has now become laden with ambiguity that finally breaks the meaning of the image. Nevertheless, this book will return to the tradition in order to retrieve that language in a new story that now must know of radical threat and destruction. This new story will be frightfully uncertain in its claims but it will not cower before the negativity of Auschwitz. In order to accomplish this task, I will take three steps in reconstructing the story. First, I will sketch a model for a post-Shoah Christian theology building from the work of Elie Wiesel. Second, I will turn to the passion narratives of the Christian gospels in order to form a new midrash of the Peter and Judas cycles as a basis for re-thinking Christian apostasy during the Shoah. Third, I will construct a post-Shoah Christian theology built on the pattern of midrash using the narratives images of Jesus and the specific narratives of the resurrection.

The Nature of Christian Theology

Christian theology is by no means a monolithic domain. Even those engaged in Jewish-Christian dialogue represent a full range of opinion about what is essential to Christian theology. Most of Western Christianity has built on a system of theology that is systematized around central themes, doctrines. For much of theological history, theological debate has meant the consideration of the doctrines. Aquinas gave a pattern of systematic theological argument that borrowed philosophical tools of definition but presumed the authority of central doctrines.[7] That form of theology has dominated Christian theology and still represents the most viable understanding of Christian theology even when the particular system of doctrine differs widely from that of Aquinas.

Though the shift in theology surely was rooted in earlier developments and controversies, Friedrich Schleiermacher represents for most Christian thinkers a watershed in defining the nature of Christian theology.[8] Schleiermacher defined dogmatic theology as an historical discipline that is rooted in the particular confession of a traditional community. Given this perspective, Schleiermacher could argue that the themes central to any Christian theology would differ widely depending on the character of the community of faith and its own history. Even doctrinal statements could vary depending on the emphasis central to a community's confession. Thus, three striking conclusions could be drawn that have influenced all subsequent discussions about the nature of theology. First, the task of theology is to be identified as an exploration into the historical nature of the community. Thus, the recognition of theological pluralism both in reality and in potential was incorporated into theological reflection for the first time. Second, the theologian is naturally drawn into a discussion of methods as of equal importance as content since the way of constructing doctrine represents the distinctions between different confessional communities. Third, the question of authority becomes a matter of communal assent and not of prima facie self-evidence. The task of identifying universal *sacra doctrina* that represent theological authority is made far more problematic.

Naturally, all of these developments opened the door to a reconsideration of the relation between Christian theology and other religions in a way impossible before. Even with the door open Christian theologians were not necessarily moved to greater appreciation for other religions but the necessity for making a case for Christianity came to the fore for the first time since the earliest life of the church. Though many other factors stirred this theological investigation into other religions, surely the shift in theological self-understanding remains a primary force leading thinkers in that direction.[9] In addition, the new infatuation with historical studies and its subsequent influence on the study of scripture and on theology renewed

Christian interest in Jewish studies and with that a theological evaluation of Judaism.[10] Much has been written on the relation between the growing liberal movement in the churches in Germany and the parallel political developments in the late 19th and early 20th centuries which makes any evaluation of this shift in theology difficult.[11] Nevertheless, this shift has marked the debate in theology since between those who find the arguments of the liberals incontrovertible leading to a focus on theological method and argumentation and those who find the move detrimental and seek to re-establish the universal authority of scripture and/or tradition, especially with the re-assertion of certain indisputable central doctrines. Between these poles there is surely a full spectrum of positions.[12]

Finding a place to locate our discussion within this spectrum is difficult to begin with. Attempting to introduce a new criteria of negativity—the Shoah—makes the task even more difficult. I will simply assert that Christian theology post-Shoah must have a dual nature which I will name its story and its dialogical character. The principle theme that organizes Christian theology is the story of Jesus the Christ and his followers as that can be made our own and the method used is a dialogical method.

Story as Theme

This way of understanding Christian theology is clearly an effort to draw together both elements of the developing tradition of Christian theology on the one hand and to introduce a new element into both aspects of our theological approach on the other. That first component of this theology—identifying the story of Jesus the Christ and his followers as our own story—is by no means unique to this author. The theme of story is so common in theological discussions today that our efforts run the risk of losing clarity given the host of possible meanings given to "story."[13] This approach to theology proposed here certainly owes something to recent debate over narrative, even narrative structure, and Christian confession but cannot be identified with that particular discussion. Instead, I believe that what I propose does have a unique sense quite apart from what others are saying about story.

Story can be the way that we designate the most fundamental defining tool we have in talking about our identity. Stories can be simple or elaborate. Stories can be self-evident or multi-dimensional. I submit that telling a story is the most beneficial way for Christians to answer that question "Who is a Christian?" or the family of related questions: "Are you a Christian?" "Why are you a Christian?" "How can I be a Christian?" It is the most beneficial way because through the story we are led to give personal embodiment to fundamental beliefs and we are forced to deal with the question, "How does confession impact our living?" Story is also one of the basic tools that Jesus used as recorded in the Gospel texts to speak of his identity and that of the kingdom of God. Thus, by seeking to identify a story we are forced back to the radical source of our faith, an encounter with the Jesus of the text.[14]

Our story, then, is first the story of Jesus as that story can be reconstructed for our use. We will need the aid of various scholars who have made investigations pertinent to this story—the character of the early church, the exegesis of the gospel texts, the nature of first century Judaism and first century hellenistic society. Nevertheless, the story remains the story of the gospel texts as the narrative is given to us.[15] In order to retrieve this story, we must retreat to the text and receive again in a fresh way without the inherited prejudice of tradition, as much as that is possible.

Story as Theological Reflection

Naturally this story of Jesus is embedded in a tradition (several traditions) that immediately drive us back to reconsider other texts in the same rigorous way. However, our consideration of these texts in the book will be consistently theological. That is to say, the stories are taken as a vehicle for religious meaning and require critical theological reflection in order to shape it into our own story, to make it our own. The movement from story to reflection is always a risky move that requires selective reading based on key central interpretive themes. Those themes arise from the texts under consideration but are also applied to them.

But one does not have to abandon the story to engage in reflection since the story is already theology for us. The story remains our touchstone, then, providing the basis for theological claims. We might remain on the verge of a systematic ordering of ideas, but our aim is to avoid allowing system to intrude on the narrative. No system of ideas, therefore, remains above critique, the critique of the text.[16]

Yet, this is a post-Shoah theology and that means that the negative event called the holocaust is a constant hermeneutic of suspicion.[17] Even the text is left frail in the withering critique brought by the reality of Auschwitz. Our constant fear is that the text will not survive, the story will crumble and fade in the face of the more recent horror of the Shoah. But we dare not shrink back from the critique. The negativity of the Shoah must be met with the full array of conviction and history of faith.

Dialogue as the Context of Reflection

Telling a story, even one so familiar as our own story as Christians, is a difficult task. We talk of life events, of Jesus' life, not with the full confidence that we know the meaning of the story but only with the confidence that this story provides ultimate meaning for us. The combination of those two facts about ourselves speaks not only for our personal struggle as evangelists, witnesses to the truth(s) we confess, but also the inevitable and radical surprise that telling the story is likely to bring. Telling the story is different than writing the story since telling always requires us to return to the beginning and start again. Unless we are simply machines repeating only what is recorded in our brain, that is less than human, this starting over will always mean new discovery.

The Shoah demands of us that we start again deliberately, working through the details of our story so that we recognize not only the radical surprise of meaning that David Tracy has said to us arises from a power of disclosure and manifestation, but also the radical surprise of negation staring back at us not only from Auschwitz but also confronting us from the midst of the story.[18] This shadow cast over our story is unfortunately a shadow seen in its sharpest and coldest form placed next to the harshness of Auschwitz. Telling the story with the painful effort of constructing an honest account of our Christianity after Auschwitz means that we can see radical evil constantly counterposed with what we have always proclaimed as ultimate, radical good. This is a shadow that haunts our efforts to witness and will haunt all efforts to witness to the God in Christ.

Yet, this latter fact of our story-telling, our theology, makes even more urgent and gives even greater clarity to the need for dialogue to be an integral part of all our theologizing. Our theology must hear the voices that it has so often tried to close out, to brand as unworthy or evil unfairly.[19] We must hear even before we speak. The telling must accompany a listening that begins with a listening to the voices of Auschwitz and continues to hear the voices of the surviving Jewish people in all their variety and complexity, not only as we would want to hear them but as they would want us to hear them. We have for so long, even the best of us, formed views of Jews that suit our theological story. We have decided their identity for them both for ourselves and sadly and coercively often for the Jews among us. Our telling must truly begin with a listening.[20]

This means that this book is partially a farce. There is no way that my theology or the theology of others can be authentic after Auschwitz outside of dialogue. Those words carry much that must be explored further in these pages. Let me say though that this book remains preliminary to an authentic theology in which the audible voice of my Jewish partner(s) in dialogue will also share on these pages. If listening is the beginning of theology, then the best I can do is to bring the voices of Jewish critics, some widely known others known to me, into this effort to shape a Christian theology after Auschwitz.

Still, the necessity to do theology in dialogue is more than an exercise to right wrongs of the past. And the value of doing theology in dialogue can be seen even without turning to the shadow and horror of Auschwitz and the urgencies they bring. For Christians owe their existence and the basic content of their story to Judaism. This is not to say that Christians are merely Jews in disguise, what a travesty that claim would be. This is also not to say that Christians have listened well in the past to their Jewish teachers, even the prime Jewish teacher for Christians, Jesus of Nazareth. What it is to say is that Christians are bound now to listen to their Jewish brothers and sisters because we can learn so much even in radical surprise about ourselves by hearing their view of our tradition, scripture, theology, story. We have only just begun to listen and learn but the results are already remarkable.

A third reason for making dialogue critical for theology lies in the very nature of theology after Auschwitz. Doing theology after Auschwitz confronts us with not only the real failure of our past theologizing but also with the radical challenge to theology as such. The language of our various theologies is if not obscene in the face of Auschwitz wholly inadequate for facing up to Auschwitz. The language is broken with regard to this event; it does not work to provide meaning to an event that is likely to escape all attempts to provide meaning. Surely naive efforts to thrust absolutist theological positions at the problems of the Shoah are vain and destructive. We not only need alternatives but a theology that structurally creates the inevitability of alternatives. We need a theology in dialogue.

This sort of theology is, however, radically unsettling in its ambiguity. Theologians, above all, like to be certain, to make claims with authority. Religions thrive on being right, on having the truth. No religion save a very few admits that other religions have the truth or even some truth. Surely even the admission that theologians are not sure of the truth of their own faith would be a radically unsettling position to take. We naturally want answers from our religious heritage, answers that set all things in their place, that resolve all serious problems, that promise certain conclusions. A theology in dialogue is radically unsettling and out of character.[21]

Nevertheless, it is this unsettling experience that promises the sort of radical response to radical evil that is called for in this post- Shoah age. Indeed, our story will always be in some way post- Shoah. Our theology must always provide a radical response, a response that shakes the roots of faith to rediscover the possibilities of faith. We must enter once again into the fire, now a new fire, that beckons us on without assurance of redemption but rather promises of destruction. But we cannot turn back because then our theologies, even our stories will have no sense and no purpose. That is the challenge that faces us.

Notes

[1]I use Shoah rather than holocaust here. Some claim that Wiesel first used this word, holocaust, which can be disputed in that the word was already current in sporadic use during the Shoah, but Wiesel has specifically introduced the term in post-Auschwitz thinking, as he said in a lecture at Michigan City, Indiana, in 1984, because he thought no one knew its root religious meaning. He has also stopped using the term choosing rather to speak of the kingdom of the night, the phrase used most regularly in the opening of this book in the discussion of Wiesel's thought. John Roth and Richard Rubenstein engage a brief discussion of the appropriateness of terms in their recent text but a far more significant discussion can be found in Zev Garber and Bruce Zuckerman, "Why Do We Call the Holocaust 'the Holocaust'? An Inquiry into the Psychology of Labels" in *Remembering for the Future* (New York: Pergamon Press, 1988), volume II, pp. 1879ff. See also John Roth and Richard Rubenstein, *Approaches to Auschwitz* (Atlanta: John Knox Press, 1987), pp. 4-7.

[2]Surely many have spoken in these terms, but I was first led to think in this way by David Tracy, "Religious Values After the Holocaust: A Catholic View" in *Jews and Christians After the Holocaust*, Abraham Peck, ed. (Philadelphia: Fortress Press, 1982), p. 92.

[3]Again, the phrase "radical evil" I first heard from Ken Seeskin. An interesting discussion of his current thinking on this subject is found in Kenneth Seeskin, *Jewish Philosophy in a Secular Age* (Albany: SUNY Press, 1990), especially pp. 134, 193, 195-6, 208-9.

[4]This theme is developed in one of Wiesel's most fascinating essays: Elie Wiesel, "Art and Culture After the Holocaust" in *Auschwitz: Beginning of a New Era?*, Eva Fleischner, ed. (New York: KTAV, 1977), pp. 403ff.

[5]Arthur A. Cohen, *The Tremendum* (New York: Crossroad, 1981).

[6]My first encounter with this theological challenge came through Irving Greenberg, "Cloud of Smoke, Pillar of Fire: Judaism, Christianity, and Modernity after the Holocaust," in *Auschwitz: Beginning of a New Era?*, Eva Fleischner, ed. (New York: KTAV, 1977), pp. 8-13.

[7]Aquinas describes the nature of the systematic discipline in the early part of Thomas Aquinas, "Summa Theologica" in *Basic Writings of St. Thomas Aquinas*, Anton Pegis, ed. (New York: Random House, 1945), pp. 5-17.

[8]See especially Friedrich Schleiermacher, *The Christian Faith* (Philadelphia: Fortress Press, 1976), pp. 3-93.

[9]Many thinkers have attempted to analyze this shift in Christian thinking. One of the more enlightening texts both for the author's analysis and for the extensive bibliography is Brian Gerrish, *Tradition and the Modern World* (Chicago: University of Chicago Press, 1978).

[10]In fact, all of the prominent thinkers of the nineteenth century began this reassessment of Judaism: cf., Schleiermacher, *The Christian Faith*, pp. 60-61.

[11]Franklin Littell has done much to uncover this dimension represented, for example, by Franklin Littell, *The Crucifixion of the Jews* (Macon, Ga.: Mercer University Press, 1975, 1986), especially pp. 100ff.

[12]A recent, even if not fully acceptable, analysis of these polar positions in Christian theology is found in George Lindbeck, *The Nature of Doctrine* (Philadelphia: Westminster Press, 1984).

[13]While varieties of approaches are available, two influential thinkers have shaped distinctive and dominant counter positions in current debate: Paul Ricoeur, *Time and Narrative* (Chicago: University of Chicago Press, 1984, 1987), and Hans Frei, *The Eclipse of the Biblical Narrative* (New Haven: Yale University Press, 1974).

[14]Such apparently naive reading for the historical figure behind the text is not what is intended. Rather, I intend to encounter the Jesus presented by the text as that can be reconstructed. Naturally, various forms of the quest for the historical Jesus have intrigued scholars for at least the past two centuries. The shape of this quest follows more the pattern of David Tracy, *The Analogical Imagination* (New York: Crossroad, 1981), pp. 248ff.

[15]I do not intend by any means to discount important work being done in social/historical biblical scholarship [e.g., Eduard Lohse, *The New Testament Environment* (Nashville: Abingdon Press, 1976)]. However, the approach in this book aims for a theological interpretation and moves in a different direction from such other work.

[16]The source and purpose of this rule of theology is manifold and the voices that support such a hermeneutic after Auschwitz are equally numerous. Again, a thorough stating of the character of religious thought after Auschwitz is dramatically stated by Greenberg, "Cloud of Smoke, Pillar of Fire...", pp. 7ff. The rule of ongoing critique is, however, as ancient as midrash and undoubtedly characterized religious thought in the early church as well.

[17]Long a theme of David Tracy's work, the connections I make here are especially well presented in the last chapter of David Tracy, *Plurality and Ambiguity* (New York: Harper and Row, 1987).

[18]David Tracy, *The Analogical Imagination*, pp. 154ff.

[19]I echo here the pattern of Wiesel's appeal in Elie Wiesel, "Art and Culture after the Holocaust".

[20]Wiesel, p. 403

[21]This is not to say that such a theology has not been attempted. Any number of examples of such efforts will become consistent resources for this study. Perhaps the most dramatic statements of this vision are Irving Greenberg, pp. 34ff. and Johann Baptist Metz, *The Emerging Church* (New York: Crossroad, 1986), pp. 20ff.

CHAPTER 1:

THE KINGDOM OF GOD AND
THE KINGDOM OF THE NIGHT

Elie Wiesel's compelling, chilling image of his experiences at Auschwitz in the book *Night* has left us with memories that are not our own but have become ours. Such is the following first experience of the camp:

> Never shall I forget that night, the first night in camp, which has turned my life into one long night, seven times cursed and seven times sealed. Never shall I forget that smoke. Never shall I forget the little faces of children whose bodies I saw turned into wreaths of smoke beneath a silent blue sky.
>
> Never shall I forget those flames which consumed my faith forever.
>
> Never shall I forget the nocturnal silence which deprived me, for all eternity, of the desire to live. Never shall I forget those mountains which murdered my God and my soul and turned my dreams to dust. Never shall I forget these things, even if I am condemned to live as long as God Himself. Never.[1]

The symbols of faith and darkness fill this picture of horror. Side by side they speak of the complete breaking of a world of meaning on the rocks of nightmare, the Kingdom of the Night. There is no turning back from this experience. Never shall we forget. Thus, no passage in all of literature is so complete in its hold over me, in its message for me. My living memory will always set the image of horror alongside of images of hope that extend from the story of my faith. The Kingdom of God is shadowed by the Kingdom of the Night.

If God were murdered by this event, dying in Auschwitz on the gallows as the child of Wiesel's story, then the pain would be less. Then God would have been the victim fully. But what of a God who survives, who must live with the memory of the little children who became ashes in that place. For if God lives, then every face of every child is impressed upon His/Her memory. The fear, the pain, the questions, the innocence must resound to a noise so deafening to the ears of God that He/She must weep daily. Can there be a corner of God's Kingdom that is free of this memory? If this memory cannot be driven away, then all of our expectations for a future kingdom free of pain and sorrow must be changed. Dare we so easily set aside the Kingdom of the Night when even God Her/Himself must daily hear again the cries of the one million children slaughtered only because they were there because they were alive.

If this is our present fate, and how could it be otherwise, then our theology must be a reflection of the truth about this. We must write about the Kingdom of God in all of its meaning in the context of the Kingdom of the Night. Our theology must weep for the one million. We must never forget. Even our words, our abstract reflections, our proclamations must convey this memory, even if we are "condemned to live as long as God Himself."

How do we write such a theology? We can begin by returning to Wiesel, by using the text to recreate the images there and translate them into the theology unfolded in those pages. If we do, then we are thrust back into the Kingdom of the Night. We will see our theology in that darkness. It will be our struggle to come to terms with a view of the Kingdom of God that arises out of the deepest pain, even pain beyond pain. Our first images of the Kingdom of God, then, will be the cries to God, the questions that break apart hope. And this is as it should be for our theology.

Wiesel's Image of the Kingdom of God from the Kingdom of the Night

As might be expected, there are at least two levels of meaning carried in the text of *Night*. First, we see the personal level of Wiesel's struggle to re-think his own faith now shattered, the faith of his childhood. This experience is not simply the shattering of first naivete as is the case with many of us but the shattering of a world of naivete to which there is no return. To be aware of the shattering and of the eternal loss is the first level of meaning in this book. Second, we see the theological level in which the tradition stretching beyond mere naivete of faith is shattered, the language is broken. Wiesel's craft and the intensity of his experience has made for us a great test of tradition itself because we not only face again the eternal questions of human curiosity and doubt but the complete emptiness of answers brought to the brink of completeness and real destruction. We take little comfort in the fact that the community of faith survives, but the community has survived and is now commanded to face the brink again before the memory of these questions has been lost. This is the power of Wiesel's images.

Wiesel's personal struggle is shaped by his background. Other victims tell different stories; thus we cannot assume that re-living Wiesel's story will tell all that needs to be said about the Shoah. This is one story, but its power and honesty has the effect of challenging us in ways that prove necessary for our theology. Wiesel's background can be reconstructed from the text. He was a child. He is a Jew. He came from a small city on the border of Romania which at the time was in Hungary. His family was reasonably prominent in the community. He studied Talmud continuously with an Hasidic teacher, a Mystic. The story of *Night* unfolds at the time of his Bar Mitzvah. Even more, the path seemed prepared for his becoming a Hasid as well, a teacher and student of the tradition. He clearly had the aptitude and the desire to do this. These short phrases are far too little to imagine this world, this life, but they serve to give us hints of the faith that was brought to destruction on that first night in the camp.

If we return to the passage quoted above, we can learn much of this personal struggle. "Never shall I forget that Night..." Clearly, Wiesel, as with many before him, had been trained to remember. Memory was and is the power of the tradition that overcomes the passing evidence of the moment. Memorizing Talmud and then studying more to memorize more is the training ground for the mystic, the wise scholar of the tradition.[2] Now we know from the simple words of this phrase above that Wiesel's skill, his memory has become the first of the challenges. This phrase printed at this point in the text, a phrase itself of recollection and reflection from a later time, is not an appeal to later generations. It is the depth of personal struggle with a memory that should not be, should not have been, would be best forgotten, but cannot be forgotten. Even before we say it must not be forgotten, we must say that for Wiesel and many others like him it cannot be forgotten.

Then the images of the tradition come cascading down onto this child, the child of destiny: "seven times cursed and seven times sealed." This image carries so much in its mystery—the image of creation, of the sabbath, of the messianic age. Indeed, the picture thrusts all of these integral parts of faith into the smoke that trailed to the skies—one long night. If creation signifies the order of God's hand, even providence, then this night signifies the obliteration of order, even God's order. This is chaos turned loose. If Sabbath signifies rest and devotion to God, then this night signifies the loss of rest, restlessness, and the absence of God. If the messianic age signifies the ultimate rule of God and ultimate human hope, then this night signifies the ultimate devastation of God's promise and the loss of human hope. The stark reality of this event destroyed a world, a faith, a God. If this night could be and God did not act to save God's people, then we see only the long night, the eternal night into which light does not shine and hope diminishes with every passing moment of darkness. The rule of God destroyed, this is the kingdom of the night.

Of course, to the child the first question is "WHY?" How was this possible? But the question cannot last long, not at least in the immediate necessities of survival. The child could not even ask why. There was no rest, no time for contemplation, time to make it all stop so that answers could be found. This was time when mere instinct takes hold and fear rules. For Wiesel, instinct also included the instinct of a life of devotion. Even without the reality of God, that instinct would lead Wiesel. Is there hope in that? What can we say? His instinct and his "luck" played into his survival. It also added to his personal struggle. Instinct led him to cling to his father and that brought him both survival purpose but also the never ending burden of guilt that plagued him and perhaps still does.

This personal challenge is one of religious depth but it is more than that. Elie's struggle is the struggle for life and its meaning. The text of *Night* is a reflection back on the immediate experience. It is an expression of the struggle which continues. The personal struggle is the merging of the intense experience of evil gone mad, radical evil, and the strength of the hope of faith. In the immediate experience, faith loses to the shock of mere survival, a reduction that is shocking in itself. In the moment of reflection, naive faith loses to the reality of that which should not even have been thought which nevertheless had become actual. No more can we on a personal level naively believe that humans have benevolent instincts. Humans left to instinct, even the most devoted, act out of fear and desperation. The shattering of our basic belief in human goodness (even minimal goodness) is a crushing blow, one that leaves us feeling incredibly alone. We wonder justifiably whether the selfishness of the camp is the norm we ought to follow. If that were not enough, the faith that God will act on behalf of Her/His people has died with the one million children who cried for help from someone, from somewhere and heard no reply. Which is more devastating, the loss of faith in humanity or the loss of hope in a God who will act? Whatever we say about the event, and Wiesel says much more in this small text about the place of God, we know that our childhood faith has broken upon the rocks of Auschwitz. We cannot expect that God will act to redeem us from this evil, some evil perhaps but not this evil.

This brief summation of the personal challenge level of this text cannot claim comprehensive understanding even of Wiesel's words. Is that even possible? The point is that any theology that quickly moves away from the personal level cannot be a post- Shoah theology. All theological questions arise from the depths of the personal and are judged by that. Any treatment other than this can only be false. A post-Shoah theology is a word for the community to be sure but it is a community that has undergone the transformation of a people reduced to mere individuals in a fearful world without promise. We, too, must stand at the gates of Auschwitz for awhile and see the smoke, hear the cries, feel the anger, be overcome by the revulsion and doubt and fear. We can never again be too comfortable in our thinking either about God or humanity for where did they who were brought to their deaths at Auschwitz find comfort?

The Theological Struggle

The story of personal devastation is at once a story of the transformation of a child and a story of the annihilation of a dream. That dream for the young child was sufficient to sustain life even in uncertainty. However, the dream could not even be sustained in Auschwitz. What brought survival at the same time brought a direct challenge to the dream. Trust in humans and in God became a threat to life and yet these were the very strands upon which the dream had been woven.

Without question the personal struggle became a theological struggle that later upon reflection could be set into the framework of faith for all to consider. Covenant, revelation, redemption, obedience that were the material of faithful living had become the nightmare of living in Auschwitz. The two struggles meld together into one only to be separated in our minds as we try to hear the story of this child. Covenant means responsibility, promise, trust, relationship all of which became targets of destruction in the Kingdom of the Night. Revelation stands over against the stark reality of the world to help us glimpse God but a glimpse of God in Auschwitz only served to heighten the starkness of that reality. Redemption has always meant new life but life that continues on after this means a life of painful, unimaginable memory. Obedience is given to preserve the order of a good world but obedience in a world that is only evil means either folly or collaboration in that evil.

Naturally, the faithful one who wants to sustain the fabric of faith, is reluctant to let go. Even the one who reflects later wants to sustain the faith in order to erase evil, to still the pounding questions of doubt. Wiesel uses the basic pillars of his own heritage and the fundamental instincts of Jewish life to shape his story of terror. This is his theological struggle.

First, Wiesel takes hold of the image of night. This image invades the whole of the story like a literary framework that reminds the reader constantly of the setting of this story. But night is also an image of faith. Abraham set out early in the morning (literally, at night) commanded by God to offer his son. Jacob stayed the night and wrestled with the angel of God before meeting his brother. Moses led the people of Israel from Egypt at night, the night when the angel of death passed over the homes of the Israelites.

Christians who read Wiesel's story will know that this image is also an image of faith for Christians. Jesus goes to the garden to pray at night and is arrested and tried at night. Indeed, the whole scene takes place at night, even the last supper. And the women come to the tomb early in the morning (literally, at night) to embalm the body. These latter images are not Wiesel's images but surely any reader Jew or Christian would know from instinct that the image is a reminder that God cannot ever be fully known and even actions of God's redemption come under the darkness of night so as not to be openly seen and become an occasion for human arrogance.

There is little wonder then that the child of faith would see the night as an appropriate time for God to act. Indeed, the night when Elie and his people were moved to the ghetto was the night of preparation. Thus, the story leads us to the very heart of our problem, our struggle. We return to this page again as we now know the story as it is fully told. The people are led away by whose hand? Who is it that really holds the fate of this people? If this is a time of revelation, then what are we to see? The shock is the revelation not of the hand of God but of the absence of God entirely. At least this is the absence of the God we can obey, worship, follow. And in this knowledge we are faced with the terrible truth that obedience, worship and faithfulness are what is at stake. That way of life and thinking is the target of destruction.

We know that the destruction extended haphazardly but with malicious intent beyond just those who could know what was at stake or even those who cared. Every representative of this way of life no matter how committed or how clearly identified with Judaism they were became victims. Every woman, child, mother, grandmother, man, son, father, daughter were automatically sentenced to death simply because they were Jewish even in the remotest connection as having just one Jewish grandparent. Who could escape the implication? If the Israelites had stayed in Egypt, then no one would be a victim here. If God had not proclaimed that I will be your God and you will be my people, then no such people called the Jews would have existed to be destroyed. These people were victims because God had singled them out and made them a people and every succeeding generation and the last three of these generations suffered the horrid impact of that choosing. This is double irony. These people were given no choice because choices had been made long ago. Who could not think that God was responsible? Who else is ultimately responsible for this people?

Thus, Wiesel takes the imagery of faith and sets it into the Kingdom of the Night as a way of talking about the ultimate struggle of faith. This image of night that bears the promise of hope is transformed in this story into nightmare and even more since then it would only be a dream. And God did not act to redeem his people. We might all be like Abraham crying to God to save the faithful in Sodom and Gomorrah, the children. How many cries does it take before God hears? If the cry of one was enough before, how deafening is the cry of one million children who were murdered brutally? And what of the brutality inflicted upon the child who survived and lives night after night with the memory?

The second image of Wiesel's story, therefore, must be the central image of Judaism, the covenant, the redemption from Egypt. This was of course not the first time that this people had faced the brutality of others and the stinging questions to God. This people had known the disappointment of the past.[3] Still, never before had their existence as human beings been denied. They had been called different, dangerous, cunning, murderous but they had never been called vermin before in this way. In every time of persecution, the centrality of the covenant had been a reservoir of hope for this people. The questions would remain but the firm belief that God had chosen them for a purpose gave strength and courage. Indeed, even in the Kingdom of the Night, the covenant was a resource for courage. Only the child who looks back begins to wonder about the source of hope. There is a point somewhere in the story that is a watershed over which the last ribbons of hope fade away and God becomes for us a tragic figure who can only weep for his people. What can redemption mean for those who have such memories?

Emil Fackenheim argues that the redeeming voice of God was not present at Auschwitz.[4] That seems to be the contention of the Wiesel who wrote *Night* since traditional images of redemption that are used as elements of the story are turned around and inside out. The night of Passover was a night of fear to be sure but a night in which the people were led out of bondage. The night of relocation, that night of Passover, was the night in which people were led into the ultimate bondage. The smoke and fire represented the presence of God in the wilderness for the ancient Israelites. The smoke and fire of Auschwitz represented the absence of God, the darkest of evils. In that first passover, the angel's passing gave hope for life to the children of Israel. In this passover, the various angels of darkness, having nothing to do with God, condemned the children of Israel to death. These are the real ironies that the boy who remembers tells us. The striking, eerie presence of these images clashing against our sensibilities cannot escape us. The redeeming voice of God was not present at Auschwitz in this story.

Naturally, if the redeeming voice of God was not present there but instead only gave way to a mockery of redemption *(Arbeit Macht Frei)*, then how can the redeeming voice still be heard. Indeed, Fackenheim questions whether the voice can be heard over the screams of those who died.[5] We face yet another gulf between our memory of tradition and our memories of Auschwitz. Irving Greenberg argues that we should say nothing that could not be said in the presence of the one million children who died.[6] Can we say the words of redemption in their presence? This question is merely one among many but an important one. *What we ask is whether the Kingdom of God can ever escape the shadow of the Kingdom of the Night.* Surely our language about God's redeeming voice has been broken in the shattering of the lives of the six million, only time will tell whether that pain can be comforted.

A third image comes rushing at us as of vital importance in *Night*. Wiesel sees his own relationship with his father as both a prime reason for his survival and an eternal burden. "Honor your father and mother so that your days may be long in the land where you will dwell." There is likely no more important commandment for us. The honor offered by the little child was simple. Fear led him to cling to his father as a source of strength. But as all strength ebbed away, the command became a burden of extraordinary weight. The responsibility of caring for his father threads its way through the pages of the text as perhaps the single most important issue outside of survival. If nothing else, he struggles to keep his respect and care for his father. The tragic ending to this line of the story (another tragedy added to so many others) sharpens, deepens the burden.

But this is a theological issue that extends beyond the critical relationship of father to son. The struggle of a child to save his father is only a miniature of the larger struggle of the people to save their God. "Out of Egypt have I called my son." Even more, the story of the *Akeda*, Abraham and Isaac, shouts out of this text. Yet another critical text is challenged by the ironies of this tragedy. If superimposed on this story, this story of the *Akeda* becomes a revealing and centrally important challenge in post-Shoah theology.

If we recall the story from Genesis, we note the particulars. Abraham is approached at night by God and asked to rise early in the morning and take his son, his only son, the one whom he loves so much to the place where God will lead him to offer his son as a sacrifice. This story has been the subject of any number of extraordinary commentaries; it is central to both Jewish and Christian tradition. The challenge to Abraham is an ultimate test of his faith in the promise of God. The story, however, is ironic in that the command is as much a challenge to God as to Abraham. It is a challenge to God's commitment to the covenant with Abraham. In that sense, the challenge seems nonsensical, open to much question. If every character in the story fully expects Abraham to carry through with the command, the command appears sadistic. If God is not serious about the command, then he is arbitrary. If Abraham is only play- acting, expecting the Lord to intervene all along, then Abraham is not really tested (that is, unless God does not intervene). The story makes no sense in itself, but it does make sense in the context of tradition. The covenant between God and Abraham does mean that the enemies of God will make every generation of the children of Abraham targets. If this is so, then simply binding the child to the covenant is already a sacrifice. The children will often suffer from the decisions of their parents. The real test of faith is time and generations.

Of course, the truth of this image is never more horribly displayed than in the Shoah. The full impact of this horror is that grandparents in the nineteenth century already sealed the fate of their grandchildren simply by continuing the covenant, by being Jews. And if these grandparents, like Abraham, knew the consequences of their actions, would they do the same? Each succeeding generation of post-Shoah Jewry will face this question now haunted by the reality of the past. The irony is that the test is now as it was then, a test equally of God and God's covenant promise. If that is the case, then this radical evil of Auschwitz is for us a revelation; one that we must come to terms with.

Wiesel's story fits into that mold as well. Unable to act independent of his father, the young Wiesel is taken with the father into the camp forever after tied to him. Whatever fate the father is to have will be extended to the son. The difference, however, is striking. Eliezer's father has no choice at this point. To cling to his son means the son will suffer the same fate as he. To let go would likely mean to sacrifice his son on the spot. There is no real choice. We assume that Abraham could choose. Elie's father could no longer choose.

The story, however, takes an unusual turn. As the story progresses, the issue becomes whether the son will sacrifice his father. Indeed, the issue becomes more what is the mind of Isaac rather than what is the mind of Abraham.[7] Does the son have a choice? The son does have a choice in that he can hang on or let go. Either choice brings devastating consequences. To hang on, the son must struggle to keep two people alive. To let go, the son must accept the end of pure selfishness. Even more, the son is bound by the command of God. This is the command of God, to hang on, to honor your father. Even if obedience comes as instinct and not commitment, what does that matter? This is the burden that the son carries because he chooses to hang on.

Thus, through this image, we are confronted with the real theological struggle—to hang on. And why do these victims hang on to their beliefs after all that had been done to destroy these beliefs. Berkovitz is correct, the Nazis not only desired to destroy Jews but Jewish life, Judaism itself.[8] The entire onslaught was aimed to destroy every reason to believe, to live out the tradition. Thus, the ending of the story and its reality culminates this struggle—the father is removed during

CHAPTER 2:
THE SHAPE OF CHRISTIAN RESPONSE

The Christian Looking On

Elie Wiesel's judgment that it was not Judaism who died in the Shoah but Christianity is a bitter epitaph.[1] It is also a strange irony in terms of Wiesel's own biographical story,[2] for if Wiesel is the one who authors both the story and this judgement on Christianity, then Christianity occupies a place in the story comparable to Wiesel's father. The question of interpretation is tricky since Elie's view of the naive acceptance of tradition after the Shoah may or may not be symbolized in this death scene (or the lack of a death scene as if tradition has vanished without notice) even though it appears that it does. The point is that both Jewish tradition and traditional Christianity die at "Auschwitz" even if for radically different reasons.[3] Christians perpetrated the Shoah, at least they called themselves true Christians. Christians stood by as bystanders looking on; but Christianity was the victim who disappears without much notice in the actions or inaction of those who believed they were carrying the banner of Christianity. The literary figure of Eliezer's father vanishing without a trace silently in the night matches the figure of Christianity also dying silently. This is irony. If history tells us that Judaism was the parent of Christianity, then history speaks incessantly of the rebelling child lashing out to destroy the parent. But the Shoah reverses this story as well. A renewed Judaism is born out of the brutality and indifference of a failed Christianity and the source that ultimately gave birth also to this brutality in spite of itself has perished.

All these are images that lead us toward some of the meaning of our post-Auschwitz world. In actual fact, traditional Judaism almost apparently undisturbed by the horror of the kingdom of the night and traditional Christianity unaware of its dissolution in the flames of Auschwitz still survive—the gap between the two wider than ever, each claiming complete knowledge of the other but in fact continuing a dangerous ignorance. The threat to the survival of Judaism continues unabated in such a world of ignorance and unacknowledged participation in Auschwitz. In this sort of world where the story of the kingdom of the night is seldom heard, the mood is not naive innocence but an unbelievable blindness that reiterates the fears of those who believe that no lesson has been learned, no story heard. This fear emanates from the despair even of Elie Wiesel.

Emil Fackenheim claims that no healing *(Tikkun)* can take place in Christianity until the rupture is acknowledged.[4] In Fackenheim's view, traditional Christianity (represented by the "teaching of contempt") can escape its imminent death only by realizing that it has already taken place. If that sounds like gibberish, then it is the language that has been thrust upon Christianity by the kingdom of the night. What we expect is not a resuscitation of Christianity but a resurrection. That is the sort of healing that Fackenheim is speaking of.

If this challenge is taken seriously, then Christianity is thrust into the position of the bystander by necessity. Christianity cannot claim continuity with a tradition that produced the hatred that led to genocide. All the rationale that can be given to defend traditional Christianity cannot escape the literal truth that Christians found in the Nazis the distorted but logical conclusion of a long held wish—that Jews and Judaism be eliminated from the world.[5] But Christians cannot have hoped for that end if they were to be true to Christianity. Still, we say that only after the fact. We know Christianity cannot mean that in reality only now, after the Nazis nearly succeeded in eliminating Jews and Judaism from Europe. Thus, there is a radical break with our past, a gulf between us and our ancestors not only in perception but in the stark reality of what happened because of us, in spite of us, with little we could do to change the end. We are in danger of being made bystanders in relation to our own tradition in spite of ourselves. We can claim these as our Christian ancestors only with difficulty even though we know they were accepted by others as Christians.

There is still yet another gulf that is at least as wounding to us. Christians claimed the role of missionary to the world before the kingdom of the night. Many still do not realize that the voices of Auschwitz have almost drowned out our witness.[6] Above all, Christianity claimed to witness to the Jew. We, in our ancestors, claimed the heritage of Jewish tradition, to be the true Israel. In our boldest moments, we might have been led to claim that simply speaking the "gospel" should convince the other of truth, the truth. We could, then, in our arrogance, claim that those who refused to listen were deaf to the truth, agents of the anti-Christ. We could even relegate them to hell. Ironically, the majority of Christians did indeed relegate the Jews of Europe to a "hell," even a million children who could claim no real knowledge of Christian witness.

And what is the gulf I am referring to here? Surely we say again that Christianity in so blinding itself to the evils of arrogance before God became unwittingly the tool of evil even while we were still accusing the so-called deaf of being the anti- Christ. That is, of course, the ostensible background to the failure of Christian witness during the Shoah. Whatever the reason, the failure is sure. The witness to the truth failed in its own territory, failed to sustain the believers in moral behavior spawning instead the seeds of the most horrible of evils. But this is not all. This gulf is still the rupture we experience with our own past. The much more devastating rupture is the realization that we Christians can never again assume the posture of the "true" Israel in relation to the "living" Israel. Even if our claims were (are) true, what credibility do they have with the Jewish people.[7] Even if the Jewish people were prepared to accept truth in Christianity at one point in time (e.g., Franz Rosenzweig),[8] how is it possible for them to do so now. Our claims are hollow. They do not restore the six million. Above all, they do not erase the memory of brutality, suffering, death. We are condemned for as long as the healing needs, a thousand years or more, to stand on the outside wanting to share just even in the pain and the memory to restore some of the credibility; but we might stand on the outside looking on now regardless with our only hope being the unlikely invitation to come in except that as unlikely as everything else we have talked about, the invitation that has come despite all odds.

So how does the one looking on tell the story of the kingdom of the night? Despite the disadvantage of being on the outside looking in, it is essential for us to tell a story. We too belong to the generation that must bear the burden of assuring the Shoah does not happen again. We can bear that burden only if we tell the story. Nevertheless, what we say will be our story. It will be the story of the one standing on the outside looking in, shaped by our experiences and perspective. This story will most assuredly have three components: (1) the story of the bystander, (2) the story of the collaborator, but also (3) the story of the resister/rescuer. This is the complexity of the story of the kingdom of the night for the Christian, each character with a separate view of the horror, a separate picture of the victim and a separate set of values that justified their actions.[1]

Notes

[1]This remark came in an interview with Harry James Cargas as noted by Cargas in Harry James Cargas, *A Christian Response to the Holocaust*, (Denver: Stonehenge Books, 1981), p. 31.

[2] Actually, I refer to that portion of his story published as *Night*, (New York: Bantam Books, 1960).

[3] This claim is built on a reading of the conclusion of *Night* (p. 106) in which Elie's father symbolizes the forced break with tradition even as he dies.

[4] Emil Fackenheim, *To Mend the World*, (New York: Schocken Books, 1982), p. 280.

[5] Again many have reviewed this connection, but we are reminded especially of the now familiar analysis of Raul Hilberg, *The Destruction of the European Jews*, (New York: Harper and Row, 1961), pp. 3-4.

[6] Again this idea comes as a paraphrase of the challenges that Irving Greenberg thrust before us nearly 15 years ago in "Cloud of Smoke, Pillar of Fire:...", p. 13

[7] Greenberg, p. 13.

[8] Rosenzweig's conciliatory position can be found in Franz Rosenzweig, *The Star of Redemption*, (Notre Dame: Notre Dame Univ. Press, 1985), pp. 337ff. Even so, Rosenzweig's position is no capitulation of Judaism but a renewed mission for Judaism. We are now quite familiar with Emil Fackenheim's critique of Rosenzweig, as for example in Ibid., Emil Fackenheim, *To Mend the World*, pp. 149ff.

CHAPTER 3:
MIDRASH AS THE FORM OF RESPONSE

The Shoah is the most profound shaping event for Christian theology in the twentieth century (perhaps for many centuries). Johannes Metz has said:

> What Christian theologians can do for the murdered of Auschwitz and thereby for a true Jewish-Christian ecumenism is, in every case, this: Never again to do theology in such a way that its construction remains unaffected, or could remain unaffected, by Auschwitz.[1]

Even if theologians recognize this as true, few seem to be prepared to take the challenge seriously. That is to say, Metz' view not only means that theologies must somehow account for the meaning of Auschwitz (if that were possible) theologically but also that the event must shape the very doing of theology hereafter. All theodicies, all discussions of sin, evil, suffering, redemption, christology, morality, eschatology must be viewed in the light of Auschwitz so that all Christian theology will become post-Shoah theology.

Theologians who have taken the challenge seriously (and there are any number of important contributions)[2] have created important initial steps toward fashioning a new kind of Christian theology. This theology will conceive new terms for Jewish- Christian relations (from the Christian perspective). This theology will seek to eradicate the "Teaching of Contempt"[3] from all theological claims and the teaching of those theologies. This theology will focus upon critical areas not only of specifically Christian concern but also of Jewish concern that can bring new light to Christian theologies. This theology will be done in the context of Jewish-Christian dialogue. The efforts thus far have been impressive even if tardy in the light of Christian theological history.[4]

Nevertheless, the challenge that Metz presents us with (and many others for that matter[5]) is more profound than just the isolation of significant themes or the designation of particular work. The challenge is to the doing of theology as well as the content of the theology. What sort of new method might both make appropriate space for the story of Auschwitz as theologically integral for Christian theology as well as turn our attention to the re-doing of the whole of Christian theology? I propose, generally at the suggestion of a number of colleagues in dialogue, that Christian theology after Auschwitz be a midrash, a new Christian midrash. This midrash now must account for both the insights of reflection on the Shoah as well as provide a new basis for interpretation of Christian texts for the doing of Christian theology.[6] The following chapter will sketch a brief rationale for just such a theological method and offer an extended example of its application to Christian texts.

What is a Christian Midrash?

We strike out on new ground, in a way, by suggesting midrash as the form of our post-Shoah theology. Indeed, it is somewhat presumptuous to use the word midrash for our own, a word so characteristically identified with Rabbinic theology and interpretation. I would not do so if I were not encouraged in that direction by Jewish thinkers such as Daniel Cohn-Sherbok and Blu Greenberg. What we do not have is a similar body of Christian literature. Thus, the shape of this theological approach must be borrowed from Jewish tradition, perhaps using Barry Holtz' description as a guide.[7] Holtz argues that there are two ways that the word can be understood. First, the word refers to an approach to interpretation characterized by a long history of Rabbinic study (4th-12th Centuries C.E.). This approach can be rather specifically defined but also reflects a great diversity of approach that has more or less produced rules of interpretation together with a range of possible theological positions. Midrash is, thus, characterized by some plurality and with that ambiguity in meaning that represents a view of interpretation that is always perceived to be open-ended.

Our theology cannot simply reproduce the various rules and patterns of Rabbinic midrash; however the midrashic literature together with a style of theological reflection represented by this literature even into contemporary Jewish thought from Hasidic literature and modern Rabbinic interpretation can be a model for the type of theological interpretation intended in this book. Holtz argues that midrash ought to cover both traditional *halakah* and *aggadah*, both legal prescription and theological/moral storytelling. As such, midrash represents a broad range of possible readings of any text that enhances even more the current of ambiguity in this theological approach. The aggadic material of Genesis can produce legal pronouncements (such as with the *shofar*) and the legal material of Leviticus can be food for theological stories. The point is to provide an interpretation for the community so that ways of understanding the Torah for each new generation can be established.

The second meaning of midrash is as a designation of a body of written material (eg., the Mishnah). Thus, particular texts become models of interpretation for any new interpretation creating a link between the rabbis of each era, a link of interpretation. Thus, even with the character of open-endedness that introduces both plurality and ambiguity into what is meant by midrash, the tradition becomes a context that limits and guides new interpretation. This conception of a growing body of interpretive literature represents as best as we can note the basic principle of "Oral Torah" that has operated within Rabbinic interpretation since the beginning of the common era. This notion of Oral Torah establishes a style of theology built on hermeneutics, an interpretive relation to written Torah as the way of producing theology for the community.

Indeed, this style of doing theology has long been present also in Christianity as a residue of the Jewish roots of our faith tradition. Interpretive theology only gradually became replaced by categorical theologies in the medieval period; nevertheless the tradition of building theologies directly out of an interpretation of scripture has always been present in the history of Christian thought even if somewhat mixed with a dogmatic, philosophical, categorical tradition. Thus, even though the suggestion of a Christian midrash is a new road in many ways for Christian theology, it is also a very ancient road for Christian theology—a style characteristic of most of the early church fathers (Justin, Ignatius, Iranaeus, eg.). In fact, the divisions of *halakah* and *aggadah,* though clearly Jewish in their definition, can be seen in some ways in the writings of these early Christian thinkers.

Even more than that, Christian scripture has the character (the style is intentional) of midrash in that nearly all of this text is aimed as a specific interpretation of Torah and the life of Jesus. If this fact is recognized in our own reading of the Christian texts, then meaning of various texts can take on new light. Part of what will happen as we pursue this task of forming a new Christian midrash will be the discovery of new meanings in our texts simply because we read them now rather specifically as Christian midrash.[8] Thus, we gain much by returning to a new reading of the Christian scriptures as midrash rather than to read them through the theological traditions and layers of interpretation that have been produced in the dogmatic/systematic theological traditions.

In order to lead ourselves back into a midrashic interpretation of the Christian scripture, then we are required to strip away dogmatic assertions as necessary elements of our theologies. We must retreat behind Nicea and the subsequent theological tradition in order to retrieve the texts in a new light. As such, we are identifying this Christian midrash with exegesis, Biblical theology if you will. Still, the entire exegetical tradition in Christian circles has been sifted through certain kinds of theological presuppositions that make a simple identification of midrash with exegesis rather difficult.[9] Almost no Christian commentary on texts is free of these theological presuppositions (for example, how to view the Pharisees of the gospel narratives) that feed any and all interpretations of individual texts. The only way to escape this is to envision a theology done outside of the exclusively Christian circle of interpretation, that is, *to make Jewish-Christian dialogue the context for post-Shoah Christian theology.*

Once we have established this rule of post-Shoah theology, we are drawing closer to a rationale for a new Christian midrash. That is, we not only know, now, what such a theology might be like but also why this theology, this midrash, must be new. Three factors make this newness imperative for us. First, all of Christian theology of the past has been riddled with an integral teaching of contempt for the Jews. This teaching of contempt is at least as viral among the early church fathers (that is, those who might be models for a Christian midrash) as in later centuries. There is little evidence to show that we could be successful in culling from the church fathers a philo-Jewish theology as the teaching of contempt appears to be a central principle of these early theologies. Since the eradication of the teaching of contempt is a primary goal of post-Shoah Christian theology, then this theology (our midrash) must be a new effort than what we have seen in the past.

Second, the Shoah presents us with a radically new event that could not have been a matter of reflection for a past generation of Christians. The character of the challenge of the Shoah to Christianity has been quite adequately presented by any number of scholars. Thus, the radically new era that we now live in demands an alternative interpretation of Christian scripture, even as that is the very character of midrash itself. We need theologies (as Metz has challenged us) that account for the Shoah as a shaping factor in our theologies. Determining how the Shoah shapes our midrash is a central concern for this new Christian midrash.

The third factor is really an implication arising from the presence of the first two. Eradicating Christianity of a teaching of contempt for Jews requires a theology that makes religious pluralism central to Christian self-understanding. To accept pluralism theologically means that we become prepared to accept levels of theological ambiguity. These two principles of our theology need further explication but are now introduced as vital elements of our new Christian midrash (indeed, they are, as we have seen, characteristic of midrash and become new for Christian theology as Christians have attempted to systematically eliminate both pluralism and ambiguity in our theologies until the very recent past).

Pluralism and Ambiguity as Central Theological Principles

This process of re-interpretation can develop from the recognition of the plurality of meanings in the text, itself. Any text bears a host of possible readings depending on authorial intent, general context (in the text or in the social world of the text), the intended audience, and the view of the reader (or any combination of these factors); and new readings of the Christian scripture (e.g., the passion narratives) have received direction from one or all of these factors rethought or reconceived. The recognition that the social world of the narrative story was both the Hellenistic setting of the early church (and gospel author) and the Jewish world that formed the context of Jesus' teaching and life already provides a plurality of possible readings (and greater ambiguity in interpretation).[10] Surely, the recognition of the Jewishness of Jesus and, perhaps, of the early Christian authors sheds new light on how certain texts ought to be read.

In like manner, the audience presumed by the narratives is at least both Greco-Roman and Jewish. Given that, the texts can also be read differently depending on who might be the perceived audience. Again, this point is not a new one but can become a source for new thinking if set into a post-Shoah theology together with the influences upon just such a theology already mentioned above.[11] Three decades ago, Krister Stendahl suggested that the gospel of Matthew represented a teaching document for a school whose leader used rabbinic teaching and interpreting techniques—that is to say, a Christian midrash.[12] Jacobus Schoneveld much more recently has suggested that the pattern of the gospel of John indicates that the gospel writer took Jesus to be "the oral Torah." Thus, the gospel can be seen as the foundation for a midrash on the tradition focussing on Jesus' teaching as guide for that midrash.[13]

Now, that claim that Christian scripture is itself a sort of midrash linked with the possibility that the Christian texts can become a source for alternative interpretations leads us in a direction that is, on the surface, quite different from much of the Christian interpretive tradition. In fact, the church has argued through the centuries that insofar as the gospels are true revelation they are a light to interpret the ancient teaching of the law and the prophets. Schoneveld's argument is not in form strikingly different from tradition. Instead, the substance of the interpretation becomes the real innovation as post-Shoah thinkers begin considering Christian scripture as a contribution to a larger rabbinic tradition rather than in opposition to it; to take seriously the notion of Jesus as "rabbi" rather than as opponent of the rabbis. To argue that Jesus is the oral Torah is to demand, post-Shoah, that this teaching be tested in the context of dialogue and in the light of the Shoah by Torah (together with the complex Jewish Tradition of interpretation of the Torah). This claim pushes us one step further—to recognize that the principal focus is once again the written Torah (in its broadest sense) rather than the gospel narratives themselves. Jesus as oral Torah still points to the written Torah as the locus of authority, as the center of God's revelation. Even if we, as Christians in this post-Shoah world, still feel that we must argue that Jesus is new revelation, this revelation must be understood in conjunction with the principal revelation in Torah.

The gospel narratives, eg., are, thus, not primarily stories of Jesus but are taken to be commentary on Torah, and such is the case with the passion narratives. The passion narratives are historical in character in that they convey a view of certain events, but these are events taken to be revelation—that is, expanding our understanding of Torah, most particularly on the question of theodicy. As such, we as readers are invited to set the narratives alongside of other historical efforts within the tradition to understand theodicy—the *Tanach*—that are also commentary upon the Passover-Sinai discussion of theodicy among others within written Torah. Nevertheless, these are more than just commentary but represent new insight into how the tradition should be read and understood.

It is not surprising, then, that for Christians the passion narratives represent a conclusive, new advance in the understanding of Torah, of covenant, of the presence of evil and suffering, of human frailty and sin. The problematic for us, post-Shoah, is not that Christians regard the gospels as scripture (how could they treat them otherwise?), as conclusive revelation, but that this revelation was cut off from its connection to Torah and made to stand isolated as revelation—as Rosemary Ruether has argued, the event was reified,[14] thus denying the text its initial legitimate role in favor of the status of "new testament." Jesus, rather than being oral Torah, was transposed into the eternal logos.[15]

All of this history is familiar to those involved with dialogue. What has not been thoroughly recognized yet is that this reification of the text also effectively shut off the openness to plurality that is born by the text itself when the text, now as isolated revelation, becomes the principal resource for theology. The post-apostolic era of Christianity was not only left with a fundamentally gentile understanding of the gospel narratives but also with the narrow task of focussing on Jesus as the only source of truth—the nature of Jesus, the principal character in the narrative, became the sole preoccupation of Christian theology. Most post-Shoah theologies, despite their differences,[16] have sought to reintroduce the possibility for openness in the text by reaffirming its dependency upon Torah as the principal source of revelation.[17] I suggest we move one step further, from the plurality of options available in contemporary Christian thought in this work, even beyond the admission that certain views can be judged more adequate than others in our post-Shoah world, to the development of a post-Shoah midrash of these texts of the gospel passion narratives that can provide rules for reading the texts as midrash on Torah.

Notes

[1]Johannes Baptist Metz, *The Emergent Church* (New York: Crossroad, 1981), p. 28.

[2]cf. James F. Moore, "A Spectrum of Views: Traditional Christian Responses to the Holocaust," *Journal of Ecumenical Studies*, 25:2, Spring 1988, pp. 212-224.

[3]cf., Jules Isaac, *The Teaching of Contempt: Christian Roots of Anti-Semitism*, (New York: Holt, Rinehart and Winston, 1964).

[4]Among the most impressive is the three volume work of Paul van Buren, *A Theology of the Jewish-Christian Reality*, Parts 1-3 (New York: Harper and Row, 1980, 1983, 1988).

[5]cf., Irving Greenberg, "Cloud of Smoke, Pillar of Fire: Judaism, Christianity, and Modernity after the Holocaust," in Eva Fleischner, ed., *Auschwitz: Beginning of a New Era?* (New York: KTAV Publishing House, 1977), p. 13.

[6]The rationale for this proposal can be found in James F. Moore, "The Holocaust and Christian Theology: A Spectrum of Views on the Crucifixion and the Resurrection in the Light of the Holocaust" in Yehuda Bauer, ed., *Remembering for the Future*, 3 volumes (New York: Pergamon Press, 1989), vol. I, pp. 844-857.

[7]Barry Holtz, "Midrash," in *Back to the Sources*, (New York: Simon and Schuster, 1986), pp. 177-211.

[8]cf., the related work of Gerald Bruns, Midrash and Allegory: the Beginnings of Scriptural Interpretation," in Robert Alter and Frank Kermode, ed., *The Literary Guide to the Bible*, (Cambridge: Harvard University Press, 1987), pp. 625-646.

[9]While midrash can almost be identified with exegesis in a general sense, the way that exegesis and Biblical theology that has developed from Christian exegesis has been limited to aspects of historical criticism—source, text, form, redaction and literary—would be too limiting for a new Christian midrash as envisioned here or for an understanding of traditional Jewish midrash.

[10]Any number of texts can be suggested as support for this claim such as Eduard Lohse, *The New Testament Environment*, (Nashville: Abingdon Press, 1971).

[11]This direction of thought already suggested in three previous papers is initially adapted from the work of David Tracy, "Religious Values after the Holocaust," in *Jews and Christians after the Holocaust*, Abraham Peck, ed., (Philadelphia: Fortress Press, 1982), p. 92.

[12]Stendahl's work is well known and can be found in Krister Stendahl, *The School of St. Matthew*, (Uppsala: G.W.K. Gleerup, 1954). Naturally, the conclusion that the gospel is midrash is

CHAPTER 4:
APPROACHING THE TEXT

Focussing on The Text

The task I have suggested is far too massive to assume in this book, but a beginning can be made to show how to shape the foundation for a new post-Shoah theology. Such a theology can develop through a series of stages that move gradually toward a narrower focus on the specifics of the narratives. Three stages, two on which I have already written—are evident in the logic of the development of this theology. The last of these three stages leads us directly to a focus on the Christian scriptural texts (especially the gospel passion narratives) and to a more fully developed constructive proposal than I have made to this point—to the hints of a post-Shoah midrash.

Any initial venture into a Christian response to the Shoah opens up the obvious—that there is a full spectrum of responses even if limited to those who take the Shoah seriously as a challenge to Christian theology.[1] Responses can range from those who leave the tradition intact as the resource for making an adequate response to the Shoah to the opposite trend of leaving little of the tradition to stand before the challenge of the Shoah. Naturally, each position along the spectrum produces different strategies for interpretation of the tradition and different criteria for judging whether a view is adequate or not.

If this discovery is obvious, then we can learn much about the plurality of possible readings of Christian scripture simply by following basic patterns for each typical position on the spectrum. For example, traditional Christian theologies which perceive the passion narrative as the foundation for a theology of reconciliation still attribute universal reconciliation to the suffering of Jesus on the cross as described in the narratives. This is not to say that such positions find the task easy or untroubled but are still framed to use traditional Christian categories and theologies for an understanding of the suffering not only on the cross but at Auschwitz as well.[2]

On the other hand, a radically restructuring of the texts of the passion narratives might emphatically deny to the narrative any normative position for understanding suffering or even reconciliation. Instead, the narrative may be read by these as a principal source for the long tradition of the teaching of contempt, thus, calling for not only Christian repentance, not only for a Christian position of stark humility before the "unthinkable" of the Shoah, but also for radical surgery of the text denying aspects of the narrative that imply Jewish complicity in crime and/or rejection of the Jews by God. Indeed, for these thinkers the Shoah becomes a critical tool brought to bear on a Christian tradition woefully inadequate to meet the challenge of the Shoah.[3]

We can see in this not only a full range of possible readings of the text but also the potential for developing criteria of relative adequacy—judging whether certain statements, certain interpretations, even certain full positions are no longer tenable in a post-Shoah Christian theology. Indeed, the position that holds that we are punished for our sins (Jewish or Christian even though the two perspectives are clearly different views) is considered by most post-Shoah thinkers to be completely unacceptable as a way to understand the suffering of the Shoah. Such a judgment affects both our reading of the passion narrative and the theologies that develop from that (such as satisfaction theories of atonement).[4]

Most Christian responses to the Shoah can be set along this spectrum and understood on those terms even if these theologies often cross between types in moving from issue to issue. While such a discovery provides a clue for moving forward from our present point (that there are a host of alternative positions) of thought, such movement depends on rising above the spectrum in order to incorporate the fact of Christian plurality (and with that, clear recognition of textual ambiguity)[5] into a post-Shoah theology.

Thus, a second stage of the process toward constructing a post-Shoah Christian theology is the application of these principles (the notion of plurality of views and the ambiguity of textual meaning) not as a device to establish yet another firm position on the spectrum but rather as a way of reading the texts. As significant as the theologies of Van Buren, Littell, Eckhardt, Tracy, Ruether, and Pawlikowski[6] are, they provide only a beginning point toward a new kind of theology and are all too easily trapped in the form of pre-Shoah theologies; and there is little to suggest that any such theology will not be subject to the same abuses that have occurred in the past despite the good intentions of present thinkers. Our interest is to counteract the teaching of contempt effectively,[7] which means that we must approach both the material taught and the means by which it is taught.[8]

This second stage leads directly to a study of the Christian Biblical texts[9] which can allow the texts their own ambiguity, searching all the while in this study for help from various contemporary thinkers who might provide vehicles for enhancing the ambiguity. The point is not to suggest lack of direction but rather to open up new direction. For example, the passion narrative understood theologically can render a series of, at the very least, ironic claims. The troublesome story in the gospel of Matthew of the confrontation between Pilate and the crowds is fraught with irony even as the gospel writers superficially attempt to whitewash Pilate by laying full blame on the Jews (on the chief priests and pharisees). The figure of Pilate is by no means completely innocent. The ritual acts of abiding by tradition and washing his hands make Pilate appear as a weak figure; yet it is he who retains the power of execution and gives the order to crucify. The whole interchange appears no more than a show. This is irony in that the incident is by no means read this way normally, nor is the narrative necessity of including the incident sufficient reason for providing definitive theological meaning to the text. In fact, it is at least one portion of this narrative that demands being left as theologically ambiguous.

Naturally, this ambiguity is more critical theologically when the text is considered in relation to the events of the Shoah. We cannot pretend an historical continuity between the story of Jesus' passion and the stories of mass genocide in the Shoah as if the reasons for the murders were the same. The entire context of reasons surrounding these two disparate events are different. How, then, can we pretend theological continuity as if one event so completely different can be used to explain or give meaning to the other? Our tongues are literally tied in this matter and the Biblical text fails to provide ready meaning to help us understand the "unthinkable" of the Shoah. That is, this text that has so often been used to rationalize contempt for the Jews is rendered silent, speechless.

Nevertheless, the text remains central for Christian confession and as such cannot be used anymore as if the meaning it bears is unambiguous, but there are no ready rules for interpreting these texts except for the theological tradition that has now been rendered silent. The tradition of theological thought can no longer be used to read the texts of Christian scripture authentically without a transformation of the perspective of that theology. The text, now isolated from the theologies of Christian tradition, can be read on its own now in *all* of its ambiguity. The interplay of the images of the suffering servant and the sacrificial lamb which give theological background to the interchange between Pilate and the people (the text is, in part, a midrash on these traditions and symbols) bears the very ambiguity we speak of given the flow of the text rather than a pre-determined theological framework. Even the statement, "His blood be upon us and on our children," bears an unmistakable irony in that the imagery holds that the blood is precisely that which sanctifies. Pilate's very act of washing his hands is an open, symbolic act of rejecting this redemption. He is both innocent and guilty. Can that be? We have not uncovered a new reading to replace the old but rather we have laid bare the ambiguity in the original text which, in itself, renders unambiguous theologies of contempt of Jews untenable, unchristian. How can we hold the people in contempt who by their very actions, admittedly according to this very Christian viewpoint, fulfill the will of God? We cannot answer this question other than to say that we no longer can read this narrative in the same way as before, not even on the basis of a steadfastly Christian understanding. We will refuse to give foundation for a teaching of contempt in the text despite our interpretative tradition.

This second stage of developing a post-Shoah Christian theology is an open attack on the mechanics of a teaching of contempt which can thrive only on an unambiguous reading of the text, only among those who are sure of its truth. Even more, we can see that the text need not be the source of this teaching. Quite the contrary, the teaching itself has been imposed from the outset upon the text as a way of assuming unambiguous meaning in a narrative that is essentially ambiguous. The teaching is a theological perspective that is imposed eisogetically upon the text and has little warrant from within the text itself.[10]

Having progressed to this point, we cannot aim to formulate a new theology to be imposed upon the narrative no matter how inviting that might be. We aim instead to generate rules for reading that enable the ambiguity of the text to be fully utilized in our Christian teaching—that is, we need a new Christian midrash of the text. This midrash would accomplish two things at least—(1) we could provide the foundation for a tradition[11] of a teaching of respect, and (2) we could provide a means for reclaiming the texts as scripture—as sources of theological meaning— even on the themes of redemption and suffering so difficult in our post-Shoah age. This task, then, becomes the principal focus of the rest of this book.

The midrash I aim for is not strictly of the classical type of rabbinic midrash with its rules but rather like that modelled in the work of Elie Wiesel (surely Wiesel's work is fully within the tradition of midrash even so) in his efforts to reclaim his own tradition post-Shoah. Nevertheless, there are some basic rules to establish before we can proceed. First, the context for any Christian theology post-Shoah is, at least, the Jewish- Christian dialogue.[12] That is to say, the community of interpretation and adjudication is not simply the Christian academic or ecclesial community but also a presumed Jewish community in conversation with Christians (potentially at various levels of engagement and with differing goals). To expand the principle further, we can use a modification of Irving Greenberg's familiar dictum—we must not say anything theologically post-Shoah that we could not say in the presence of the one million children who died.[13] This rule means literally that our theology is done in the context of a memory and also that all of our theology must speak in the way that we would in the presence of our Jewish colleagues. This is a principle of formulation that implies that all theology (even that done in relative isolation) is done in the presumed context of dialogue.

A second set of rules develops from a fundamental view of the relative Christian relation to the Shoah. It is possible to think that Christians and/or Christianity can be aptly called victims of the Shoah. Now on a certain level that may be true. However, there are serious difficulties even with talking about the Jewish people as victims of the Shoah. Still, we know that Jews were victims in a far more profound, far different, far more central way than were any Christians or Christianity as such. Even the blessed who acted as righteous gentiles were victims in a very different way than were those they tried to save. If we are to use the Shoah as criteria for examining the Christian narratives, therefore, we cannot presume that we as Christians can draw direct implications from the idea of victim in the biblical texts to the real victims of the Shoah. Can we presume to render judgment about what it means to be a victim from a Christian theology? Our perspective is rather that of the outsider, at first: one whose relation to the Shoah is being outside of the center looking in. The question for us is rather how Christians responded in that context—how they thought and then acted on behalf of, in indifference toward, or in animosity to the Jews.[14]

These rules naturally confine the possible readings of the narrative (although we can allow the text its full ambiguity and plurality). They are, nevertheless, essential rules, criteria for interpretation that remain in place as essential elements of a post-Shoah theology. They may help lead us to select certain possible readings to form a judgment about meaning but are not intended to exclude possible readings except insofar as those readings transgress the memory of those who died.

A Christian Midrash Taking Shape

The particular texts that have formed the basis for theologies of redemption in the gospel passion narratives are too numerous to give full attention to in this paper. Thus, what follows is a selective example of how a new midrash can be developed on the Christian texts. The selective tool I am using is developed in the next section of this book as a schema for reading possible Christian perspectives of the Shoah. I do so because the elements of this narrative sequence confront us with the most serious problems we, as Christians, have in retrieving our scriptures post-Shoah. The narrative sequence also presents us with ambiguities that are resident in the texts as they conflict with one another in narrative detail. Our interest is to suggest the plurality of ways that the texts present for us images of the various figures of the passion narrative insofar as those images form a foundation for Christian perspectives on indifference, betrayal, resistence and rescue.

Notes

[1] Moore, *Journal of Ecumenical Studies*.

[2] Among the most prominent of such thinkers is Juergen Moltmann, *The Crucified God*, (New York: Harper and Row, 1974).

[3] cf., Ruether, *Faith and Fratricide*.

[4] Probably the most thorough and persuasive critique of such positions can be found in A. Roy Eckardt and Alice Eckardt, *Long Night's Journey Into Day*, (Detroit: Wayne State Univ., 1982), pp. 82-110.

[5] Hints for this conclusion stem from a reaction to David Tracy, *Plurality and Ambiguity*, (New York: Harper and Row, 1987).

[6] Van Buren, *A Theology of the Jewish-Christian Reality*. Eckardt, *Long Night's Journey Into Day*. Ruether, *Faith and Fratricide*. Franklin Littell, *The Crucifixion of the Jews*, (New York: Harper and Row, 1975). David Tracy, "Religious Values after the Holocaust: a Catholic View," in *Jews and Christians after the Holocaust*, Abraham Peck, ed., (Philadelphia: Fortress Press, 1982). John Pawlikowski, *Christ in the Light of the Christian-Jewish Dialogue*, (New York: Paulist Press, 1982).

[7] I refer to the pointed perspective of Haim Macoby, "Antisemitism and the Christian Myth," in *Remembering for the Future* - Volume I, (New York: Pergamon Press, 1988), pp. 836-843.

[8] The first effort at this task can be found in Moore, *Remembering for the Future* - Vol. I, pp. 844-857.

[9] Cf. Moore, *Remembering for the Future*.

[10] The argument presented here is given fuller treatment in Moore, *Remembering for the Future*. Obviously, others have given different views such as, Ruether, *Faith and Fratricide*.

[11] Again, the use of the word "tradition" presents problems in this context. The point here is that only tradition can sustain any reform in scriptural interpretation as is suggested in these pages. I hearken to the work of Clark Williamson, *When Jews and Christians Meet* (St. Louis: CBP Press, 1988).

[12] I realize already that there is no readily identifiable community of dialogue participants. Many different forums have been designed to facilitate dialogue, each with a specified purpose and natural limitations. Still, the conference "Remembering for the Future" which met in Oxford in the summer of 1988 demonstrates that there is a dialoguing community that could represent the context

for the kind of work suggested in this paper. Cf., the volumes of the conference, *Remembering for the Future,* Volumes I-III.

[13] Irving Greenberg, "Cloud of Smoke and Pillar of Fire: Judaism, Christianity, and Modernity after the Holocaust," in *Auschwitz: Beginning of a New Era?*, Eva Fleischner, ed. (New York: KTAV, 1977), p. 23.

[14] We have any number of historical texts designed to map these behaviors each designed to reflect an historical perspective. The recent text by John Roth and Richard Rubenstein sketches a fair picture of the theological context of this set of responses (see Roth and Rubenstein, *Approaches to Auschwitz*).

CHAPTER 5:
THE BYSTANDER

The Bystander

Elie Wiesel never tires of repeating the phrase, the enemy of good is not so much open evil but indifference.[1] Evil openly done can be resisted but indifference remains only an unfathomable puzzle. And no matter how rational the reasons given, the bystander will always appear to be indifferent. The bystander may choose not to act out of fear, out of ignorance, out of bias, out of misguided loyalty or warped values. Whatever the reasons, the final result is that the bystander has implied that he/she chooses to make this none of their business, or can make this none of their business, or dare not make this any of their business. Abandoning the opportunity to save, to rescue, the bystander in indifference makes the terrifying difference of lending support to evil by refusing to resist evil.

Of course, indifference is then a form of collaboration. It is another factor in the formula of destruction, undoubtedly predictable. Large proportions of a population will simply choose not to act to resist and thus allow our plan to go forward unabated, the perpetrators will say. They could depend on this is easily as on the small groups of collaborators in each occupied area. And, if terror assures continued indifference, what could be easier to instill? Surely in the decades after the horror we are even more convinced of the ease and success of terror at all levels of society. We know how easily we can become prisoner of terror, even extended by our self-imposed fears.

Emil Fackenheim has argued that the form and intent of the Nazi "Final Solution" could not have been anticipated by any general view of morality, history, politics, or human nature.[2] He, in effect, says that we were trapped by our innocence of such horror and thus by the terror that was integral to the Nazi ideology. Surely we recognize the implications of Fackenheim's conclusion. If our past did not give us the essential wisdom and courage to resist no matter who we might have been, then the whole of our past stands reduced to failure before this great challenge. We can so easily agree with this realizing that so many were pawns in a game that they could not anticipate let alone play.

But we are talking of bystanders who were also professing Christians. We are talking not just about individuals who are so susceptible to threat not only to themselves but also to all who might be affected by their actions. We are also talking about institutions of Christianity with resources of both moral and political influence. These leaders also chose to make this event none of their business or chose to hide behind rationales of all sorts—of ignorance, of lack of means, of unclear moral choices, of fear for others, of misguided loyalties, of ancient stereotypes and prejudices.[3] No single category of explanation can be brought to this fact. The result may not be surprising to many, but we are forced to admit that even the church can be made a prisoner of terror, an admission that strikes at the core of Christian witness to the redeeming and freeing power of the grace of God. "There is no fear in love, perfect love casts away all fear." (I John 4:18)

And what story can we tell to begin to understand this fact of our most recent past. We have one story that stands at the heart of all we profess. This story is the foundation of understanding for all other things in our existence and now receives a great test when confronted by the enormity of the Shoah. Might we reach the same conclusion as Wiesel did when he drew the great stories of Jewish identity into his story of the kingdom of the night? Surely, the questions that come to us now betray our wonder. How could a generation of Christians, despite a history of anti-Judaism, simply stand by and watch as a people were massacred? Can there be meaning found in our story to give explanation to this more recent tragedy? We are tempted to say no; Yet we must tell the story nevertheless because it is our story (both the story of the crucifixion of Jesus and the story of the "crucifixion of the Jews").[4] Our telling of the story must first be directed at the Christian community even as we hope to engender sensitivity to both the Shoah and Jewish-Christian dialogue. Thus, the dialogue voice of the Jew will be heard as we re-think the Christian story, but this will not yet be true dialogue. Still, even as we do this in each of the remaining chapters of this book, points of insight will appear where dialogue can take place as an invitation to carry forward the work done here toward a full conversation.

The story is complex in its telling.[5] Not all are merely bystanders, though most are. We can give focus to our story, however, by concentrating on the disciple, Peter. This is appropriate in the gospel context since the gospel writers surely accounted for the central role that Peter would later play in the new church. The gospels all mark Peter as a significant character in the whole gospel story giving him greater coverage than most except Jesus himself. Peter is quick to act, impetuous, often unthinking. Yet, he is bold and courage marks him as a leader of the twelve. He it is who steps out on the waters of the lake to greet his master. It is Peter who steps out to acclaim Jesus as lord. Peter is the one who refuses to let Jesus wash his feet only to be the central example for a lesson from the master. Peter refuses to believe that he would desert his teacher at the point of greatest threat. Still it is Peter who denies openly even knowing Jesus, refuses to associate with him, even as his boldness led him to the courtyard of High Priest, where according to the story he knew precisely the fate of his master. Listen to the text:

> But Peter was following him at a distance, as far as the courtyard of the high priest; and going inside, he sat with the guards in order to see how this would end... Now Peter was sitting outside in the courtyard. A servant-girl came to him and said, "You also were with Jesus the Galilean." But he denied it before all of them, saying, "I do not know what you are talking about." When he went out to the porch, another servant-girl saw him, and she said to the bystanders, "This man was with Jesus of Nazareth." Again he denied it with an oath, "I do not know the man." After a little while the bystanders came up and said to Peter, "Certainly you are also one of them, for your accent betrays you." Then he began to curse, and he swore an oath, "I do not know the man!" At that moment the cock crowed. Then Peter remembered what Jesus had said: "Before the cock crows, you will deny me three times." And he went out and wept bitterly. (Matt 26:58, 65-75)

This story has it all, drama, suspense, intrigue. It is a story that in the telling captivates the listener. It is the story of the first Christian bystander. I do not mean that Peter is the first to stand by watching when action would have been more appropriate not that this was the first time or opportunity for action that is passed up. Rather, I mean that Peter through this story becomes a symbol imbedded in the Christian story of the bystander. It is ironic that the story itself talks of the bystanders one of whom Peter eventually becomes. The first reference to the bystanders in the translated text simply means those who were there. The second clearly means those standing around idly, though it appears in the translation that the same word is used for both, actually two different Greek words are used to mean respectively standing firm beside someone or standing with someone. Peter ironically has the chance to do each of these but chooses by his own words to be one of those standing around idly vehemently denying any identity with Jesus.

Thus, the story portrays the failure of friendship at the time of crisis. Ideals are lost and personal safety protected. What makes this text so powerful to the

Christian is the central figure. Peter is the impulsive, courageous one. To deny, to back away is out of character for Peter. And we might say, if Peter refused to act, then can we be so sure that we would act? The intent of the story is clear. We do not in our humanness have the courage to lay our life on the line for a friend. The gospel writer intends that we listeners place ourselves into the story as Peter. Could we honestly expect to do any better?

Of course, the hypothetical question is just that. For each of us, each moment of decision is new. Peter's actions do not determine ours even if we cannot claim to be facing the same choice. The same options that confronted Peter as he stood by confront us. Our choice is our own; our failures our own. That challenge is also clear from the gospel text. If decision is the key matter for the presentation of the gospel message (and surely it is for Matthew's gospel), then this short episode becomes an important element in the intent of this gospel writer to challenge his readers to courageous action, to hold fast to the faith.

But Peter faced this moment that in many ways is not and cannot be ours. Peter is a symbol of decision, of the bystander, and not the mold our of which all are made. It is Peter's story that we tell first, and not succeeding generations who might learn from the story. Peter forfeits his chance to rescue Jesus or at least to stand by Jesus. He lives with the bitterness of the recognition of his failure, a guilt that we cannot share with him even if we might compare his failure with our own failures. And Peter, having sealed his fate, remembers. He remembers only after and in remembering is reminded of his own bold claim now brought to ruin in his equally bold denial. This is Peter even in action to deny, and he wept bitterly.

This is the story that is told so often and in the telling has created for us a memory bank that has become our story. If we cannot claim to be Peter, we still must claim Peter as a part of our story. Of all the embarrassments of this narrative in the collective failure of the collective failure of the disciples, Peter remains the symbol of the bystander. No matter how bold we might be in claiming discipleship, to be the actual followers of Jesus, this story is part of our history. We cannot deny Peter his place, Peter the bystander, a place that challenges our boldness and humbles us in our boldness. We cannot be so sure that we are really disciples, not in what we say or do.

But wait a minute! This story has other levels that are not so often told yet must by told. The narrative depicts a Peter who weeps over his own failure. Even so, the narrative contains another twist. Jesus predicts Peter's failure. This irony at is highest form. Peter's choice is his own but it is not his own. On the most minimal level, Peter's denial becomes a proof of the validity of Jesus as master. Could Peter have acted otherwise? Wasn't he a pawn on the stage of a play that was not of his own making? Or was it that Jesus knew Peter so well that he projected this scene out of that knowledge? But, then, why warn Peter of his coming acts? Is it to drive Peter to tears?

This dimension of the story is rarely told. The implications are not nearly so positive, nor are they so dramatic. We prefer to read the story in the traditional fashion thinking of Peter as a type of disciple of Jesus. We take some comfort in realizing that we small people surely cannot do any better than the great disciple, Peter. But what comfort is this gained at the expense of one driven to tears in a drama that he could not, would not control? Surely we know that on a more complex level that the narrative tells ultimately of a story that was historically necessary. Not one of the gospel writers would deny this even as they weave images as lessons for us. Peter's denial is seen as part of the whole story that would proceed as planned. Peter, in effect, had no choice. The options were false options. If Jesus death was truly the intended plan, then no action by Peter could have avoided this conclusion. Indeed no action at all, save that of God, not even the denial by Peter of Jesus, could change the outcome. All of the characters are depicted as actors on God's stage, acting at God's choosing.

Even more that this, if Jesus is depicted as unique in his death, then Peter could not, even by his own choosing, actually stand beside Jesus. Jesus must have by the full theological intent of the narrative been cast into complete loneliness. "My God, my God, why have you forsaken me?" And for this Peter weeps. This is irony as well. How can we weep for that which God intends? And good are our tears when it is God that determines finally our failures? Peter walks into this drama unaware except in the warning of a teacher. And his tears are wept bitterly because he knows that he could do nothing before God. He is helpless to change what God ordains and all that might be humanly hoped for comes to nothing in this realization.

But these might angry tears, not only of our own failures but anger that our world has left us no choices and we are confronted by a God who acts in ways we cannot understand. So we cower into our corners as Peter did. We weep for our world and the insanity that has become our experience still waiting for a word from God that can let us in on his secret. What are you doing to us Lord? What is the meaning of all of this? And our questions like peter's fade into the darkness of the moment and perhaps never are voiced except when we are alone, and then only in tears, bitter tears.

This is also our Christian story, part of the narrative that we have so usually claimed with little trouble. The first framework of the story fits comfortably into our experience, even if we are confronted by life-threatening decisions. The second framework fits nowhere in our experience since it reduces us to confusion, despair, and bitter tears. The Christian thinker, Roy Eckardt, has said often that the one thing that we Christians and Jews have left to us to do together is to weep together.[6] Are these the tears that he refers to. Not the tears of our own failures but the tears of despair in which we know God is involved but we have no word from him to give us hope, except the warning to Peter, we will deny him. But, of course, Peter's denial is not the same as the indifference of the bystanders during the Shoah. We will not claim that God planned the death of the six million. But does this mean that in the story of the Shoah God becomes the bystander?

It seems so trivial to say that Peter's denial is the first fruits of centuries of Christian denial of God. It is even more trivial, perhaps blasphemous, to claim that Peter's denial is echoed in the voices of the countless bystanders that time and again denied knowing their Jewish neighbors, who refused the option to stand by them instead of standing to the side looking on saying I do not know them. Standing idly by as trains were loaded and people were made cargo for destruction. Yet, could we claim complete ignorance of this destiny for our people with Peter as part of our story. We are bold to confess but cannot live that confession. We are constantly on the precipice of denial that drives us to the sidelines thus forfeiting our chance at discipleship. For this part of our heritage we weep bitter tears. They are all the more bitter because we know that they do nothing to erase the past; they cannot restore the dead or recreate hope. They are tears that flow simply because we recognize that nothing else is appropriate.[7]

But tears are not enough. We say this all the more since we know the other part of this story. We are also perplexed by God's own part in this. It doesn't help us to say that God has warned us of our own destructive tendencies, of our tendency toward failure. It doesn't help if God has set the stage and we, like Peter, are players in a drama not of our own making. Our cry has to rise to God. Our cries of despair that this could happen. But my cry is different than the one voiced by Elie Wiesel. My cry is that wonder, how could God allow the failures of the masses of Christians to be such a contributing factor in the mass destruction of the Jewish people? Surely, the narrative of the crucifixion and that of the Shoah are linked in a far more significant way than we have yet uncovered. But we weep bitter tears even more so because in the first narrative the plan of God is spelled out, given meaning. In this second narrative, we are not even so bold to claim just how God is acting or was acting let alone claiming some kind of plan. We are fearful of suggesting a plan that includes such massive destruction of human life. We instead weep bitter tears as did Peter who knew that after the fact he could do nothing to change what has happened. After the fact, we cannot change what Christians did not do during the Shoah. Indeed, in this latter narrative, can God do anything to change what has happened?[8]

But Peter is not left to his tears. This is the same Peter that becomes in discipleship to Jesus of Nazareth. How is it possible for the narrative to take such a turn? It is possible only in the two stages that we find in the extended narrative of the gospel texts - the empty tomb and the confrontation with the risen Jesus.

We ought not be surprised by the overwhelming treatment of the narratives on the empty tomb and the resurrection appearances.[9] These two pieces of the puzzle explain for us the sudden transformation of the disciples in the narrative. The question is not so much one of proof but one of understanding. Peter is brought back from despair and anger by his meeting with Jesus as the resurrected lord. We must leave the scientific believability of this narrative to the side for the time being. In terms of the narrative, the question of proof is quite irrelevant. The narrative makes sense only given the dramatic impact of Jesus reappearance. The whole of Christian narrative makes sense only in the light of this narrative event.

The event is really two. For Peter, the first part is again a moment of disappointment. Peter finds the tomb empty (or is left to receive the message that the tomb is empty whichever gospel is source). Peter is witness to the empty tomb but the tomb's emptiness leaves Peter not only with shocking disbelief and lack of understanding but also with continued guilt. The empty tomb cannot speak a new word of forgiveness for the tomb is empty and Peter was a bystander. He is outside of the circle in even more significant ways that the others because he personally refused to do anything. he was afraid, yes. He was caught unprepared, yes. He was openly challenged and in that challenge failed his opportunity. Even more, he denied his opportunity.

Empty tombs give no forgiveness. They are no less cold and harsh. They are even less than discovering the body for in the emptiness there is the threat that the pain and guilt will not end. Peter was a bystander who denied knowing Jesus and at the tomb is denied the chance to say farewell, to say words of grief and sorrow, to say *Kaddish*. Peter can be nothing but amazed and stunned. Words fail this in the darkness of deep despair. Peter was a bystander and he remains on the outside looking in.

The irony of this part of the resurrection narrative is so often missed. An empty tomb despite the words of promise is still an empty tomb. The first experience is still separation from Jesus, still assumed death. Why is the tomb empty with no risen lord to greet these disciples? The triumph of the narrative is postponed and the possible exaltation is dampened. We are greeted with one more disappointment that is only alleviated by the resurrection appearances. Human experience is such that the empty tomb (despite pointing to some meaning) does not bring joy or even belief. The message and the messenger at the tomb is greeted with surprise and fear not with relief and excitement.

Then we have an even greater irony. The gospel of Mark, the earliest written gospel, undoubtedly concluded with the story of the empty tomb. This gospel apparently does not attempt to enforce the hope of the resurrection with stories of resurrection appearances. How odd this is. Indeed, the impact is stunning. The conclusion to this narrative as it stands strikes us, powerfully presenting an entree into the Christian confession quite different from the traditional image of the triumphant, risen Christ. Hear the words:

> So they went out and fled from the tomb, for terror and amazement had seized them; and they said nothing to anyone, for they were afraid. (Mark 16:8)

There are two implications of this verse critical for our present story. First, the verse concludes with only the deep image of despair that I have just painted. The bystanders are left with nothing to say at this. They do not even have a body and a grave over which to say *Kaddish*. They tremble and are astonished for this is a conclusion that goes beyond expectation. Can it be that a murder can take place, an execution, that ends in this way, with no trace of the body? There is an eerie sense of deja vu here whose head rises again at Auschwitz. Forget for a moment the usual moderation of this passage. Yes, surely Mark knew of the resurrection narratives that gave accounts of appearances. Yes, the witness was given and Peter and the other disciples were told. All of this can be said, but what remains is this stunning narrative in this the earliest gospel. The emptiness is not in the tomb but in the heart of those who are denied a moment of grief whatever the ultimate outcome.

But there is a second matter to be recognized in this conclusion. In this story, Peter, the representative bystander, is left on the outside. He is not at the tomb and the women who were there told no one about their experience. Again, even given the possible modifications, we conclude that this early gospel leaves Peter without forgiveness, without confrontation with the lord whom he denied. How can that be in a story so fraught with the need for healing and forgiveness? What can be the meaning of a narrative that ends with this very central matter unresolved? Peter, the representative bystander, remains on the outside.

Naturally, we are left with the task of resolving this perplexity ourselves. Not given other resources in the text, we must decide what a narrative of this character must mean. It is possible that the storyteller intended precisely this striking encounter with the empty tomb. It is also possible that the evangelist intended to portray a Christianity growing out of the experiences of encounter with the empty tomb given in this text. Such a Christianity cannot be a triumphant church or a bold power in the world. Such a Christianity cannot boast of its purity or of its worthiness of the mission it takes on. Such a Christianity is one seeking forgiveness, humble before others, utterly incapable of bringing judgement on the actions or belief of other people. In short, *such a Christianity is quite different from the way Christians have been portrayed, have been seen in the intervening centuries.* If Peter is the rock (the meaning of the Greek name), then this church (represented by the bystander Peter) is still a bystander to God's actions of redemption waiting for this same God to welcome us back in.

Can we be so bold as to make the final leap to talk about the church as bystander again? We speak not of a church that fell into collaboration or those who could not be bothered by the church that received the mantle of Peter. Those who in the midst of the greatest challenge facing the church went to the door of execution and then denied knowing the victims. This is a church of both compassion and conviction; yet a church that could not even given that conviction, follow through to protest, to rescue, to resist the Nazis. These are Christians that we cannot blame in our supposed position of superiority. These are rather Christians with whom and for whom we weep since we know that faith, value, even commitment to love could not prepare them for what was to be and for what they would do. We weep because we have seen in them ourselves and cannot bear to face the truth of ourselves. Instead we are left with empty tombs, millions of bodies that have disappeared without the opportunity for friends, family or Rabbi to say *Kaddish*, even *Kaddish*, for them. Can we imagine not mourning those who died in such anonymity or those who grieve for not being able to mourn.

But can the empty tomb remains a symbol of hope for Christians even as I portray this image of the fate of the bystander? Jesus' death as it is understood in the context of this narrative cannot and must not be confused with the deaths of the victims of the Shoah. As a narrative that has been told over and over again, the death of Jesus and the empty tomb remain embedded in a tradition of belief that through this comes redemption and hope for the future. Can we say that about the deaths of the six million? Even asking the question, as necessary as it is, seems obscene. These latter day deaths bring no hope and they cannot, must not be used as a symbol of hope. They remain empty of meaning for us only to be greeted with the eternal question, why?, and the eternal obligation, remember.

And what is the death of one man, even set into the narrative of Christian faith in the Christ, in the face of the deaths of six (no twelve) million?[10] Indeed, this question opens the door to see that the death of the twelve million is a negation of the Christian narrative. In the death of one is to come hope. In the death of the millions, despair reigns. In the juxtaposition, the empty tomb cannot carry even a little of the meaning of hope that it does in the context of the Christian narrative. It is a symbol cut off from is potential meaning left with little more that the bitter memory of what might have been. This cross is too much to bear.

This strikes us as an impasse unless we recognize that the image of the bystander just does not fit the Christian narrative really any more than it fits the expectation of Christian response in the face of Nazi horror. We cannot read Peter's action as a deliberate work of God to produce His end especially now. Despite our inability to effect our salvation from the messes we have created, God's grace is not an excuse for moral numbness and inaction. If we are to see Peter as symbol, our hope is not in the belief that God will always make right what we have wronged or failed to do. Peter is symbol of our reality not of our ideals. We are not called to emulate Peter, despite our possible envy that Peter met face to face with the Lord. Peter as bystander is only a first symbol of the greatest human tragedy, that those with moral courage can be terrorized into abandoning their ideals and practical wisdom for the sake of self-preservation. It is the symbol of highest despair that the best of us can be so susceptible to cowardice becoming unwilling accomplices.

What we say regarding this recognition is that Peter is a symbol of human fact that we see made even more evident in the Shoah. Religious hope cannot mask blatant human failure to other humans no matter how human that failure. Can we erase the memory of our past simply through the stroke of hope in God's redemption? Perhaps this is why Peter is the one in some accounts that is the first disciple to come to the tomb. Even if that redemption were to come in our time, the tears for our failure could not be turned to joy so easily. Even the God who authors such redemption continues to weep for those who perished even while they might have been saved but for greater human diligence. "Never shall I forget these things even if I am condemned to live as long as God Himself. Never."[11]

The Risen Lord

This touch of irony that complicates the narrative of Peter's betrayal is most striking in the Gospel of Mark. As we have said, that gospel leaves the matter disconcertingly open not allowing for the closure that appearances of the risen lord provide in the other gospels. That the other gospels modulate the harshness of Mark should not lead us to reduce the irony of the narrative that is still there in all the other gospels. That touch of harshness is still there in the other versions even if adjusted. Peter is condemned to remember even as he is led to see a new hope. Even more, the irony of the symbol of the empty tomb infects the rest of the narrative if allowed to hold its proper place in the narrative. The finished narrative of the risen lord also bears an irony in the face of all this that only continues the duality of this narrative especially for the symbolic bystander, Peter.

Nevertheless, the narrative of the resurrection appearances are of a different character than the empty tomb, a matter to be treated separately. Peter is treated differently in these narratives. In the narrative in Matthew, Peter receives no special treatment being simply a part of the group of disciples who are met by Jesus in their hiding place and later gather in Galilee for the commission. This particular version needs further development which will be taken up later (chapter seven below). The Gospel of Luke includes a more extended set of appearances in which Simon (undoubtedly intended to be Peter) is said to have seen the resurrected lord individually. Even so, Peter is described as running to the tomb only to see nothing but the grave cloths and in the general appearances described is again included only generally with the other disciples. This gospel has a complicated narrative extended into the book of Acts of the Apostles in which again the disciples as a group receive the risen lord. All we know from this narrative is that Peter, for whatever reason, assumes a leadership role in the early Christian community.

The narrative that is most instructive for our purposes is the one in the Gospel of John. This gospel is most extraordinary among the four. The author depicts Jesus in clear opposition to "the Jews", meaning the Jewish leadership, for their inability to accept his ministry. The words of this gospel are as harsh as any in the Christian scriptures and are less discriminating in labeling "the Jews" as the ones opposed to Jesus. Set into that context, the narrative of Peter as bystander presents a perplexity far more troubling that ordinarily is evident in commentaries on this text. Is there a distinction to be made between collaborators and bystanders? Can we accept this acceptance of Peter at narrative's end and the apparent rejection of the Jews by the gospel writer? This is the problem that stands before us even as we attempt to understand the confrontation between the risen Jesus and Peter.

The resurrection narrative itself presents a fascinating set of possibilities. Peter is only one of the group until a final appearance, the climax of the gospel. Peter leads the group back to fishing with little success. While coming to terms with their frustration, Peter along with the others is met by a "stranger" who invites them to throw their nets in one more time. This effort brings an enormous catch. Peter is finally led to recognize Jesus as the stranger; he leaps into the sea and runs toward Jesus. Nothing could be more appropriate. This is Peter's reprieve. he has another chance to atone for his failure at the trial, and this opportunity overcomes him. he more that the others is moved to rush toward Jesus. This is not ordinary exuberance even if the other accounts had implied his presence among the group as Jesus appeared to them. The issue of Peter's place, of his failure, had not been resolved.

But could it be resolved? Of course, all had run away; but Peter explicitly denied knowing Jesus. His tears could not remove the fact that he had become the symbol of the bystander. In face. even this appearance could not remove that fact.

Even as Peter rushes to meet Jesus, the reality of this must have come to him that nothing Jesus could do could take away the guilt of the past denial. He would remain the symbol of the bystander even if Jesus welcomed him back into the group. The only possible alternative for Peter would be if Jesus (and the others) were prepared to say, it does not make any difference. It is okay to be a bystander.

It is not okay to be a bystander. The very heart of the message of the extended gospel narrative and of this final passion narrative is to say it is not okay to be a bystander. One stroke of a wand at this moment does not change that. To say that would be to say that the event of Jesus and the revelation of God that comes through claimed by Christians means nothing, is simply an aside. To say that it is okay to be a bystander would deny the thrust of Jesus' message about love, a message that in this fourth gospel is central and according to the Jesus of this gospel is both new and old. The point of the message of love is that being a bystander contradicts our commitment to the God of the covenant; there is no way out for Peter by this route and to believe that forgiveness for him and for any other bystander means this is to utterly miss the point of the gospel narrative and to distort the meaning of forgiveness. Though, of course, this focus on Jesus makes this a Christian reading, the conversation is open to dialogue about the God of the covenant.

Of course, Jesus could have said the word of forgiveness to Peter and to the other disciples for that matter, but he doesn't. He extends the word of peace to them as a word of hope for their relationship in this new time. He approaches Peter and accepts him into the group in this general way but does not address the matter of forgiveness in any specific way. Nowhere is this situation viewed as a matter for discussing forgiveness. We do not know what was said otherwise; only that Peter does not receive the word of forgiveness in this narrative nor in any of the gospel narratives for that matter. Now we can rationalize this point or attempt to find something that is implicit but to do so would be to erase the tension in the narrative and its implications for us. No indeed, there is no word of forgiveness in this narrative.

The word is one of challenge for Peter. *The question is not whether Jesus forgives Peter but whether Peter loves Jesus.* Frustrating as the question is for Peter in this time of great remorse, the issue has moved beyond simple words. Peter's actions or inactions have left a mark for the time tainting his relationship with Jesus. Thus, even the word of forgiveness cannot address the issue at hand. The only resolution of the issue will be Peter's actions now and in the future. Peter's desire for forgiveness hangs in the balance between Jesus' willingness to accept him and Peter's willingness to "feed Jesus' sheep."

Now this reading of the gospel seems in keeping with the gospel itself. Jesus is portrayed in the gospel as the Shepherd and his sheep are those who hear his voice and know him. This image is somewhat different from similar images in the synoptic gospels (e.g., the parable of the lost sheep in Luke) since the image is applied indiscriminately to all the sheep who are already in the fold. This Johannine imagery fits with the broad sweep of the view of Jesus' mission according to this gospel which is clearly the "world". Thus, the call to love through "feeding my sheep" is a call for indiscriminate loving care. That is to say, Peter's challenge is not just a specific call to love Jesus and those especially close to him but to love all people. We have to read this text as a conclusion to the consistent theme of love in the gospel (e.g., Jesus' so-called new commandment).

The call to indiscriminate loving is a deflection of the human need for Peter, the need for present security that might be offered in a word of forgiveness. Peter, the representative bystander, is called into an ongoing life of loving that surely means little more than a renewed call to covenant relationship with the God of Israel. The linking of love of God and love of neighbor is the long held tradition of covenant that becomes the open-ended commandment that culminates John's gospel (John 21:15- 19). Thus, we are led to see that the clear implication of Jesus' resurrection in this gospel (and in Matthew's gospel as well) is the call to mission on the terms of the covenant of Israel. The claim of Christians to be sole inheritors of this mission is made dubious since Jesus deflects specific adoration for himself in favor of love of neighbor as a mission for humanity (*Tikkun Olam,* to mend the world).[12] The text suggests that Jesus puts himself and his disciples squarely back into their own tradition in understanding the mission of Jesus' disciples.

Again the notion of bystander is taken to be a contradiction of the basic terms of discipleship. A Christian by definition cannot be a bystander. To be a bystander is, like Peter, to deny Jesus, to deny my discipleship. The only resolution of our guilt is not forgiveness, then, but love for the other, love of neighbor. The issue is always how much love; the answer always is open- ended, love never ends. Love, by definition does ask the question how much or how risky or for whom or in what circumstances. Love is rather the basis of a view of the world that determines the whole of what we do and think.[13]

It is precisely for this reason that Peter stands out in the text as contradiction. We cannot be lulled into thinking that because we potentially all can be Peter that thereby he is us and we are thus excused from the call to love. It is precisely for this reason that the Shoah is a contradiction of Christianity. It is for this reason the Shoah challenges the validity of Christianity. The gospels portray Jesus as a Jew who advocates the religion of the Jew, indeed advocates the Jew. The gospels portray the religion of the disciples as Judaism with Jesus as rabbi. Even this alternative understanding of the resurrection continues this picture despite the alarming claim of the resurrection itself. Above all, the gospels portray discipleship in such terms that the convenient separation of ideal and practice is not possible, even before God, and, thus, leaving no covenant place for the bystander.

Now, let us take this notion to the tradition that has become Christianity, especially the tradition of "gospel" that makes forgiveness, and thereby justification, the centerpoint of Christian faith. The interpretation of the narrative on Peter I have just offered seems to be in direct contradiction to this tradition of justification. How can we understand this opposition? How can we reconcile the two themes that seem so integral to Christianity? Are we talking about a conflict that has arisen because our midrash is taken from the gospels with specific focus on the narrative of Peter, the bystander? That is to say, have we created this conflict because there is a real conflict between the gospels and the Pauline literature. This issue is central to any further development of a post-Shoah Christian theology such as our own. The only way to fully reconstruct this issue is to lay Paul's understanding of the crucifixion and the resurrection alongside the full midrash of the gospel narrative (that completion awaits further development at some later time).

One issue is clear, however. If justification is understood to be offered through God's grace alone and by faith alone (is this how we understand Romans 3:21ff.?), then strictly speaking all of us are made bystanders in relation to God. If Paul intends this message then there is a direct conflict between Paul and the gospels, the religion of Paul is not the religion of Jesus nor of the disciples of the gospel. The issue is as obvious as this. The bystander has no lasting place in the covenant religion of the gospel texts.

Part of the conflict arises when the Christian scriptures are read as doctrinal statements rather than descriptions of Christian life. Even the Pauline literature suffers when this mistake is made, when midrash is made theology proper. When the latter is imposed on the text, then the words justification, grace, gospel, law, works are made into theological categories rather than left as word pictures of Christian life. The problem lies principally in the desire to fix tenets of faith rather that to read the full narrative of the life of discipleship. The claim that the bystander has no place in the covenant religion of the gospels is not a categorical statement of exclusion if it is taken to be consistent with the gospel narrative, and only if that narrative is read as categorical doctrine can this statement be taken to reflect "law" as has been doctrinally defined in Christian tradition.[14]

In like manner, the words "justification," "grace," "works," "forgiveness," "alone," become categories for a theology only when they are divorced from the narrative of the crucifixion and the resurrection (that is, the gospel narrative).

Naturally, the categorical statements set-up a tension in understanding that leaves the reader baffled by the tradition and leads to the supposition of a contradiction. Justification is not a theological category in Paul. It is rather a word describing the covenant relationship between God and God's people. Paul argues that the only possible relationship between God and God's people is one in which the people have been elected to be such by God's initial action. The whole of covenant relationship hangs on this notion of gracious election because the covenant is dependent upon the faith conviction that God imposes a perspective on history that can be known only through God's revelation.

Now, for Paul, this revelation is principally given in the crucifixion and the resurrection. That is to say, God's acts on behalf of the world that now determine the election of the people of God can be seen most clearly in the "story" of Jesus, his death and resurrection; thus the claim of the specific revelation of God in Jesus as Christ is in concert with the gospel narratives. This notion of justification does not exclude the call to mission of God's people for *Tikkun Olam* simply because it is part of the whole narrative of the crucifixion and the resurrection.[15]

We are still left with the question about the bystander, however. We have only said that our previous claim is a narrative claim—that the bystander has no place in the covenant religion of Israel, the bystander has excluded him/herself from the covenant by their actions. But that is not a theological claim but a legal claim that is met with the same challenge as always—"do you love me, then feed my sheep." The challenge is a critical matter that must be left as part of a narrative. Jesus does indeed accept Peter into the group. Peter is not left outside but is given the chance to once again be part of God's people. In the same way, Paul's claim that we are justified by grace alone and not by our own doing is, in terms of the narrative, the same word of description. Peter can be made a member of the group only by being welcomed back by Jesus. The acceptance that Jesus' shows is an example of the very love that he later calls Peter to take as his mission in life. This love of acceptance is the kind of love that Paul means to describe by the word 'grace.'

Surely, this rendering of Paul's thought makes greater sense of what Paul will say in other texts about obedience, love, discipleship, etc. Surely, this note we have gained by setting our midrash alongside that of Paul is an important addition to our rendering of the gospel narrative about Peter, the bystander. On the other hand, the bystander is the symbol of the worst possible distortion of Christian belief and life. The only possible response can come from a re-commitment to the covenant call to love neighbor. Nevertheless, the bystander, such as Peter, is also welcomed back, given that opportunity not with mere blanket approval but with the belief in humanity as such and in God's judgement, His selection, of His people. This aside comes under heavy critique when placed into the context of a theology after the Shoah. In this context the words 'grace,' 'judgement,' and 'selection' bear meanings that throw the traditional images into some turmoil. The grace of God seemed utterly lacking in this kingdom of the night and especially one wonders about such grace offered to the bystander when so many innocent victims were apparently denied. It is one thing that Jesus accepts back the bystander. It is quite another thing that we accept (or more appropriately, the Jewish community accept) this bystander on behalf of the victims. And judgement is also a problem for us since judgement implies justice and that is just the factor so utterly missing (or at least distorted during the Shoah). Finally, God's election must now be considered next to the Nazi selection in which the fate of God's people was sealed. Can we be sure that God's election means promise given what we have now witnessed?

All these things we say not to dismantle Christian confession but to safeguard that confession. The Shoah brings that confession to meaninglessness if we attempt to use traditional categories in an attempt to understand the Shoah. It is especially the matter of the bystander that negates essentially what Christianity is and claims. Even more, the extent of this denial finally brings to question Jesus' acceptance of the first bystander, Peter, a question and negation that our confession cannot survive. We must believe that Jesus' accepts, that the family still holds, that God's intention is benevolent. We are stunned by this quandary that undermines our very claim for justice, God's justice; but we cannot deny now what must be the truth of God, that justice is to accept the sinner who repents. Thus, we continue to believe in spite of our lack of understanding because there really is no alternative (or rather we have seen the alternative and shudder before it).

Notes

[1] Among the various places that Wiesel has said this, among the other lessons he says we have learned, is Elie Wiesel, "A Message to the Second Generation," in *The Holocaust: Forty Years After*, Marcia Littel, Richard Libowitz, and Evelyn Rosen, ed. (Lewiston, NY: Edwin Mellen Press, 1989), p. 13

[2] Emil Fackenheim, *To Mend the World* (New York: Schocken Books, 1982), pp. 262ff.

[3] The actions of Christian leaders and their motives are discussed any number of places but are given an interesting and provocative treatment in Harry James Cargas, *A Christian Response to the Holocaust* (Denver: Stonehenge Books, 1981), pp.53ff.

[4] I take here the language of Franklin Littell: Franklin Littell, *The Crucifixion of the Jews* (Macon, GA: Mercer University Press, 1986).

[5] In fact, the telling is best supported by work such as that of Nechama Tec in order for us to make judgments about the complexities of actions and motivations: Nechama Tec, *Dry Tears* (New York: Oxford University Press, 1984) and Nechama Tec, *When Light Pierced the Darkness* (New York: Oxford University Press, 1986).

[6] While this sentiment may be expressed by him in various places, I heard him say this in a lecture opening the conference, Remembering for the Future, held in Oxford, England, in the summer of 1988.

[7] It must be said though that Emil Fackenheim echoes the sentiments of many that the children of the generation of perpetrators need not bear the burden of guilt. The birth of a new generation does present itself as a possibility for hope even if too late for a generation past. For this effort to "bridge the abyss" as Fackenheim puts it, we can be grateful: Emil Fackenheim, *The Jewish Bible After the Holocaust* (Bloomington, IN: Indiana University Press, 1990), p. 92.

[8] Again, Fackenheim's comments are very much like those of others. Like the return of children to Job, we dare not imagine that even this gift of God can replace those who died: Fackenheim, *The Jewish Bible...*, pp. 94ff. see also, Elie Wiesel, *Messengers of God* (New York: Summit Books, 1976), pp. 211ff.

9 These themes will be treated in greater depth in chapter nine of this book.

[10] The numbers are in some cases magical symbols. Still, the attempt here is to recognize the scale of non-Jewish victims as well both to show our investment in the event as well as to be accurate. A discussion of the various groups of victims can be found in John Roth and Richard Rubenstein, *Approaches to Auschwitz* (Atlanta: John Knox Press, 1987), pp. 178ff

[11] Elie Wiesel, *Night* (New York: Bantam Books, 1960), p. 32.

12 I am indebted to Fackenheim again for instructing me on this theme: Fackenheim, *To Mend the World*, pp. 250ff.

13 In fact, for a more thorough treatment of this theme see my: James F. Moore, *Sexuality and Marriage* (Minneapolis, MN: Augsburg Publishing House, 1987), pp. 39ff.

[14] It is, of course, a distortion to assume that even this doctrinal tradition can be defined as a single way of thinking. Each splinter group within the Christian world of thought and even various theologians within those groups have offered differing perceptions of "law" as a theological category.

[15] See the extension of these themes in chapters 7-9 below.

CHAPTER 6:
THE COLLABORATOR

The Collaborator

There are those who can respond to the evil of any moment and did respond to the great evil of our age not simply by turning away from the victim and, thus, their basic beliefs but by twisting those beliefs to mean something quite different, even to become the ally of evil itself. This twisting surely occurred within the camps of evil with spite of intention driving an ideology that was at war with religion and God. These would speak as Christians, even be portrayed as prophets, who claimed authority from God but drew authority from the darkest elements of their ideology. Still, these were so-called prophets easily unmasked. Tradition gives us models for challenging the false prophets and we can say with complete conviction, these people of evil ways were not Christians.[1]

The collaborator is another matter. Many confused emotions drove Christians to work for the Nazi persecutors—fear, misplaced devotions or concerns, bias and prejudice, ignorance or envy. All of these are unbecoming to God's people but are human nevertheless. Under normal circumstances, these very emotions can be excused together with the actions as long as true repentance is evident. In fact, we can be led to offer such leniency with the proviso that again we are not the ones who can truly offer forgiveness. Such acceptance must come at the very least from the living representatives of the many who died. This is a question difficult to resolve. The question is not the one who misplaces actions based on fear or related emotions.

The question is more the one who is convinced of the very truth of a distortion of Christianity and in that belief acts to distort Christianity.

Now it is difficult to single out these figures since we can hardly tell if actions result from fear or misplaced devotions or from blind and distorted belief. In addition, so many also stood along the side as bystanders who also did so because of either these same emotions or because of deep belief in the distorted view of Christianity floating through the air at that time. And why not? Such views were merely pieces of a long tradition of hatred that is the unfortunate part of Christian history that so many of us would like to ignore but cannot, at least not now. We are perplexed by this history; how can hatred be substituted for love? What twisted sort of manipulation could allow this and now has born itself out in its fulness through the lives of many who threw themselves into the Nazi effort of destruction because they saw truth there, aligned Christianity with that.

Our midrash of the passion narrative can be a foundation upon which we can make comment to this response to the Shoah as well. Our confusion about the collaborator is like the confusion expressed in the gospels about Judas, the one who betrays Jesus. Even though the gospels are uniformly critical of Judas, they are not uniform in the eventual judgement upon Judas (that is the narrative judgment). The gospels are themselves a midrash on this story evident through the different versions of the tale, and the return to this story will confront us, Christians, with a deep challenge to our tradition—the tradition of accusing Judas, Judah, of the most devious betrayal of Jesus, for Jesus' death.

The Judas Narrative

In fact, there is not a single Judas Narrative. The gospels present fragments that can be pieced into a story but each provides a twist that changes the character of the narrative itself.[2] The Johannine narrative identifies Judas with Satan. The Matthean narrative tells of a remorseful Judas who at the end discovers his awful mistake which drives him to suicide. The Lucan narrative (in the book of Acts) tells a similar scene but in such a way that Judas appears simply mad. The Marcan narrative, the barest of all, leaves Judas' betrayal a mysterious event with no apparent motive and no ultimate consequence for Judas. In fact, this last of the narratives is the most curious of the four. Mark apparently saw Judas' actions as only a vehicle for the story. Again, we are led to surmise that Judas is little more than a pawn in a larger struggle undefined by his own actions. Only this supposition can make sense of the lack of detailed concern for the figure himself in a gospel that so completely aims concern toward the one who betrays the community. And if we assume that Judas had no choice, then none of the other narratives make sense.

The four narratives, thus, when placed together seem to counter the each other. If Judas is consumed by Satan, then he is the enemy to be destroyed (or is he?) If Judas repents his sin even in taking his own life, then are we compelled to have sympathy? If Judas is mad, then he cannot literally be held responsible at all. If Judas is a pawn in God's plan, then God authors this act and not Satan. This is not narrative, but confusion, and we are inclined to argue that the four versions must be held together in some way in order to be genuine to the gospel midrash. Yet, let us first consider them separately.

The Matthean narrative is a good beginning to trace the full flow of this narrative piece. Judas appears in the gospel in only one place prior to the passion narrative section—the list of the disciples in which Judas is already identified as the one who betrayed Jesus. Thus, the narrative concerning Judas is almost entirely connected with the passion narrative as a piece with it. Judas' identity could not, on the account of the gospel text, be separated from the full intent of the passion narrative. Any reading of the Judas narrative must, then, be placed within the context of an interpretation of the full passion narrative. In that way, some of the differences between the various gospel versions can be understood.

The Matthean narrative is matter of fact about Judas' action simply stating that Judas on his own accord went to the chief priests asking what they would give him for betraying Jesus. There is no mention of motivation for Judas' actions and no indication that the chief priests sought out Judas. The event is simply a piece of the flow of the narrative with little preparation or explanation. One would think that such an act would receive more profound treatment, the deed exercising emotional anguish in the gospel writer. Why is there no deep concern over the turn of a faithful disciple against the master? Why is there no explanation of this event that turns the narrative in a radically different direction? Instead, the short section reads as if it is of little distinct importance, only one additional detail in the telling of the story.

The next appearance of Judas in the narrative also is puzzling. Jesus speaks of his betrayal obviously knowing it will take place, and the reaction of the disciples seems almost ritualistic as even Judas joins in asking "Am I the one?" There are two striking points about this interchange. First, Judas seems to act the part still of the faithful disciple even while plotting betrayal. Second, even when found out, Judas makes no move to leave the supper and Jesus makes no effort to turn him away. Judas stays with the group through the supper!

All this suggests another agenda that is the context of the telling of the narrative. Why does Matthew handle this enormously important narrative detail in such a matter of fact way? This could only be true, it seems, if betrayal like that of

Judas was, in fact, commonplace in the early church. Judas is not treated differently or with shock because he is not so unique, his action was no longer shocking. Indeed, Judas has become the metaphor, the symbol of the betrayer, of the many betrayers in the early church. A church threatened by persecution undoubtedly had grown used to the experience and the fear of betrayal.

If this is so, then the gospel writer is obviously using Judas as a symbol and the narrative as a means for commenting on this experience and the fear of betrayal. How is it that the betrayer is to be treated? He is surely to be exposed so that the threat to the community is taken away, but the betrayer is not to be expelled from the group, from the Lord's table. Surely, this story exemplifies the extreme command of the Sermon on the Mount, love your enemies, do good to those who hate you, even when the enemy is within.

Jesus' action at the forefront of accepting the betrayer even as the betrayer plans his deed, even before, is striking in itself. The point is graphic, that the community of the church, like Jesus, continue to live the life of service (as earlier in the gospel, lording it over another is not the way it is to be with you). The dramatic acceptance taken, as it were, in stride is ultimately the message of the passion narrative that no longer can we live in such a way so as to divide our world into friends and enemies. This is the radicalness of the Matthean Jesus. We are to love our enemy as well.

Ah, this profound passage leads to a most joyous turn on Christian history, a turn so infrequently heeded. Christianity has all too often defined itself so as to necessitate enemies, opponents. When opponents could no longer be found with ease outside of the faith, after the wedding of church and empire, enemies were found within. How is it that the church has so often defined itself in such a way turning its back on this most central of Matthean themes? We cannot know what motivates the necessity to find scapegoats. We only know that when Christians start looking for scapegoats they almost always have turned on the Jews. We cannot escape this history, but we can emphatically state the truth of Christianity. Followers of Jesus are called not to seek out enemies but to love them, not to place blame but to accept people. In that we have the clearest motivation for finally saying that the Jews are not the enemies of God but our brothers and sisters in faithfulness.

Indeed, there are many who suggest that Judas (Judah in the Greek) has all too often represented an image of the Jew. What that has often meant in the past is that as Judas was the most wicked of men to betray his Lord, Judaism is the most wicked of people for rejecting Jesus as messiah. What can this mean for us, now is that just as Jesus accepted Judas and welcomed him, the church can do no less than accept the Jewish people without blame.

This matter, however, is attached with irony in our post-Shoah world. If Judas is truly the image of the betrayer in Christian scripture, then what does all of this say about those who became betrayers in the Shoah? The contexts are not the same. Even if the image is extended to envelop all those who from within betrayed members of the early church, the image does not speak to the issue of those who betrayed the principles of their faith by associating with the evil one. Matthew's narrative loses strength in this context. Can we so easily say that the betrayer ought to be accepted by the community of the betrayed? We cannot here say that as Christians for we are not the community of the betrayed. I do not claim here that Christians weren't betrayed or that sympathy for them is not as important as sympathy for the Jews. I only say that it was the Jewish community who felt the full brunt of this massive betrayal of Christian principles, of those as Christians ignoring the essentials of Christian morality and aligning themselves with the Nazis. We cannot offer forgiveness since we were not the ones betrayed.

Even more, the tragedy is that millions died, many without full awareness of the massive betrayal of the community around them. How is it that they can forgive now? How is forgiveness possible under these circumstances? Indeed, the communities, the tables that could have been opened up for welcome even of the betrayer are now gone, wiped from existence never to return. Jesus sat at table and accepted even the betrayer to eat with him. For the millions now gone there is no longer any table for the meal.

This is undoubtedly a harsh stating of the situation. The surviving communities are slowly moving toward a level of acceptance and even sharing tables. There is a level on which the community that fostered the betrayer, like Judas, now is finding acceptance in the surviving Jewish community. Surely that acceptance, however, has arisen from the dialogue that includes Christian awareness both of the history of a teaching of contempt and Christian collaboration in the Nazi effort. What an irony this is. Who is Judas now? Can we even read the passion narrative anymore without also hearing the echoes of the Shoah and the irony of this question, who is Judas now? In this, we play out the narrative of Judas in a different fashion post-Shoah.

Still, there is another lingering problem. The problem lies in where we began this exercise. As betrayer, Judas represents an image of one of the ways that Christians acted in the Shoah. It was one of the choices that Christians took in large numbers. The nagging problem that will stay with us is the question I first heard from Irving Greenberg—"Hasn't the Shoah so tainted the Christian faith that the taint can never be removed?"[3] How can we be sure that the massive betrayal during the Shoah is not the dominant character of Christianity? We hope and pray that this cannot be, but we can no longer be sure of this. And, how long will it take before we can be sure again? Who can tell? No telling of the Judas story least of all the Matthean version can deal with this nagging question of uncertainty about the character of Christianity.

And so the Judas story already presents to us an ambiguity even in this Matthean version, the most sympathetic reading. The fate of Judas ultimately is suicide. Again, the textual judgment on Judas is suspended. The betrayal scene is marked by irony with Judas greeting Jesus with peace addressing him as teacher. In return, Jesus simply says, be quick about it friend. Jesus still refuses condemnation. In the Matthean text, Judas received more personal acceptance than the bystander, Peter. Judas having fully grasped the implication of his deed (still with no specific condemnation from Jesus), repented his deed, gave back the silver payment and hanged himself in remorse. Indeed, Judas appears to have intended something other that the death of Jesus through his act according to this narrative. Thus, the betrayer is not really a betrayer. The betrayed does not seem to be betrayed, but both die.[4]

The ambiguity is far more obvious when this sympathetic version is set alongside the other gospels. What are we to make of the Lucan text in which Judas is depicted making arrangements with the chief priests who, it is said are pleased with the opportunity? In this text, we have Judas acting only to greet Jesus with a kiss. Nevertheless, Jesus responds with a much more poignant accusation—Is it with a kiss that you betray the Son of Man? (Luke 22:48) And Luke tells of the death of Judas not as one who repents but as one gone mad, falling from a cliff. By this text, we have no clear picture of how to deal with the betrayer, only that he ultimately received death as a consequence of his deed, a deed conceived, apparently out of his personal madness.

Again, we are left with a perplexing narrative to lay open to the critique of the Shoah. On the one hand, Judas has symbolized (for Christians) the fate of Judah, blindly following their madness in rejecting the messiah. Can we really continue this tradition in which death ultimately is seen as an appropriate end for the betrayer? Isn't this version one among many traditions that stand behind the "teaching of contempt?" Still, when the Shoah reverses the narrative so that Christian collaborators are now Judas, prepared out of madness or evil to betray their Christian ideals, what do we say then about fitting justice? And isn't this the point in this narrative—the problem of justice?

The issue at stake for the Christian has always been the issue of justice. What separates Judas in the narrative from the others who simply stand on the sidelines is that Judas is shown as the betrayer—he rejects Jesus. In that is found the essence of justice for the Christian tradition. The ultimate justice is determined on the basis of the one accepting or rejecting Jesus. Thus, the Lucan Judas is a type of all the others in the narrative who have set themselves outside of God's grace in Jesus. Judas had a choice and made the wrong choice.

The Lucan text (chapter 22), however, cannot finally justify this tradition. Judas is portrayed as one gone mad not as one able to make responsible choices. In fact, the whole of the guilty who betray Jesus (reject Jesus) are depicted as mad with power or ignorance or jealousy. These are not ones who make responsible choices. On the other hand, we do hold such people responsible. Judas' madness does not relieve him of guilt. Thus, the new Judas, the mass of Christian collaborators, cannot escape judgment simply because they were afraid, jealous, mad with power or some ideology. The choice was wrong and the judgement swift. Justice is death for the betrayer.

More centrally, Judas' deed was a choice only on the surface. Judas may have chosen differently but in that case another betrayer would have to emerge. Judas, like Peter, was a pawn on God's stage plan of redemption, a necessary element. We cannot presume that this justifies the betrayal but we are at least left with doubt about how God ought to judge. Even more, if Judas does represent Judah in the gospel text, we cannot so quickly conclude that Judah is thereby condemned to death by God. Our tradition has fallen apart on its own terms even before the horror of Auschwitz gave us the reality of the extension of our teaching.

However, Auschwitz was not Gethsemane. Even if the latter day Judas may be Christian collaborators, no such redemptive purpose can be attributed to this event (notwithstanding Ignaz Maybaum).[5] The collaborators were not pawns on God's stage even if some thought they were. They were pawns on the evil stage of the kingdom of the Night, nightmares made real by Hitler and the Nazis. No such rationale of justification can emerge here that portrays in the farthest stretch of imagination that these were doing the work of God. This narrative collapses in the face of the Shoah, left bare to the horrible injustice thrust on an unsuspecting people, the people of God. And in this context, can the question still be what is justice? We cannot know what is the fitting recompense, only that twelve million deaths cannot go unpunished. Mad or not, the Lucan narrative portrays an end more fitting than the ambiguous, repenting Judas of Matthew. But surely the text from Luke 22 must be applied with caution. Judas of this text cannot be compared with the massive apostasy of European Christianity during the Shoah.

Both are needed in the conjoined ambiguity so that final judgments are left wanting. The two narratives that pull at each other as equally compelling truths each telling only a half truth, each on its own a distortion of truth, left to its own ultimately a terrible lie. Both are needed to allow for the word of God to be born by the narrative.

Even as the harshness of each of these narratives leaves us with little sense of compassion, only a possibility of sympathy, the picture is made more startling by the inclusion of the Johannine text (John 18:1-10 linked to John 13:27). This gospel writer includes no picture of the betrayer plotting to expose Jesus. Still, Judas' motivations are made clear in the earlier text in which he is described as an uncompassionate thief. Judas is pictured as one who is already wicked. This imagery is a prelude to the scene at table in which Jesus predicts his betrayal. That scene orchestrated by Jesus focuses full accusation on Judas and describes the turn of events vividly, Satan at that moment entered into him (John 13:27).[6]

The gospel narrative here extends what has already been said—that Judas was a thief, already wicked. That Satan enters into him is only a culminating image of Judas' wickedness. Still the image is more, for Judas is no longer simply an image of human weakness but of incarnate evil.[7] Judas is already beyond the power of Jesus' love, beyond what Jesus could do for Peter, for example. This Judas is Satan's representative and as such portrays that larger battle that could not be waged on the human level. Judas as a human character is no longer significant to the narrative for he is no longer the symbol of the betrayer but rather is the tempter par excellence.

But this is precisely the problematic of this version of the tale. If Judas is no longer a figure of human weakness except in that humans can become vehicles for ultimate evil, then Judas cannot become a symbol of any people. The rejection of Jesus in confession is not the same as the open deed of betraying Jesus to his enemies. Surely, if a generation of some Jews were to be viewed as heirs of the Johannine Judas, this text is the best of all possible arguments against the extension of the deicide charge to succeeding generations of Jews. There is no pretension of some form of original, hereditary Judas-complex here. The deed is part of a unique, particular drama that for the sake of the meaning of that drama cannot be universalized - every rejection of Jesus is not a new murder of Jesus.

Far more significant in this line of thought is the ultimate thrust of the narrative in John, the portrayal of the Jesus in full control. In fact, in John, Judas is robbed of his chance to betray since Jesus betrays himself (cf., John 18:4-8). More to the point, Satan is robbed of every form of victory by the Jesus who is pictured in control of every event, every twist of narrative. Whatever Judas was, whatever the plot, all that fades before the Jesus who wins at every turn. In fact, the death of Jesus in this narrative is not a tragedy at all, certainly not a sin but the victorious plan of God. Judas, the pawn of Satan, is shown ultimately as Judas of God with even more certainty than in any of the other texts. This conclusion only fits the entire scene in which every potential accusation against Jesus is turned by Jesus into his triumph. In the end, the accusers are tools of God fading to the background with no ultimate judgement made about their fate.

This image of the triumphant, controlling Jesus makes our midrashic interpretation even more difficult and ambiguous. The ultimate meaning of this tale in John is unmistakable though. The whole narrative despite appearances is determined by God. What appears as the power of evil becomes the tool of God. God wins over evil despite what things look like. This image of the God in control (if it is John's image) is even more shattering in the face of the Shoah. We have no way to draw lines between events. The Christian collaborators of the Shoah may well have been tools of absolute evil. Indeed, we have in our memory images of the satanic that are vivid enough for us to say we now know hell. But can we say that God is ultimately in control? Can we actually say that despite appearances all these who collaborated were tools of God? There is no simple response to this for we must say both no and yes emphatically.

Our emphatic no is a cry of what really cannot be true of our world. We cannot make sense of any of this if God who is good is also the author of such evil. The words good and evil would lose any meaning in such a claim even if on the surface the claim makes sense in a traditional way. Even more, can we say and for what reason would we say that the collaborators, tools of Satan, were tools of God as twelve million die? Such good-intentioned but wrong-headed theology does not give justification let alone justice. The plan of God finally has to have boundaries if the whole of our tradition is to make sense. God finally will refuse to do certain things in the name of his purpose. And whatever that purpose might be, it is dubious to say that its fruition would make up for the horror of Auschwitz.[8]

Thus, we say emphatically that the narrative of John cannot work in the face of Auschwitz. The line cannot be drawn from Jesus and Judas to the Jews of the Shoah and the Christian collaborators. The parallels when attempted on this level are not only dumbfounding, they border on the obscene making a mockery both of Christian belief in Jesus and in the deaths of the twelve million. Auschwitz is the revelation of absolute evil and not Judas. Whatever else the narrative from John might mean for Christians, we can no longer see Judas as the symbol of incarnate evil. Auschwitz has now replaced Judas as this symbol. In that discovery, we are truly answering to a new thing in the Shoah for which our narratives nearly always fall short.

But we must say also an emphatic yes. Even with the rejection of the lines between the Judas of John and the collaborators of this century, the ultimate image of the gospel is one that cannot be rejected even if we have every reason to do so.

To presume that God is finally at the mercy of evil, that good cannot prevail is to give ourselves over to despair. The narrative may sound too bold in the face of what we now know, but the claim must be as emphatic as the gospel writer intends. The meaning of the claim may dumbfound us, but we must still say for the sake of humanity that God prevails not evil. We have no other wager to make that makes sense in the face of radical evil, even if we cannot finally say that history is then a pawn of God's purpose.

So then what do we say of the betrayer? From our interpretation we gain no clear picture either of the motivations or the fate of the collaborator. Even if we must say emphatically that God prevails in spite of everything, we are left with an ambiguous picture of the betrayer that for the sake of a humanity, a Christianity more humane must remain ambiguous. And for those of us who are among the ones standing on the outside looking in, we only say that we cannot any longer arrogate to ourselves the position of condemnation, of looking for enemies. Yet, we are now given the eternal task of assuring that Christianity survives this greatest of challenges. If we still can reclaim our Christianity from betrayal, we must do so with ever present diligence.

The Jews in the Narrative

Indeed, including a section on the Jews of the passion narrative is clearly odd if not out of place given what we have said thus far. Even so, our project aims not simply at a reinterpretation of the texts but at rules of interpretation that enable us to guard against distortions in the light of the Shoah. In this regard, the Jews of the passion narrative must be considered for the role that these figures have played in the "teaching of contempt." These Jews are clearly seen as the principal perpetrators seeking the death of Jesus.

First, we argue that nearly every Christian group has rejected the explicit teaching of deicide that placed blame on the Jews for the death of God (Jesus). That this claim has persisted in Christian teaching (and for some still persists) is an extraordinary puzzle for us post-Shoah. The teaching is devised in complete disregard for the text itself in which the Jews are (except for the possible exception of the gospel of John) seen as a pluralistic society (with many groups competing for a place of authority). The brash claim that the Jews were responsible for the death of Jesus is, at least, a naive ignoring of the basic plurality of first century Judaism (even as portrayed in the Christian gospels). The teaching also neglects the central thrust of the theology of the narratives that God is the one who wills Jesus' death. To presume Jewish accountability in the light of this position is to presume that the Jews (again, whoever of this group might be made party to these plans) were doing God's will. Also, the claim simply makes the false extension of the narrative that because some Jews according to this narrative might have sought Jesus' death that all Jews are accountable. The fallacy of this argument is clear and is sufficient to reject the broad teaching of deicide.

However, we hope not merely to absolve Jews of guilt[9] but to note that the foundations for assuming guilt to begin with are slim. That is to say, the whole question of Jewish guilt for collaboration in Jesus' death is wrongheaded and improper to begin with. Add to this contention that the Shoah confronts us with a striking historical irony (that Christians were clearly collaborators in the murder of Jews in this century) that dwarfs all bases for this teaching of deicide in a post-Shoah theology. The Jews were not responsible for the death of Jesus and the narrative as well as our post-Shoah sensitivity leads us to reject the teaching of deicide as a particularly horrid and obscene statement for Christians to make.[10]

We can reinforce this rule by returning to the text and examining the text as we have with regard to the figure Judas in order to give further warrant to a different reading of the passion narrative. In the texts, the Jewish leaders (the gospels specifically refer to the chief priests and scribes and not to the pharisees even though the pharisees are included as part of plots in earlier sections of the gospel narratives) are shown in the same light as Judas with some of the same implications. They are in one text recipients of Judas' offer (Luke 22:3-5) while in others initiators of the plot Matthew 26:3-5). In some texts the leaders are seen as protectors of the interests of the nation (John 18:14) while in others they are perceived as being filled with Satan (John 8:44). Thus, what we have said of Judas can also apply to the Jews of the text.

On the other hand, we recognize that the Jews of the passion narratives cannot be identified as images of Christian betrayal. Judas may be perceived as the one who betrays but the Jewish leaders are never seen as disciples of Jesus (at least not the chief priests and scribes). In addition, unlike the Pharisees of the earlier texts, the Jerusalem leadership is not portrayed as engaged in open conversation with Jesus. Jesus' teaching appears to disagree with the principal views of the Sadducees and the scribes. Thus, they do not become models of discipleship for the gospel writer (as the pharisees are in Matthew). Because of this twofold argument, the Jews of the text cannot be perceived as models of mistaken Christian behavior without a complete distortion of their relation to Jesus. We cannot talk about these Jews even as a type of betrayal like the Christian betrayal during the Shoah.

No indeed, to understand these Jews we must understand them as Jews on their own terms. In spite of their disagreement with Jesus, they would have perished with Jesus in the Shoah for the very same reasons if both had been characters of the twentieth century and not the first. Thus, whatever we conclude about the Jewish leadership we dare not transform them into models of bad Christians. What a travesty that would be.

If we read the Jewish leadership in terms of their Jewishness and not just how Christians have understood Jewishness of the first century, then we have reason to believe that these leaders had cause for disagreement with Jesus and fear of his intentions. But that was an inner Jewish debate and not a debate between Christians and Jews (for Christians did not yet exist). Jesus represented a radical reform in Judaism (some of which was to take hold in later Judaism) that challenged central aspects of the Jerusalem/temple cult and early pharisaism. Nevertheless, there is little to suggest from what we know of first century Judaism that such disagreement would have led to plots against Jesus' life let alone legitimizing a trial and execution of Jesus.

In fact, there are elements of the passion narrative (especially of the trial scene) that imply that the gospel writers knew that the pretext of Jewish plots was a farce. Statements purported as coming from the mouths of the Jewish leadership are most unlikely statements from Jewish leaders of the time (such as we find in the 8th chapter of John's gospel in the claim that we are children of Abraham and we have never been in bondage to anyone, a most unlikely statement by a Jew of any age). Thus, there are elements of the narratives that might suggest to us that the inclusion of the Jewish leadership is regarded as literary farce—perhaps that the writers knew that the Romans were chiefly responsible from the outset but could not dare open condemnation of the Romans.[11] Given this, it is highly unlikely that we should read the inclusion of the Jews in the narrative as an historically accurate accounting of events. The point of inclusion must be for some other reason than to accuse the Jews of killing Jesus. The narratives suggest that the issue was one of Jewish self-identity, that Jesus was a party to the vigorous debate about what the very character of Judaism ought to be (probably aligned most directly with various pharisees). The issue is not the life and death of Jesus but the life and death of Judaism. That issue was a serious one that surely represented a bitter dispute that could rather strikingly be portrayed through the image of the trial.

Still, this matter of the central question of Jewish identity is far removed from the actual concern of what brought about Jesus' death. It is an important question even in relation to the Shoah, but any attempt to conclude that the debate can be universalized as a battle between Judaism and Christianity and the debate is the central theme of the gospel narratives on Jesus passion is a distortion of the text. Christians find no models for Christian self-understanding by casting the matter as a question of who is a Christian unless we see that as being derived from a prior struggle of deciding what constitutes the identity of a Jew. In that, we might be led to see Christians in common struggle with Jews to sustain a genuine commitment to covenant in any age that threatens to weaken that commitment.

In the same manner, the Jews of the text (including those who call for crucifixion at the gates of Pilate's residence) cannot be seen as representatives of Satan. The language of the text is an intensification of the inner Jewish debate but is not a legitimation of Christian hatred of the Jews (even of the leadership referred to in the text.) As for now, we are left with a basic rule that the model of the collaborator in the text is not the Jewish leadership (judgments on Jewish collaboration in any age including in the kingdom of the night are not ours, that is Christians, to make). Judas remains the principal image of the collaborator, and even he must be seen in the ambiguity we have already brought to this text.

The Instigators—Pilate's Spite

Christians confess in their creeds that Jesus suffered under Pontius Pilate. No mention is made in our confession of Jews—even though the gospel stories make the Jewish leaders prominent in the story of the passion of Jesus. Even so, our confession is simply that Jesus suffered under Pontius Pilate. There is a clear twist of irony in this confession. On the one hand, Christians in so confessing attempt to distance themselves from the perpetrators. We are the heirs of God's Kingdom, we might be led to say. Instead, Christians are almost all gentiles and not Jews. We are instead heirs of the gentile world with more in common with Pontius Pilate than with the Jews of the first century. Jesus suffered under us.

The irony sweeps over us even more as we think about the impact of this recognition. The Christian story ultimately claims that the Jews suffer at the hands of non-Jews. Pilate was at work murdering Jesus even in the first century of this era. Has the story changed over the centuries? Gentiles have been at work oppressing and murdering Jews throughout the centuries. There is little wonder that gentiles in the twentieth century could be encouraged again to persecute and murder Jews. Let's get the story straight. The Roman procurator Pontius Pilate was responsible for the death of Jesus.

And, Pilate was no Jew. Pilate was also no Christian. Even more, Pilate seemed to despise the Jews and their territory. Even the passion narrative makes Pilate out to be one who cares little for the religious passions of the people of Israel. Jesus was no more than a nuisance, a troublesome nuisance. And, Pilate clearly showed little patience or compassion with such nuisances. Pilate represented the imperial authority and brutality; power that acted swiftly to eliminate opposition. And this is the one that the gospel texts wish to whitewash, or so goes the normal reading of the passion narratives?? Indeed, Pilate held authority over the fate of Jesus and he made sure that Jesus was made victim to his power, the power of Rome.

Now both Judas and the Jewish leadership are shown as collaborators, but with Rome. The motives of the Jewish leadership appear to be principally religious and communal. Their fears can be justified at least on that basis. Judas appears to be one who is confused and misled. His motives are at the very least ambiguous in the story. Only Pilate dismisses Jesus for death even in spite of knowing that Jesus was innocent. We must know and say whenever these texts are read that the story is fraught with ambiguity and irony. Pilate, nevertheless, is responsible for the death of Jesus and principally because Jesus was a Jew and for no other legal reason.[12]

Our Midrash on Judas

Now the pieces of the Judas narrative can be put together. Judas is the symbol of the collaborator but the symbol remains ambiguous for us. Judas can represent the collaborator in a host of different ways with different motivations. As such, Judas can represent even the images of the Christian collaborator in the Shoah. Whatever the motivation, the judgment we make about Judas must be partially left in ambiguity as only the one betrayed can forgive. Only Jesus can make judgment in this matter and not us.

If we must make comment about the collaborator Judas as a symbol, then two critical rules of reading arise from our midrash. First, if Judas is read as Judah (symbolizing Judaism's rejection of Jesus), then we gentiles cannot make judgment on that matter. Whether Christianity is worthy of Jewish respect is a matter still open to determination. Even so, we gentiles cannot and must not make explicit or implicit judgment about Jewish collaboration. We have no right to presume that Judas in our story represents eternal condemnation of the Jews for their rejection of Jesus. And this corrective is especially important when we realize that gentiles and not Jews were the perpetrators of this crime (in so far as this is a crime).

Second, if we read Judas as a universal symbol of collaboration that includes gentile Christians, then we must recognize the prophetic power of this symbol—that gentiles, especially those falsely influenced by Christianity and those influenced by other ideologies, have long been persecutors and murderers of Jews. Judas, then, becomes a symbol of the long, horrid history of Christian anti-Judaism that forgot along the way that Jesus was a Jew. To continue to forget would be to betray him and his people. To remember that Jesus was a Jew would be to open the door to dialogue. Such is the prophetic word on even this last episode of our collaboration—the murder of six million.

Naturally, Christianity, like Judas (mad or filled with evil?), has long been misguided in their actions, motivated by disappointed expectations perhaps. Our motivations do not mitigate the end result, but at least we can say that Christianity, like Judas, has another choice. The collaborators had another choice even from the foundations of their Christianity. Those Jews who died had little or no choice, but Christians had a choice. Christians have a choice. We can choose to resist collaboration in Jew-Hatred in all its forms. We can choose to work for a Christianity that tells its stories in such a way so that Jews are our brothers and sisters on the stage of our story. We can be prepared to declare both in word and deed that our God will not be overcome by evil. We can at least act as if we believe this even if the signs make such a judgment tenuous at the very least. We can choose not to be what we have been before. We can repent, even if our repentance now seems all too weak. Still, our repentance, like that of the Matthean Judas, can lead us to see that Christianity is at heart and soul philo-Judaic rather than anti-Judaic. That can be fully recognized only if we learn to tell the story of Judas differently than we have before.

Notes

[1] Again, our assertion comes after the fact and is appropriately challenged by Emil Fackenheim in another footnote in *To Mend the World* where Fackenheim speaks about his use of the phrase "Nazi Christian" (p. 281).

[2] I refer the reader to the appendix of this book where the full texts of the individual gospel narratives can be found.

[3] Greenberg, p. 13.

[4] We are, of course, brought face to face with a key question for Christianity after the Shoah. Is anti-Judaism an essential element of Christianity? That is to say, ought we despair that Christianity will necessarily side with those who would kill Jews because the demise of the Jews is, after all, always an implicit hope of Christianity? I think not and this midrashic interpretation is a beginning attempt to show an argument for thinking otherwise. The Judas narrative does provide (in this Matthean reading) a credible way of understanding our relationship to the betrayal of the Shoah—that death was not the intent of historical Christianity even if it was the ultimate end of our collaboration.

[5] Ignaz Maybaum, *The Face of God after Auschwitz* (Amsterdam: Polak and Van Gennep, 1965).

[6] The text from John is a confusing text given our contemporary experience. Even more for our theology in dialogue that completely rejects an association of Judas with the Jewish people, this text must be understood as a metaphor for Christians. Even so, the contention that Satan enters into Judas pales in light of the massive apostasy of Christians during the Third Reich. We follow the narrative line here but will, as the chapter develops, suggest alternative readings of texts such as this one. Above all, any reading of this text requires some form of commentary in our post-Shoah world.

[7]The notion of incarnate evil does create a polarity of types in the Johannine narrative between Jesus (the word become flesh) and Judas. Such a polarity creates difficulty for us since neither can we be comfortable with the polarity even as a narrative tool nor can we accept the symbol of Judas as incaranate evil if the Nazis must be seen as bearers of radical evil. Any discussion of Judas requires this renewed discussion of how we talk about evil in a post-Shoah Christian theology.

[8]This point, I take it, is the reason for the uneasiness that Elie Wiesel feels toward simplistic messianic theologies after the Shoah or the reason that Emil Fackenheim finds locating the redeeming voice of God at Auschwitz to be, itself, an atrocity.

[9]That phrase is extraordinarily awkward given the events of our time and the content of this paper. We have no right to arrogate to ourselves this role of forgiver of the Jews. I mean here more that we have a duty to tell our narratives so that there is no room to suppose that we still teach a contempt for the Jews.

10 Ellis Rivkin's fine work, *What Crucified Jesus?* (Nashville: Abingdon Press, 1985) gives sufficient clues to assist our re-thinking the tradition of Jewish guilt.

[11]This view is the one clearly advocated by Roth and Rubenstein, *Approaches to Auschwitz*, pp.31-35.

12 The eerie connection of this narrative on Pilate and the latter day Aryans in the Third Reich is not to be overlooked. The condemnation of Jesus comes from a perspective shaped by neither Judaism nor by the views of Jesus' disciples. I do not wish, either, to pass responsibility on to the Romans even though Roman power is actually responsible for Jesus' death. The point is that a perspective fed by general cruelty and shaped by lack of respect for anything spiritual will make the Jew (here, the Jew Jesus) a target of that cruelty.

CHAPTER 7:
CHRISTIANITY AND
THE KINGDOM OF THE NIGHT

A Christian Midrash Taking Shape

The particular Biblical texts that have formed the basis for Christian theologies of redemption are too numerous to give a fully developed interpretation of these texts in this chapter.[1] Thus, what follows is a selective example of how a new interpretation (what we have called a midrash) can be developed on these Christian texts. The selective tool I am using is the image(s) of Jesus presented in these narratives. The texts can, then, become a resource for the plurality of readings that we seek in this new approach looking at the Jesus of the "Last Supper," the Jesus of the Trial sequence, and the Jesus on the cross. Naturally, the narrative flow suggests that these textual pieces are interlinked and thus present the same Jesus but that, as we know, cannot be presumed. In addition, the plurality of narratives already presents us with ambiguities that are resident in the texts as they conflict with one another in narrative detail. Our interest is to suggest the plurality of ways that the texts present for us images of Jesus insofar as those images form a foundation for theologies of redemption.

1. Jesus of the "Last Supper"

Not only are we familiar with difference in detail that have intrigued generations of Biblical scholars, the narrative pieces connected with the last supper give interesting new clues to a reading of Jesus' image as a vehicle for the narrative. The simplest form of the narrative in Mark portrays Jesus as teacher, Son of man, Sacramental sacrifice, and shepherd. The narrative is usually read as a focus upon the image of sacramental sacrifice. In this, Jesus forsees his death as an inevitable part of the covenant relationship he has with God. *The Oxford Annotated Bible* records that Jesus' words make him the mediator of a new relationship between God and humans.[2] That is to say, Jesus is seen as the propitiatory sacrifice initiating a new covenant. That Jesus apparently introduces this idea by speaking of himself as the bread and wine (in all three synoptic gospels) endorses not only his acceptance of the role of mediator but also his view that God is working through him to establish a new covenant. But the text does not speak of a new covenant. The text (in the case of each of the synoptic gospels) reads as if Jesus sees his place as a part of a larger significance of the present covenant with Israel. In that reading Jesus is made a piece of the fulfillment of that covenant. Thus, what is the meaning of the supper for the reader?

The text is more complicated than this for the Jesus of the narrative is beset not only with the burden of the role of mediator but is seen as a referee in the midst of group that will betray him, deny him, and abandon him. In fact, this complex of imagery is similar to the portrayal as given in Matthew and Luke. Given this, the image of sacramental mediator slips to the background behind other images—teacher and shepherd. Jesus the teacher is a frustrated person in the face of possible failure. Even more, the teacher is resigned to this fate. When the shepherd is struck, the sheep will scatter. Thus, the meaning of the text becomes murky. Do we have the confident mediator of a covenant—this *is* my body—or the resigned teacher— "For the Son of man goes as it is written of him,..."?(Mark 14:21)

But this text is itself a commentary. Both Matthew and Mark point to Zechariah 13:7 (cf., Mark 14:27 or Matthew 26:31 in the *Appendix*) as the foundation of meaning for the events yet to happen. Is this merely passing reference to a justifying text or is it midrash? If it is a midrash that speaks of the terrible testing of God, then we tremble at its meaning for us. The words of Zechariah are words that haunt us in the light of the Shoah—that two thirds shall be cut off and one third will tested *with the fire.* Surely the words mean that the path that Jesus takes is a path that will bring this dreadful consequence, that the prophecy of Zechariah is linked intrinsically with Jesus' own understanding of his betrayal and death. Yet, how can we say this now, now that so many were cut off out of pure hatred not by the hand of God but by the hand of evil. And to this we are left struck dumb. Surely, the death of Jesus cannot mean this judgment on Israel.

But are there alternative readings that can be offered at least to give a way out of this dilemma? The Jesus of the last supper is an image that can be seen as the midrash upon Zechariah. Indeed, the tradition has seen the sacrament as an exclusive claim but principally because we have read the word "new" into the text of the narrative. Surely, looking at this text anew can offer another way (or ways), looking at the text in the context of Israel's covenant. This Jesus is the one whose blood is intrinsically connected with that covenant. His death is emblematic of faithfulness to that covenant; this death is the reassurance of the validity of that covenant. Indeed, the interpretation here is a commentary that keys faithfulness to that covenant as the best way to read Zechariah. For this Jesus, the clue to Zechariah is not the judgment (two thirds shall be cut off or that even the remaining third will be tested with fire) but rather that the point of the prophet is covenant faithfulness. That is what Jesus dies for.

This means that Jesus openly attacks the conclusion that human tragedies are a part of God's covenant plan or that we can see with ready eyes that these tragedies are a sign of God's judgment. The whole tradition of we are punished for our sins is rejected as a way to read Zechariah. Instead, the way to read Zechariah is to focus on the prophet's appeal to covenant faithfulness. This means that Christians cannot read this text as the institution of a new covenant or even as the sign of God's judgment on Israel. To read the images of the betrayal of the disciples, even, as a declaration of universal human guilt also misses the point. This Jesus calls simply for covenant faithfulness which is worth his giving his body and blood for.

But Jesus is the frustrated teacher who knows even as he appeals for courage in commitment, for the disciples to cast their lot with him, that these disciples will betray, deny, and abandon him. He also lives with the strong conviction that he is bound to accept this fate by his own sense of mission. In fact, Jesus is portrayed even in this narrative section as the one who boldly steps forward as one ready to stand fast in faithfulness before forces that would challenge the roots of that faithfulness. Our midrash for that is complicated. How do we read this self-image of the Jesus of the last supper and gethsemane?

Indeed, how do we read this text as such now that we know what we know? The Jesus of the text is not alone in this matter. Surely, so many others have been abandoned to stand for God even those who would not, could not choose that fate. Of what comfort is it for those who died in the Shoah but could not choose to say "For the Son of man goes as it is written of him,...?" The naive belief that the response must be covenant faithfulness sounds hollow before the cries of those who died even as it sounds noble in the mouth of Jesus of Nazareth. Do we dare say that this Jesus who dies for the sake of many dies for these victims of the Shoah? Can we say that without mouthing an obscenity? But dare we not say it for these are

surely worthy of such compassion? But dying for them seems to be the essential
obscenity in a world where death was stripped of any dignity.

Surely the text does not seek this solution either to our theologies of
redemption. Must we be trapped by this reading of the text that so wishes to
universalize the Jesus of the last supper into a figure who dies for everyone even
those whose death dwarfs the meaning of that of Jesus. Surely, we will condemn
the text to hollowness if we persist in that direction. No, the text has another
direction that makes of Jesus truly a sacramental figure that divinizes not his death
but rather sees Jesus as one who ultimately points to the author of the kingdom of
God as the only possible hope in the face of all this. I will not eat and drink with
you again until the day when I eat with you in the kingdom of God. This proleptic
vision that sets the kingdom of God as the point of view which alone can counteract
the kingdom of the night is the final word of this text. For us, this may be an
invitation to dialogue about what can be our hope. Nevertheless, not my will but
thine be done is Jesus' prayer in the garden. Redemption comes not in Jesus blood,
not in his mediation but in the God who works to bring his kingdom in the fulness
of time, who calls us to covenant faithfulness. This, like other texts, is an invitation
to dialogue about what we can say is God's will.

Even this reading rings empty at times to our ears as we puzzle about what
can possibly be the "fulness of time." Still, this reading which also comes from the
text closes our mouths about the finality of Jesus and opens another vision, that of
Jesus, which draws us back in respect to God's people, Israel for whom Jesus lived
and died. This reading is bound to be ambiguous in that it is openended looking for
a hope proleptically; nevertheless this reading does provide a principal rule for
reading other texts, that Jesus who stands at the center of Christian faith remains
fundamentally Jewish in his self-understanding and no reading of texts is fitting
(especially post-Shoah) that breaks this vital, unbreakable connection between Jesus
and the Jews.

2. Jesus of the Trial Sequence

In fact, our earlier discussion avoids for a moment the image Jesus the lamb
that the tradition has often imposed on the passion narrative (we will return to the
Johannine text in our comments here). The tradition has most prominently offered
up the image of Jesus as lamb as the principal meaning of this text which means that
this text has always been used as a midrash of the tradition as well. On the other
hand, the synoptics do not cast this narrative into that imagery. Jesus the lamb is
the theology of the tradition principally derived from the gospel according to John
and not explicitly found in the synoptics. How is it, then, that we continue to read
these texts in this way setting them into this theology of sacrifice and expiation

drawn from the imagery of the sacrificial lamb (in John, this imagery is also muddled with the image of the passover lamb, at the very least begging for a dialogue over the confluting of these images)?

The trial sequence (there are at least two scenes in this sequence) instead extends the imagery of the earlier section but in a peculiar way acts in the narrative to throw out efforts to impose an identity on Jesus. Jesus continues to apply only implicitly the image of Son of man to himself (except in the Marcan exception as Jesus is portrayed responding to the High Priest saying "I am..." Mark 14:62). Does this mean that all that need be said about who Jesus is can already be determined from the previous texts? In that we conclude that Jesus is the teacher who sees his mission as one calling the people of Israel back to covenant faithfulness and the mediator who through his own teaching and action rejects images of the God who punishes in favor of the God who promises the kingdom in the fulness of time.

Surely, this is the Jesus who is brought before trial; the Jesus who is fully in agreement with the Pharisees who sought to teach a similar message even if in different ways. This is not a Jesus who stands in conflict with the Pharisees but one who has little or no religious conflict with them at all. Matthew portrays this Jesus as the one who so respects the Pharisees that he points to them as the models of how his disciples should be and even more (Matthew 5:20).[3] Thus, we cannot conclude by the text of the synoptics that there was an essential religious conflict between Jesus and the Jewish leaders.

Indeed, the synoptic texts bear this conclusion as well. The trial before the chief priests is odd in its structure and format[4] and seems to mock the whole scene as a farce. Whether this mocking was an early Christian condemnation of the Jewish leadership or whether the mocking seems to be a subtle way to let the reader know that the scene cannot be taken seriously as a true reading of the Jewish leadership seems ambiguous given the text (eg., Mark 14:55-65). That Jesus knew (or is portrayed as knowing) this mockery seems evident in his behavior. The Jesus of the trial is an anti-person; that is, he completely absents himself from the action mentally and vocally as if the whole scene has no real impact upon real events. His responses recorded in Matthew and Luke are few except simply to say "you say that I am."(Luke 22:70)

What do we make of this? Most traditional readings of this text make the assumption that the narrator shifts attention to the portrayed accusers as if the point is that these leaders were unjustified and corrupt. In fact, one conclusion might be that they were corrupt, but then we need ask with Ellis Rivkin, "What Crucified Christ?"[5] That is, we need to recognize the portrayal as a whole to get a clue about what was happening that could make sense of this mockery outside of the usual condemnation and even mockery of the Jews that is assumed to be the point of this sequence. We can cast that aside by reading the text again looking at the Jesus of the trial sequence.

Again, we ask, what do we make of this narrative interlude? An alternative might be to take seriously the anomoly of the scene, that it is an interlude. What this means is that the trial does not decide the fate of Jesus. His decisions where already fully made; his fate was already decided (either by Jesus' choice or by God's will) before the trial begins. Jesus is the one who has decided, chosen to offer himself up to the consequences of his boldness to assert complete faithfulness to the covenant (we cannot read the Jesus of the synoptics, who accepts fully the Torah, through the prism of the Pauline shift in Christian thinking). Thus, the narrative importance of the trial is not to set it as a vehicle for the progression of events.

All of this stands as presumption to a re-reading of the trial culmination—the interaction between Pilate and the crowd. No section of the narrative bears greater irony and ambiguity than this section. We have no way to sort through this ambiguity except by the simple recognition that the story is a narrative interlude that *does not effect the course of events.* That is to say, the events have already been decided before either trial scene. This conclusion is not only founded on the recognition of Jesus' personal decision or on the ultimate vision of the plan of God (let us speak to this in the next part) but ultimately on the belief that Pilate, himself, had already set the course. The trial is a show orchestrated by the procurate for his own cruel fancy and for full justification of his actions. The great irony of the text can be explained by seeing Pilate for what he was rather than for what he seems to be according to the narrative.

But, then, why the mockery in the narrative, why do we have this elaborate narrative interlude? Two possible directions of explanation can help us unravel this perplexing puzzle. The first direction is to take seriously the section as neither merely an interlude nor a piece of the larger narrative. That is, the text is a separate piece of narrative designed to offer definite conclusions quite separate from the specific fate of Jesus. That Jesus refuses identification is more than a sorting through the Christian question of how do we understand Jesus. This sorting is also a sifting through the whole tradition to uncover appropriate ways to understand the covenant. Jesus is only the blessed "if you say that it is so." Indeed, the challenge of the text is upon the reader to determine how we shall understand at any point in time the meaning of the covenant promises. Even more, the teacher Jesus who calls us to covenant faithfulness is focussing our attention on that question of the abiding identity of Israel over against their identity in any given circumstance. We can call this the messianic age and it will be so for us.

However, the very character of the text compels us to challenge that view. The words "you say that it is so" are taken not as an affirmation of our power to shape our world by our views but of the ineffectuality of that effort when placed into the long range pattern of the covenant relationship and promises. Jesus seems to treat this question in the opposite way than we normally do—that we call this the messianic age because of who Jesus was—by indicating that we call this the messianic age because we have chosen this to be so. This challenge to our traditional sense opens even further the ambiguity of our conclusions both about the meaning of the specific events surrounding Jesus in the passion narrative and about our theologies as such as tools for bringing meaning to events.

Doesn't this ambiguity also create the opportunity to dialogue both about the viability of messsianic visions and the possibility of present hope?

The Marcan text seems to be an anomoly. There Jesus breaks silence by saying "I am..."(Mark 14:62). Is this anomoly actual? The text is ironic as well for the confession (perhaps more indicative of the challenge facing a persecuted Christian community of four decades later) immediately precedes an appeal to the apocalyptic imagery of the Son of man coming at the fulness of time. In other words, the confession is of little significance when placed alongside Jesus' personal witness that our trust is in God who in mystery and wonderment still is promised to bring a kingdom at the end of time. This is an irony not only of narrative flow—that the question to Jesus seems so monumental but is not—but of our experience. The faithful one of God is that one who looks to God in covenant in spite of what we might (meaning our time, culture, religion) say.

Thus, this direction of understanding makes the text a narrative whole that acts as more than an interlude. The meaning can be seen as the systematic rejection of any theologies of fulfillment not on the basis of the falseness of what we say or don't say about Jesus but on the basis of the very nature of such theologies in the eternal perspective of the covenant. This rule of interpretation which we now apply to all theologies is a powerful corrective to the standard teaching of contempt for the Jews that is so readily made a corallary to this narrative piece about the Jewish leaders.

Nevertheless, a second direction begs our attention. The narrative style itself might be seen as an invitation to understand the whole as intended irony. That is to say, the mockery is done in complete earnest with the full expectation that the reader will see this irony. Pilate is shown to be innocent (note the great pains of the author of Luke). But the innocence of Pilate is a mockery. Knowledge of the circumstances should have clued us that this was tongue in cheek of a serious sort that fully intended to implicate Pilate in a show. Pilate is not innocent in this drama but guilty. He washes his hands ironically of the blood of redemption (we now read that as this full investment in covenant faithfulness) while the crowds so often spoken of as the Jews receive fully the blood of Jesus. This irony is so evident in the narrative that we are now quite alarmed that our reading of the text has been so narrowly assured in the past. This is not drama as we have played it in the past,[6] but farce that carries a sting not only for Matthew's readers but for those of us who so readily see just one and only one meaning to this text. How have we missed the irony before?

But the drama is more than just farce. The implication taking this direction of reading is that the only true identity of Jesus is that which again tightly ties him to his people (I have come only to the lost sheep of the house of Israel). To claim that Jesus' death was like all those who died in the Shoah because Jesus was a Jew is obscene. However, to claim that Jesus would have suffered the same fate as his people in the Shoah because he was a Jew (by both choice and birth even though his fate in the Shoah would have been the same regardless) is a brute fact no matter what we, Christians, might choose to say about him.

Thus, we can openly say that now and hereafter we are compelled to tell this drama not as an anti-Jewish drama but as the drama of the Jew Jesus. It is our drama (those of us who are both gentile and Christian) only as this Jesus has invited us in. Above all, the drama is different from the emotion of its usual telling. As compelling as that drama has been, it has succeeded by feeding on hatred, a hatred that is missing from the narrative itself. This narrative instead bears an irony that flavors our reading now.

Still, the text now begs us into the image of the lamb for the words of Matthew (slim evidence here) do force us to see how the text is also a midrash on the tradition of the sin offering. The imagery is unmistakeable and the role of Jesus, in this view, in what the people say, is that of the sacrificial lamb. Matthew's imagery, however, is given meaning in the larger context of the narrative. The drama, if void of irony, would imply that Jesus is the expiation, that Jesus is the lamb. However, the narrative structure shows more that Jesus does not accept this as his role but rather it is yet another contextual, theological image imposed on him. The Matthean text (eg., Matthew 27:25) does demand that we read the passion narrative through this imagery of the sacrificial lamb. Perhaps, quite the opposite is suggested.

The Johannine text (John 18:19-24, 33-38) is, however, another story. This narrative has little of the irony (at least on the surface) that is found in the synoptic texts. In fact, there is no Trial sequence in John but rather a narrative structure for a series of discourses by Jesus. The point is clear from this text that Jesus is not on trial for much as with the synoptics the trial has nothing to do with Jesus' ultimate fate. Indeed, the trial scene is made a farce but in a different way than with the synoptics. It is a farce in that Jesus is portrayed as controlling events. If there is a trial here it is not of Jesus. Whatever traditions might remain common to the gospel writers, it is clear that John's is a very different kind of narrative from that of the synoptics.

John's narrative, in fact, refuses to allow blame to be a reason in any way for the events taking place. His discourses make clear that the issue is not what has been said or not said, done or not done by Jesus. Thus, this narrative also rejects any theologies that see God's actions as direct punishment for sin. The point is not that at all in this gospel. In fact, sin is of fairly minor importance as a theme. The main theme is that of truth and the commitment to the truth.

In this way, John's rendering coincides with the synoptics in that Jesus refuses to settle for labels that we give but rather sees his entire teaching work for one purpose—to bear witness to the truth. There is little doubt in this gospel that the truth is intimately connected to Jesus' teaching and life and, thus, we have the compounding of allusions to the witness of his words and actions. But this means that the truth is that which is connected to the teaching and not to his person as such. The truth is still God in God's teaching word. Jesus does not appeal to himself (i.e., what he does or what happens to him) as the witness for his justification but rather to his words and ultimately to his Father (the talk of unity and union in this gospel often confuses this matter in our minds mostly because we conceive of mystical union principally in substantial terms and not in ethical-cognitive terms as John does, truth is a corallary to knowing and loving).

But the enemies in this text seem all the more starkly drawn. The Jews are the villains in the drama by our teaching. They have been the villains in the drama at any rate even in spite of ourselves. They are the ones who steadfastly refuse to see the truth in Jesus' words. It is to them, is it not, that Jesus speaks as he appeals to his words and actions as his witness? Such has been our reading that in spite of the ambiguities of the synoptics seems to raise without question the ugly head of the teaching of contempt in the midst of our scripture. What ambiguity is there in this text that raises up to open for us a new avenue of reading?

To this dilemma we bring the image of the lamb of God. In fact, the whole gospel might be seen as a midrash on this imagery. For John, the question is one of Jewish identity. Thus, the Jesus of John's trial is the lamb of God but more the image is a tool for understanding Jewish self-understanding (in the narrative, this means both for Jesus and for the author of the gospel). There is irony in this text but of a different sort than we have seen thus far. The irony is in the very nature of being a Jew. We see this in this text, most troublesome of them all, only if we once again allow Jesus to be a Jew even in spite of the way the text is usually seen (Jesus and the Jews). Jesus' struggle for identity is the same struggle as that of the whole people (as Jesus saw himself connected to his people). The trial is then more than just confrontation of opinions about being Jewish (about being close to God), but is that occasion for sorting out the implications of being Jewish.

The implication as completely unacceptable as it now sounds to us is that the Jew is both the one chosen by God for special relationship and the lamb of God offered to the world for the sake of the world. Both of these identities expose the people to the full force of the world's own rejection of God. The two wedded together condemn the people to a fate of being enemies of the world. The one who would save is precisely the one who would be hated. Can I even say this now given what we know? Dare I not say it in the naivete that things will somehow be different in the future if I turn from the dilemma? The battle over Jesus' identity is the battle over what it means to be a Jew but not in the usual way that this text has been read by Christians, that the real Jew is the disciple of Jesus, but in this new way that the real Jew is the one who bears a fate because he/she bears the name and mission of God. The problem remains how to define who it is that bears this name and mission. At the very least, we can allow the narrative of the Christian text lead us once again into an open dialogue on who is called the people of God.

This image is, however, too much to accept in the light of the Shoah. In fact, the image appeals to similar themes that make the *Akeda* (Genesis 22) unacceptable for understanding the Shoah.[7] Indeed, this almost fatalistic view of Jewish identity while alarmingly close to the truth of our time cannot be "true" for us post-Shoah. The image, in itself, leads us to the presumption that the Jew is fatalistically condemned to be the victim. While the past may give support to such a claim, the victimization of the Jew ought have nothing to do with Jewish identity (the great abomination of the Shoah was that it did) nor with the purposes of God which the image of the lamb of God suggests. In fact, this conclusion might close the matter except that the lamb of the Johannine text is not a victim. Jesus in the trial here is the one in control. Jesus is an image of the resister who refuses to allow the forces of fate to determine the future. Steadfastly, this Jesus forges a vision of resistence through unbreakable commitment to the covenant that refuses ultimately to envision the people of God as the ultimate victims of history. Jewish identity is not that of the victim but that of the one resisting the world and its forces of destruction (yes even when those forces are a Christian world). This image of the resister arises especially out of the Johanine narrative. The image of resistance, therefore, becomes one image of Jewish identity. It is a call from the Jesus of this text to see Jewish identity linked with resistance when that identity is fundamentally threatened.

Indeed, this very political/moral image of Jesus may be the point of all of this narrative. At least the narrative can be read in that way. Also, there is no great surprise that Jesus, the Jew, is the prime (perhaps the only) model of resistence (against political corruption) in this narrative (surely, Pilate is no model of resistence!!!). In this model, John has linked with the synoptic writers approaching this theme in a way quite different but pointing to a similar conclusion—that Jesus is no victim but the image of the resister parexcellence. The great tragedy of our tradition is that we have failed to see that this strength of resistence is derived from Jesus' Jewishness and not from a war against that Jewishness.[8]

3. The Jesus of the Cross

The narrative possibilities derived thus far from two sets of narrative sections in the extended passion narrative have opened up directions in thought and helped us locate rules of interpretation enabling the heightening of the appropriate ambiguity of the text so that our teaching can be released from the disease of contempt for the Jews. We have isolated the rule that the narrative is Jewish in character demanding an inclusive vision (including the Jews) for Christians as they read their scripture. This rule frees us to see the implications of Jesus as teacher from within the Jewish tradition of that time and to see the texts as midrash of tradition (Jesus as oral torah). That we cannot anymore settle for a view of God's judgment as a punishment for sin seems evident from the text that calls instead for a vision of the God who calls us to covenant obedience and hope in the promised kingdom in the fulness of time.

The great irony that this vision itself displays in the texts has led us to see that the Jesus of the texts can be viewed as a model of the larger struggle for Jewish identity in a world where the choices might have been to succumb to the culture, or to suffer as victims of the culture or to courageously forge resitence to these pressures by steadfast obedience to the covenant and unshakeable hope in the promises of God. Naturally this vision is ambiguous in its application to experience and not surprisingly to its application to an understanding(?) of the Shoah. The vision is proleptic in character and eternal in scope. Yet, the vision is political/historical in application.

With this background already we can turn to the images of Jesus on the cross. In fact, the two—Jesus and cross—are interwoven in such a way in tradition that the cross is taken to imply Jesus. Much of Christian tradition has claimed that the full revelation of God in Jesus is found at the cross. So deeply ingrained is this view that the story of the crucifixion is and has become the story of Christianity, confessionally and theologically. Jesus so loves us that he willingly gives himself as a sacrifice on our behalf. The beauty of that imagery is so compelling that it appeals in narrative strength even to non-Christians. The ugly ramifications of this story, however, are rivalled by none in the ears of Jews. If love is the image of Jesus here, the stark brutality displayed in our story has instilled deep feelings of resentment and hatred that prey upon emotions coming from we know not where to produce violence and anti-love toward those we might most profitably love.

It is difficult to rid ourselves of the implication that Jesus is fully abandoned by everyone even though deserving none of this. We instinctively feel the injustice of this, even those of us who have difficulty fighting for injustices otherwise. Could there be a more powerful narrative drama than this? Isn't sympathy the emotion that the narrator seeks to draw from us?

But the text (especially Matthew 27:38ff.) is clearly more even other than these sentiments (sentimentalities). It is, itself, a powerful interpretation of the prophetic tradition. The Jesus on the cross as displayed by Matthew and Mark and Luke is the prophetic suffering servant of Isaiah. The allusion is so strong that we are even confronted in the words of Jesus with the complementary words of Psalm 22. And, indeed, the point is clear that the prophetic image of suffering servant is to be linked with the imagery of Psalm 22. This text (Matthew 27:46-50) is a midrashic interpretation. And if it is midrashic, then this text must be seen in the light of the texts that stand as the basic focus of interpretation—Psalms and Isaiah.

We cannot do the entire job here of sorting out this connection. Thus, we make only beginning steps in the process. Surely, the point of this midrash and the whole passion narrative is that the question of theodicy must be understood in the context of covenant. The appeal to Psalms and Isaiah certainly presumes that as the beginning point. Thus, the servant in Isaiah 52-53 is one perceived by the precepts of the commands of the covenant. The point is what makes one great—a servant of God. Isaiah's prophetic vision is much like that of Hosea 14 or Jeremiah 31 that greatness is dependent on God's choosing and on our choosing back—mutual relationship with God.

This foundation for understanding must mean that the cross as symbol is not principally to direct our attention to Jesus dying. The death of Jesus means nothing in itself. Meaning comes only in God's choosing. Thus, we are given by Matthew and Mark a narrative midrash on Psalm 22. The words "My God, My God, why have you forsaken me?" are imprinted upon the mind of the reader by repeating them both in Aramaic and Greek. The point is not a selective reading of Psalm 22 but a presuppostion that we know the Psalm and can see the intended meaning. The appeal turns on the word "why." The why automatically directs our attention not to Jesus but to God and his choosing. That the why is there in this text taken from the earlier text should alert us to the fact that the narrative is intended as a further explication of how we should understand the covenant plan of God.

Of course, the text (Matthew 27:46) is often read as just one more sign of Jesus being abandoned. But the full link to Psalm 22 cannot lead us in that direction. Instead, the why is not a cry of despair but rather an appeal to search out the mystery of God and his plan for any time. Or we could say the word thrusts us again into the ambiguity of our relation in covenant with this God. The why is both an expression of hope (that there is an answer to the why) and profound trust (that the why posed to God even in anger and puzzlement is far better than the why thrown back at ourselves in our limited possibilities).

But this seems to drag the bottom from under most of our christologies. What is there in Jesus that is unique? Rosemary Ruether may be correct in offering an answer to this question by saying the uniqueness question is the wrong one. The important question is how Jesus has successfully brought us closer to a true vision of the purposes of God. Jesus is paradigmatic then and not by necessity unique. Christology does not need to seek the uniqueness of our claims or of Jesus to be revelation for us. Instead, Jesus as oral torah, as the one who points us in greater clarity to the God of the covenant (or to us gentiles to some clarity in potential covenant), is enough for us. To understand that all along Jesus sees the Father as the source of all hope and redemption and not his actions is a most significant rule of interpretation as we create a new Christian midrash for a post-Shoah Christian theology, for now the focus shifts for Christians from Jesus' actions to the words of the text and their meaning.

Do we lose our assurance if Jesus is not the unique truth for us but points to God as the only unique truth? Perhaps John Pawlikowski is correct to say that the theme of the incarnation is truly the unique contribution of Christianity and chris-tology.[9] Perhaps in this we still have a unique perch to take. Yet, Pawlikowski does not wish to argue for the theme of the incarnation but rather the fact of the incarnation. That God was actually present in Jesus is, for Pawlikowski, the essence of the Christian perspective that in itself provides the resource for shaping a response to the Shoah. But this claim of the fact of the incarnation is not present explicitly in the synoptic narratives. The claim might be present in the Johannine text, however; and a return to that text (John 19:17-30) is a necessary road to travel before we conclude this survey of the passion narratives.

Jesus on the cross in the gospel of John is quite another figure[10] from the Jesus of the synoptics. There are three different scenarios in this text (at least)—Jesus as the word made flesh, Jesus as the passover lamb, and Jesus as the persecuted servant of God. We also see that this narrative is structured around a set of references to the written scripture set off each by the phrase "this was to fulfill the scripture." The structure suggests more than just proof-texts; the narrative is an intended midrash on a cycle of texts from the Tanach that we need to identify.

Surely this text (cf., John 19:24) shows that the claim that Jesus is the oral torah is at least as fitting an understanding of the theme Jesus as the word made flesh as the imposed meaning of ontological incarnation. The shift in this text toward a midrashic form at such a critical point in the narrative is reinforcement for the belief that the gospel writer directs the reader toward the context of torah for a proper understanding of the role of Jesus. The cycle of texts (in the gospel of John introduced by "this was to fulfill the scripture") that form the midrash clearly point us to that fact as well if we take the texts of John's narrative of Jesus crucifixion in full and in relation to one another as the narrative suggests.

Each of the texts from the Tanach integrated into the narrative are reference to God's redemptive acts. Each of these texts, individually, are cries for help in the midst of times of persecution. Each of the texts begs for a reading that remains appropriately unsettled (ambiguous) for the acts of God to redeem are set by God and not humans. Thus, each text is a piece of a theology of theodicy. This set of texts from the Tanach, I contend, is a cycle that when read together presents an interpretation of tradition. That interpretation on Exodus 12, Psalm 22, Psalm 69, and Zechariah 12 is clear. God acts in his own time to save those who are faithful. In these acts, God and God alone is the rescuer.

If this is the message of John's Jesus on the cross, then the word from this text reinforces the message of the earlier narrative sequences. Jesus is teacher who through his words and actions invites his followers (disciples) to continue in faithfulness for God, and God alone, is the one who redeems. Still, this message is firmly set in the context of Jesus' Jewishness. To be faithful for Jesus is to be a true Jew and that faithfulness is central to the invitation that Jesus extends.

Yet, Jesus is also the lamb of the passover in this narrative sequence. The imagery is made quite obvious in the textual references to the passover preparation. In this, this gospel differs strikingly with the synoptics. The intention of portraying Jesus as the passover lamb feeds our reading of the narrative and is focussed for us on the two joining texts (Exodus 12:46 and Zechariah 12:10). The one text is drawn from the set of instructions to Israel not only for the night of the passover but also for the remembrance of that night. The gospel writer uses this text as an ultimate witness to Jesus' identity—he is the one whose bones are not broken.

However, the meaning of this interpretation from the gospel of John is not obvious. The reference could mean as a whole tradition has said that Jesus replaces the passover lamb and thus the passover: that this Jesus is the new revelation that replaces the old, that in Jesus God acts to bring about redemption. Though the interpretation might fit and renders a compelling drama perhaps as exciting as that of the Exodus, this interpretation ultimately fails to hold together the other strands of the Johannine text. Unless the imagery is linked with the other lamb (Jesus as the sacrificial lamb), the picture of redemption is at best cloudy and at worst completely defeating. The victory of the moment in the narrative has no obvious evidence. What redemption does God bring in Jesus? Above all, the text does not bring the other imagery to bear. John does not make that connection except perhaps earlier in the gospel ("behold the lamb of God who takes away the sin of the world" Jn 1:29). The connection is not made here at this critical point.

The text in John 19 could be read differently with emphasis on the Zechariah reference. The twinning of the two texts suggests a tradition of reading—a midrash on the passover. Zechariah is a text that implies that the God who redeems redeems for a purpose. In fact, the text leads us in quite a different direction than what is normally read into the passion narrative. The ones who look upon "him whom they have wounded" are quite different than the assumed protaganists of the Christian tradition. The one wounded is (if Jesus) not perceived in the same way as the typical Christian reading would suggest. The purpose of the looking is quite different than the bald statement of the narrative has implied for generations of Christians.

The Zechariah text is part of a call to Israel who having just been recipient of God's redemptive blessing through their own action to ward off the enemy are asked to look with compassion on those they have wounded. The passover redemption is now viewed anew (in Zechariah), in different light. Israel is redeemed for a purpose, to be rescuers and healers, not people of vengeance and hatred or of indifference. If Jesus is the passover lamb in this sense, Jesus is a reminder of this call. If Jesus is presented in this way, then he, being the lamb, according to John, is symbol of the call to rescue even those we have wounded—the symbol of the rescuer. And, if John ties the passion narrative to the text in Zechariah, thus wedding the passion to this reinterpretation of the passover, then we have a point of true dialogue on the link between the passover and the crucifixion.

And, thus, we make sense of the third direction of the text. Jesus does not replace the passover but rather represents an alternative interpretation of it. In this, Jesus is perceived as the servant of God who suffers (Psalm 22 and 69). The point of suffering is not that either God's people suffer because they are chosen or that they suffer because they have failed. Both might be true incidentally but are neither sufficient to provide meaning to suffering. In fact, there is no meaning in suffering as such, only questions and pleas. The point is rather that any meaning must find its source in God and God's promises and God's purposes.

This invitation to faithfulness as the way to understanding the role of the servant of God not only draws from the prophetic tradition but demands our rethinking that tradition. If Jesus, the servant is victim as we are tempted to say, then the only meaning to this text is that suffering is cruel and not God's way. There is no way out for the victim (in fact, the image given to the synoptic narrative as a rule) as such except some transcendent hope in God's ultimate victory. The synoptics seem to suggest this type of proleptic vision of that day in the fulness of time. However, the Jesus of John is not the victim (and perhaps we should read this for the synoptics who also use Psalm 22) but the rescuer—the one who leads out of darkness into light.

This servant who is rescuer is surely at first a moral/religious leader who seeks to fashion the redemption of the people on moral/religious principles—to feed the poor, release the captive, give sight to the blind, etc. Still, this moral/religious leadership has ultimate political consequences. To be faithful as a servant in the way that this Jesus portrays is to seek the ultimate change of the political order for the sake of seeking justice, God's justice.[11]

Again, the ones whose suffering made them truly victims in the Shoah, victims without choices, will see little consolation in a servant figure who is also a victim. All of the religious imagery misses the mark if it is only to portray Jesus again as victim. Even more, Jesus cannot under any circumstances be seen as a victim in the same way as the children of the Shoah. To make this connection is not only insensitive, it is obscene, making a religious symbol stand for an immoral abomination. God's relation to Jesus cannot be seen, cannot be spoken of as the same as God's relation to the Shoah, whatever that might be. The only way to rid our theologies of this problem in meaning is to refuse any effort to make Jesus a victim. Jesus is not a victim; he is a rescuer.

Can we change the passion drama together with all of its emotional history in this radical way? Indeed, we can and must do this for the sake of the health of Christianity. We must make this image of Jesus that impresses upon us the image as followers of Jesus our own; the only viable response to the suffering of the Shoah for Christians was and is that we are rescuers. This invitation to be faithful as we say Jesus was in being rescuers is the only essential image of our faith that could have effectively combatted the evil of the Shoah. Indeed, it was, even in vaguest terms, the image that enabled many to become rescuers even in spite of themselves.

The multitude of meanings and images that can be brought to the texts of this extended narrative (the passion narrative) must be maintained as a resource for the kind of flexibility that can humble us and provide insight for us. However, this alternative Christian interpretation of our scripture, for the passion narrative, is now that the whole of the text with all its images be read in such a way so as to depict Jesus and his followers as rescuers. It is thus that we can look upon those whom we have wounded and know that in our zeal to be known as the chosen people ourselves we have unwittingly rejected this Jesus who in his Jewishness, called his people to a renewed faithfulness of rescuing the world as God's servants.[12]

Notes

[1]The full texts can be found in the appendix: Matthew 27, Mark 15, Luke 23, John 19. Since theologies based on the crucifixion have formed the basis of much of Christian theology, any full treatment would require a more detailed analysis of the various verses, scenes, references and interconnections in each of these texts as well as some comparative analysis. This chapter is suggestive rather than thorough.

[2]*The Oxford Annotated Bible* (Revised Standard Version), Herbert May and Bruce Metzger, ed., (New York: Oxford University Press, 1962), p. 1234.

[3]The scribes are added in Matthew and of interesting note are not included in those who are responsible for the crowd sent to arrest Jesus.

[4]Clearly, one of the most incisive treatments of this issue can be found in Ellis Rivkin, *What Crucified Jesus?*, (Nashville: Abingdon Press, 1984).

[5]Rivkin, *What Crucified Jesus?*

[6]We recognize that the gospel narratives have been literally imbedded in our experience in the form of passion dramas in scores of minor and major productions for each of us. For a critique of this dramatic tradition, cf. Saul Friedman, *The Oberammergau Passion Play: A Lance Against Civilization,* (Carbondale: Southern Illinois University Press, 1984).

[7]A critique of theological interpretations that make use of the *Akeda* for understanding the Shoah, even in ironic ways such as with Elie Wiesel, cf. Zev Garber and Bruce Zuckerman, "Why Do We Call the Holocaust "The Holocaust?": an Inquiry into the Psychology of Labels," in *Modern Judaism*, Vol. 9:2, May 1989, pp. 197-211.

[8]That Jesus represented a reform movement within Judaism cannot be denied (cf., Rivkin). That Jesus opposed Judaism is completely unsupportable given the text of the gospels. This rule of interpretation is as clearly shown in this instance as with any. Even more, by reading the gospel texts in this way (from the vantagepoint of Jesus' Jewishness), we can see that in Judaism, contrary to what has been traditionally true of Christianity, there is a foundation for resistance that is characteristic of what we are saying here of Jesus. Only a Jew, like Jesus, or someone with adherance to these principles of Judaism could have the resolve to counter with such resistance. Surely, my reading owes some insight to Emil Fackenheim, *To Mend The World* (New York: Schocken Books, 1982).

[9]John Pawlikowski, *Christ in the Light of the Christian-Jewish Dialogue,* (New York: Paulist Press, 1982), pp. 108ff.

[10]In fact, Luke also follows this pattern.

[11]I don't believe that I am suggesting something akin to Liberation Theology here but the theme does suggest why Jews might find liberation positions a more appropriate foundation for dialogue; cf. Daniel Cohn-Sherbok, *On Earth As It Is In Heaven*, (Maryknoll: Orbis Books, 1987).

[12]Here, I do intend a connection with the ancient Jewish tradition of Tikkun as recently interpreted by Emil Fackenheim, *To Mend The World*.

CHAPTER 8:
RESURRECTION AS RESCUE

If our development of post-Shoah Christian theology along the lines of a new Christian midrash has produced an outline for reading the passion narrative in a new way, we are still left with an incomplete answer to the question concerning Christian response during the Shoah. The cycle of narratives concerning Peter can give us new insight into Christian understanding of the bystander. The comparable narrative sections concerning Judas can help us see the complexity of developing a response to betrayal and collaboration as Christian response. And, the narrative sections that open up for us various possible images of Jesus within the passion narratives of the gospels can enable us to see in Jesus the model of the one who is faithful resistor. However, where can we find portrayed for us a basis for the Christian as rescuer?

Indeed, we instinctively want to say that rescue is the most natural Christian response. Jesus' command to the disciples is that they love one another and that love is portrayed as the willingness to give up one's life for the sake of the other. Our tradition sees Jesus as the one who is willing to sacrifice so that others might be saved. These are the principles that give foundation for a Christian view of rescue. These are principles that are deeply imbedded in the passion narratives, especially in the superimposed interpretation that all of this is necessary so that Jesus might in faithfulness fulfill God's plan that all might be saved. Then, why was rescue so difficult to find in the most horrendous crisis of our time? Why did so many Christians find so little motivation to risk life and limb for the sake of the Jew who was condemned to die in the Shoah?

There are naturally social and political explanations for the why. There are even moral and psychological explanations that are quite understandable. The pressures upon all who were caught up in the whirlwind of evil and threat make all of the apostasy quite understandable. We know now that the most well-founded principles and motivations can be dashed in the crucible of terrible threat and horror. People who are motivated to act with high principle normally crumbled under the weight of the Nazi machine.[1]

We also know that the high moral calling of love, even when reinforced by the image of the servant Jesus interceding on our behalf, could be obliterated by culture, tradition, antisemitism, and misplaced values of patriotism and loyalty. People could be made indifferent in a selective way. We can be made indifferent subtly and almost without knowing what is happening. Thus, the principles found in the main body of the passion narrative were not enough to risk, with abandon, the charitable act of rescue.

Yet, some did become rescuers. The reasons are not all the same or even explainable for some. The fact is that rescue is the least understandable of acts in the Kingdom of the Night. Rescue was the one foremost act that challenged the basis of the anti- value system of the Kingdom of the Night. Even resistence participates in violence even if the violence can be fully justified. Faithfulness is a defiance yet such that the anti-values of Nazi action remain untouched even as they did form a protection of the dignity of the resistor, warding off that which the murderer would hope to do. Resistence hoped to defeat but realistically expected to be defeated even as that defeat lost its ability to degrade and destroy the dignity of the victim. Rescue was an act that defied but almost with disdain ignored the anti-values and their threat so as to destroy at heart and "soul" the intent of the kingdom of the night. Some were rescuers.[2]

We cannot assume that a new Christian midrash can offer an explanation for the extraordinary efforts of the rescuer. Our midrash is an effort to attempt a theology after the Shoah, to try to say only what can be said now, to try to establish rules for talking about and reading Christian scripture. Rescue is most often a reflex action born out of instantaneous, spontaneous decision even if schooled by certain unshakable values and sympathies. We cannot imagine how a theology can become a guarantee that rescue will be more common in the future or a motivation even for those few who choose on the spot to save rather than ignore. Still, a theology can assist us in shaping our faith so that now in our awareness we can pit models of rescue over-against models of indifference or collaboration.

What model of rescue do we have in the passion narrative? Yes, we superimpose in our tradition a theology of rescue on the narrative. Yet, this superimposed theology is precisely a problem for us. The narrative, as far as it goes, can portray Jesus as rescuer only in his dying since the resurrection is described as an act of God. The rescue in Jesus' dying is attached to an image of expiation—rescuing from sin not from death. The rescue cannot be anything but a spiritual rescue that, powerful as that might be, provides nothing more than an image of faithful resistence, standing with the faithful. What we need is an image of life being snatched from the jaws of death.

The resurrection is that image of life coming from death. Surely, Roy Eckardt understood this ultimate point of post-Shoah Christian theology long before I did.[3] The resurrection is the one point of the narrative that expresses the full meaning of rescue as act that is born by the righteous gentiles of the Shoah, that certain death is robbed of its hold replaced by life. Naturally, we need to exercise great caution in offering this fourth image of Christian response to the Shoah as the resurrection tradition is problematic even as it is hopeful. Yet, the instincts of our interpretation thus far have led us to the threshold of a midrashic reading of the resurrection narrative sections of the gospels as the next, perhaps ultimate, theological word of a Chiristian post-Shoah Christian theology.

The Resurrection Narratives

Willi Marxsen, among others, has reminded us that there are at least two strands of the resurrection narratives in the gospels—the narratives of the empty tomb and the narratives of the appearances of the risen Jesus.[4] Now, we will need to ask if these are indeed two separate narrative strands or whether they are by necessity linked in a single narrative whole. That the gospel of Mark does not include (if our source criticism serves us well) a narrative of resurrection appearances, suggests that there is a distinct separation of traditions represented by the two strands. At any rate, we will look at these two lines of story separately at first. As we do so, we also note that at least a third strand is present in the Pauline tradition, the strand of the appearance of the ascended Christ. That Paul is led to talk about resurrection differently because of his encounter with the ascended Christ is also of concern for our midrash, but remains tangential to the work of this book for now.[5]

The Empty Tomb

The Marcan narrative (Mark 16:1-8) is the most streamlined and this economy of words is most noticeable in the Marcan narrative of the resurrection. The narrative begins with the burial, the preliminaries that not only set up the narrative but also give food for our own thinking. According to Mark, the body of Jesus is up for grabs after the crucifixion. Joseph of Arimathea comes to Pilate to claim the body for burial. Such things are not of concern to Pilate in this narrative,

Pilate is not even aware of Jesus' death. Having ordered Jesus' death, Pilate loses all interest in how this was done or whether this was done. Pilate certainly has no concern about whether Jesus will be buried. So Joseph of Arimathea comes to claim the body and takes Jesus to his own tomb, places the body there and rolls a large stone in front to seal the tomb.

In this story, the tomb is prepared and sealed by Joseph. There is no mention of anxiety on the part of the Jewish leaders either for actions of Jesus' disciples or for rumors about a false resurrection. Thus, when the women come to the tomb after the sabbath, they find no soldiers guarding the tomb. Their fear is not generated by the lingering and threatening power of the authorities. The Jews are not pictured as those unusually paranoid about events. The entire story is set into the context of the disciples reaction to Jesus' death—first, the action of Joseph and then the action of the women.

There is something powerfully sacred about this rendering of the tale. The death of Jesus is not used as a ploy in a larger plot (pun intended). Instead, the death of Jesus is hallowed in its finality. At least, we can hear in this narrative a caution that we do not attempt to make theological gain from the deaths of anyone, to rob the moment of death of its own hold upon us and its own sacredness. The story of the deaths of six million all the more need this sacred space so as to recognize that there is a holiness in death, even this form of death, that demands a holy response. Let it be enough that we say *Kaddish* for these six million, that we can give them a place to rest.[6] Let our response be to those who have died rather than a ploy to find some message or meaning or theological symbol in these deaths. In this, the death of Jesus is linked to the deaths of the six million and perhaps just this.

That we can escape a form of martyrology that grows from the death of the six million and with that the fears of a suspicious opposition that might even claim the ultimate blasphemy that the deaths were simply invented to serve the purpose of conspiracy, is a precious hope. We gain nothing by making the six million martyrs and attempting to create symbols of their deaths. We are sickened by those who would even dare to suggest that those who died are only a figment of imagination.[7] We simply cannot remain idle while the sacredness of the deaths of these people is once again held hostage to an idolatrous revisionism so thoroughly afraid of those who died. We cannot let those who died be robbed again of their due peace.

Thus, the Marcan narrative sets a context of simple respect for the one who has died. And the women, after the sabbath was over, "brought spices to go and anoint the body of Jesus." **The narrative does not say that they went to say *Kaddish* because there was not yet a form of prayer called the *Kaddish*, but our midrashic voice says that they went to say *Kaddish* nevertheless even before** there was *Kaddish* to say.[8] And the tomb was empty, the stone being rolled away. And the tomb was empty. The power of that phrase in its agony is barely audible in our tradition. The fear of the women surely included this feeling that they had been robbed of the moment of mourning, the time to say *Kaddish*. What comfort is there in the empty tomb? What agony is there in this shock of the empty tomb? The question that our midrashic voice asks here is, **"Can *Kaddish* be said for a body that is not there in the grave?"**

Perhaps the tradition is unable to encounter this shock fully that which is most completely conveyed in the Marcan narrative. Maybe the tradition takes too much stock in the presence of the young man at the tomb. Does the messenger really alleviate the sorrow of loss even in the message? **For they went to say *Kaddish* even before there was a *Kaddish* prayer to be said.** Surely we cannot miss the great irony of this text. Surely the image of the empty tomb set in the starkness of the Marcan narrative is at best ambiguous. How else can we understand the reaction of the women even to the message of the risen Jesus? They react with fear. Is this fear of something that is beyond comprehension—the power of God? Or is this the fear of loss; the fear that they cannot now mourn and will not be allowed to mourn? Is this the feeling of bewilderment of not knowing what this message means? **Can we say *Kaddish* when there is no body in the tomb?**

Marxsen understood the ambiguity of the text as he says that in the narrative of the empty tomb "we learn nothing about the resurrection itself."[9] If this gospel becomes the basis for a resurrection theology, then such a theology would have the resurrection only as announcement and one that is doubted at that. This is not a theme of rescue but of despair and fear even if our trained ear might be ready for a tinge of hope. This basic ambiguity of meaning and lack of closure for us is what comes from the narrative of the empty tomb.

We are struck by the way that the narrative truncated as in Mark reproduces for us an instance of *hester panim*, the hiddenness of God. Literally, we see here the absence of God and even of the body. Is this what trust is built on? But our answer depends on who we are. While the hiddenness of God is an idiom for both Jews and Christians, the very nature of the idea opens again a real possibility for dialogue. Roy Eckardt's argument that Jesus has not yet been raised as an antidote (the only one) for anti-Judaic resurrection theologies is even a moderation of this absence and claerly an opening for dialogue on this idea.[10] If Jesus were yet in the tomb, then the women could carry out their obligation and his fate becomes ours, that of anticipation for the day of the Lord. But, the gospel speaks of an empty tomb in which even the anticipation is robbed of its certainty. And, the women here cannot even fulfill their obligation.

The notion of the absence of God (there is an angel at the tomb, but what is this to the women?) does not provide rescue. The empty tomb is only an exasperating reminder of our ineptitude. We did not act in time? Even so, the image stands as a constant warning against the sort of spirtualization that makes the acceptance of death too easy. Especially for us, we want to say yes but. We want to run in with the answer, the solution, the final solution. We want to parade in with the resurrection as certainty to hail God's victory even in the face of all evidence of evil and defeat. We want to make the death go away. This is no answer. For the millions who had no grave, no comfort, no *Kaddish*, only death, this is no answer. And what is a little exasperration for us now in comparison with the enormity of the final solution? For those of us gathered at the tomb too late, what have we to say about rescue? Surely, the Christian relation to the empty tomb is not the same as the way we can relate to the deaths of the six million. Those bodies are gone, disappeared, wiped from existence without a trace. And the midrashic voice asks the question again, **"Can we who are Christians now say *Kaddish* for the six million whose bodies are not there in a grave?"**

Dare we tell our narratives anymore without pausing to throw up this cry of challenge? I think not. One of the rules of our talk now is that we are compelled by our memory to respect those who had no rescue, whose chance of dignified, even remembered and honored death was torn away in brutality. At the point of this latter day tomb, rescue is too late for us, but there is still the chance to mourn. Perhaps in the brutality of the Shoah, rescue is also too late for God there as well. Such a realization is fearful indeed. No, models for rescue are not to be found at the scene of death. God, our God, is not God of the dead (at least in this context) but of the living.

Even so, this God is, like us, one who mourns.

The Resurrection Paradigm

What purpose is there for including these narratives of the empty tomb in the gospel texts (see Mark 16; Matthew 28, Luke 24, John 20 in the Appendix)? The passage on the empty tomb is expanded in the gospel texts other than Mark to give different meaning to the story so that we can begin to speak of a resurrection paradigm—a basic model for understanding a central message of Christianity. The narratives, including the truncated version in Mark, are not just a completion of an unfinished narrative but a cycle of stories with separate purpose. This sense of a cycle of stories cannot be appreciated apart from an exploration of the other gospel texts, but before turning to that survey, we need to focus abstractly on what we think the purpose of these narratives is.

Most contemporary theologians argue that the resurrection narratives do not speak, principally, about the identity of Jesus.[11] In fact, this point seems to be a consistent, mainstream Christian perspective. Jesus' identity is not clarified nor does it emerge in the resurrection. At best, the narratives simply affirm what is already claimed about Jesus. In that sense, we need a clear appraisal of the claimed identity of Jesus that does emerge from the extended gospel narratives. We might claim that the resurrection is in some sense an affirmation of Jesus' messianic claim.

Contemporary thinkers who also see their thought molded by post-Shoah thought and Jewish-Christian dialogue have almost uniformly dismissed this purpose as neither valid or beneficial for us today. John Pawlikowski argues that both in terms of the general lack of a uniform messianic vision in second temple Judaism and the lack of any evident fulfillment of any of the particular messianic expectations that were present in this time, the claim that Jesus is to be called the messiah has no defensible foundation.[12] This view is certainly held by such various thinkers as Paul van Buren, Rosemary Ruether, and Roy Eckardt.[13] At least in relation to the tradition of the messianic hope, these thinkers reject the notion that the term "messiah" can adequately define Jesus' identity for the church.

Indeed, the development of christological thought in the early church seems only tangentially to take up the argument that Jesus fulfills messianic expectations rather arguing that Jesus defines what it is to be the messiah. With the apostle Paul, the church generally thinks of Jesus in the light of the resurrected Lord and not as the historical Jewish figure. That the whole of the gospel narrative is, then, read from the perspective of the resurrection (the point yet to be determined) seems to be the basic thrust of the mainstream Christian tradition. The purpose of the narrative is, then, despite our original claim, to give the defining element to the identity of Jesus.

With this point, we reach a perplexing juncture. On the one hand, thinkers like Paul van Buren argue as they do in an effort to protect Jewish thought from inordinate Christian distortion that happens when we believe that Christian views of Jesus fulfill Jewish messianic expectation (and when we find that Jesus does not then "we" traditionally assume that the Jews must be wrong).[14] On the other hand, the argument that the resurrection leads us to see that Christianity and its claims about Jesus must be understood apart from Jewish messianic expectation leads to a radical separation between Judaism and Christianity that appears by definition to be inevitable.[15] Not only this, this break into a separate world of thought enhances the chasm that separates Christian hope from Jewish hope in such a way so as to lead directly toward competing universal claims.

Surely, Ruether's argument that Christians think of Jesus as both paradigm and prolepsis helps to guard against a radical slip into this necessary competition (can both be right??) by making Jesus' identity both symbolic and partial.[16] Still, sharp separation of Christian theology from its Jewish roots that is threatened by this reading of the resurrection narratives raises the specter of Christian anti-Judaism that has so often been associated with Christian reflection on the resurrection narratives. We can avoid this problem only if we reject the notion that the resurrection is definitive of Jesus' identity for the church. We need to re-think the appropriateness of talking about Jesus as Lord.

Pawlikowski does seem to recognize this dilemma even as he makes the initial argument. His resolution lies in the shaping of a christology from the foundation of incarnational thinking.[17] Much has been said in recent years about whether Jewish thought has room for a notion of the incarnation; however one cannot help but see that the notion of incarnation as it is shaped in Christian thinking has also a decidedly hellenistic root that again seems somewhat removed from Christianity's Jewish roots.[18]

We are still left with the question of what is the purpose of the resurrection narratives, what is the resurrection paradigm? Given what we have said thus far, the purpose of these narratives seems far more related to God's identity than Jesus' identity. That is, the resurrection narratives are a culminating comment on the the whole tradition of theodicy. This is the paradigm with which Christians understand God's final word on suffering and evil. In that scheme of thought, the resurrection narratives connect with the Jesus' narrative principally as a way of understanding the whole of Israel's reflections on theodicy. Thus, the point of the narratives is not so much to affirm Jesus' messiahship but rather to re-affirm Jewish messianic hope.

To fully test this thesis would require a more thorough connecting together of texts from Torah with texts of Gospel. We can at least attempt to test the thesis by looking more closely at the resurrection narratives in the gospels. The narratives will be seen, then, as a separate midrash on the tradition of theodicy. What we will discover is that this midrash is also both pluralistic and ambiguous. What we should infer from this pluralism and ambiguity is that any theological answer to theodicy must be rich in this way to guard against the kinds of obscenity that would both try to deny the full reality of suffering and evil and also the full reality of God and God's promises.

The Empty Tomb As Midrash

Our problem in re-creating a midrash here is the obscurity of the text. The empty tomb text appears to stand separate from the longer narrative (since the empty tomb is not the story of Jesus but simply a claim about Jesus) and this section does not make explicit connections with the Hebrew scriptures as earlier sections do. The midrash is implicit demanding a recognition of the connections that must have been obvious to the original readers but less so to us. We have at least three options to explore, each having a feel of legitimacy as an interpretation of the empty tomb narrative. The first is simply a connection with the theodicies of the tradition (particularly, the Exodus narrative). The second is like the first, a commentary on other interpretations of the tradition (particularly the servant songs of Isaiah). The third may be the most fruitful, a finishing touch to the gospel debate about the resurrection that sets Jesus' life into the heart of the "theological" controversy between Pharisees and Saduccees.

The first of these options leaves us with only vague hints of possible meaning. The empty tomb means nothing if the the tomb and that which happens to those entombed after death is our focus. Earlier in the gospel narrative (an encounter found in all three of the synoptic gospels), Jesus is asked about marriage in the resurrection. In answer to this question Jesus appeals to Exodus 3:6 as a demonstration of the validity of belief in the resurrection which he interprets as meaning that God is the God of the living and not of the dead. The focus is on the living and not the dead. The focus must be on the living for any doctrine of the resurrection to make sense. In like manner, the event of Jesus' resurrection can be placed into this basic perspective of the gospel text.

But what of the reference? The text of Exodus 3:6 is central. The narrative there is of Moses' encounter with the burning bush. Even more, the reference is a central feature of the whole narrative of God's promise to redeem his people, Israel. The reference is an identification of God, the God of Abraham, Isaac and Jacob. This is the one God of the tradition that encounters Moses in the bush, the burning bush. What follows is most remarkable:

> Then the Lord said, "I have observed the misery of my people who are in Egypt; I have heard their cry on account of their taskmasters. Indeed, I know their sufferings, and I have come down to deliver them from the Egyptians...."(Exodus 3:7-8a)

Ellis Rivkin argues that the Pharisees, who also believed in a resurrection, applauded Jesus not simply because of his acceptance of the doctrine of resurrection but because of his exegesis.[19] What exegesis is this? Surely, what is happening here is that Jesus is putting the doctrine into direct relationship with the redemptive event of the Exodus. Indeed, Jesus argues that the text gives proof that a resurrection is necessary. What proof is necessary here? Only that the resurrection is seen as a completion of God's intent made in this early promise given to Moses. The resurrection is God's ultimate reaction to "having observed the affliction of my people...," that is, the resurrection is intended as an ultimate answer to theodicy, particularly in the Torah tradition that gives as paradigm the rescue of Israel from Egypt.

Now, the rescue from Egypt also leaves an empty tomb. The Israelites escape their fate at the hands of the Egyptians. Indeed, Jesus interprets this escape in a brief sweeping comment, that God is the God of the living and not the dead—that God's intent is to give life to Israel, whatever this may require and not simply to give this people over to death. This is what makes the resurrection necessary for Jesus, as the ultimate threat to Israel as God's people is death. The ultimate answer to this threat must be the defeat of death.

To make this argument is to say that the redemption of Exodus is not a complete event. Historically, of course, this is true. Israel has constantly faced the need for escape; the escape from Egypt might have left empty tombs but others would inevitably replace them. The Exodus is not a complete redemptive event because it is historical; thus the only ultimate redemption would be to solve the dilemma of history. Nevertheless, the Exodus is the paradigm by which all other narratives of redemption are understood—according to Jesus, God's intention is to give life to Israel.

That we should understand the gospel resurrection narrative as a midrashic interpretation of the Exodus paradigm seems likely. Jesus gives resurrection that particular place in our Christian understanding. Thus, we are led by all the gospels to see Jesus' resurrection as a fundamental affirmation of Israel's messianic hope. The resurrection doctrine is Jesus' way of understanding Israel's theodicy, particularly as based on the Exodus narrative. That Jesus specifically chooses this interpretation places his understanding directly into compatibility with the Pharisees who likewise looked for a resurrection while the Sadducees did not. The gospel narrative does little to modify this basic interpretation that Jesus gives and much to affirm it. Surely, this interpretation becomes yet another invitation to dialogue between Jews and Christians.

The problem we have is not so much understanding the interpretation of the doctrine but attaching the specific event of the empty tomb to this exegetical tradition. How is Jesus' resurrection viewed as part of this basic doctrine? Rivkin argues that this is, indeed, the dividing point between Christianity and rabbinic Judaism.[20] The Pharisees could not have accepted the resurrection of Jesus as a part of this basic doctrine of resurrection. The early Christians (and, perhaps, Paul especially) did see that Jesus' resurrection was a guarantee of the hoped for ultimate especially) did see that Jesus' resurrection was a guarantee of the hoped for ultimate redemption. The empty tomb was to be taken as a symbol of reaffirmation of the hope, God's intent, and Jesus' particular view of that hope.

Actually, this debate does not make sense if the exegesis were only a reading of the tradition of Exodus 3:4ff. If Jesus' resurrection were seen only as a reaffirmation of the Exodus tradition, we are hard pressed to see how the empty tomb marks any significant advance on the understanding of that tradition. Even the physical evidence, remarkable as such an experience might have been, does not essentially alter the hope. Even so, the effect would then be to shift focus to the empty tomb rather than onto the ongoing work of God in the world (an emphasis that is spelled out more thoroughly in the gospels other than Mark). A full understanding of this midrash seems to require more.

The Isaianic Servant

The second scenario for interpretation, listed above, may provide that "more" called for. At any rate, this approach to developing a midrash represents a separate line of interpretation that is distinct from the reading of Exodus 3:4ff. A more traditional rendering of Jesus' identity is to be found in the Christian use of Isaiah's servant songs. That Mark intends this connection is so obvious that we feel clouted with a hammer at the beginning of the gospel. Mark quotes Isaiah 40:2:

> See, I am sending my messenger ahead of you, who will prepare your way; the voice of one crying out in the wilderness: "Prepare the way of the Lord, make his paths straight." (Mark 1:2-3)

The quotation is rather loose but clearly sets Jesus (and I would argue not John the Baptist) into this role of the voice, the messenger of God. In fact, this reading makes more sense of the gospel narrative that has Jesus on center stage proclaiming the message of redemption and the kingdom. The point is that Jesus is viewed in the light of the suffering servant of Isaiah and the whole "story" of redemption of the gospel is made to fit that image.

The narrative of the empty tomb, therefore, is part of a larger midrash on Isaiah's image and particularly the powerful text of Isaiah 53:

> Therefore, I will allot him a portion with the great, and he shall divide the spoil with the strong; because he poured out himself to death, and was numbered with the transgressors; yet he bore the sin of many, and made intercession for the transgressors." (Isaiah 53:12)

Surely, the Isaiah text extends the tradition of the Exodus theodicy. It is God's intent to give life to his people, and the text of Isaiah 53 records the work of the servant as that planned by God. The intercession made was redemptive because the intercession was on behalf of God. Again the rule of interpretation that has already come from the earlier reflections—that God is the God of the living and not of the dead—is fully substantiated in this text. No Christian reading of the resurrection narrative can be authentic if the focus is on the tomb, on the dead and what happens to this dead one. The focus is still on God's intent for his people. Again, we face an opportunity for dialogue as this interpretation of Isaiah 53 can become a chance to explore together reflections on this theme.

Even so, the Isaiah text clearly introduces the fact of the hoped for completion of God's work. Perhaps the setting of the Babylonian exile created the opportunity for realizing the incompleteness of the Exodus redemption. Whatever, the Isaiah text notes clearly that the reward for faithfulness comes not in what one receives from this world but in what one is promised in the next. In that, we cannot confuse hope with naive enthusiasm for present reward. God's intent is not complete in temporal peace, wealth, status, power, etc. All these things are denied the servant even though the prophet argues that "he shall see the fruit of the travail of his soul and be satisfied." (Isaiah 53:11) Nevertheless, this midrash in Isaiah does more than extend the traditional theodicy to its logical end. The narrative of the servant sets up an identity of the servant as intercessor. In this, the special nature of this midrash might be seen. The rabbis identified this act of intercession with the fascinating even if obscure text in Numbers 25.[12] In this text, Phinehas responded to the potential challenge of apostasy in Israel by slaying the apostate Israelite and the Midianite princess with a single sword so that the rest of Israel might be spared the wrath of God. Indeed, Phinehas is called intercessor here and is promised the reward of a perpetual priesthood (taken as a symbol of the rewards of the life to come by the rabbis).

Now this connection may well be a tradition of theodicy that is reflected in Isaiah. On the surface, the tradition is rooted in a jealous protection of faithfulness to the one God. The reward of eternal priesthood (life) comes to the one who safeguards Israel for that service. Thus, resurrection is seen as ultimate answer but specifically for those who remain faithful to God's law, protected from apostasy. The intercessor is one chosen (or choosing) to protect Israel from apostasy.

Two reactions to this tradition surface immediately within the context of ancient Judaism. First, the tradition thus given seems quite in keeping with what we sketchily know of 1st century Pharisaism. Rivkin argues that the Pharisees believed that the resurrection comes for those who maintain righteousness before the demands of the two-fold law.[22] Resurrection is then a specific reward of the faithful ones and not simply a universal divine response in the intent of the Exodus tradition. That this is so, may shed light on the gospel narrative and needs to be set alongside of the critique brought by the Shoah and its victims.

Second, the text of Isaiah seems to suggest that the principal threat to God's redemption of Israel is apostasy and not simply violence from Israel's enemies. Thus, in the context of the exile, the over-riding concern is not merely the physical fate of the people at the hands of the Babylonians but the spiritual state of the people amongst the heathen. Now the interplay between these two threats to Israel represents the dialectic of the two traditions of theodicy that we have presented thus far. In this second view the answer from God comes in the midst of the danger rather than as an ultimate end of the danger. Given the different emphasis, this slight shift in thinking seems necessary.

This second perspective also needs to be brought to bear on the gospel narrative and on the narrative of the Shoah as both can be understood in light of the tradition of Isaiah as well as understanding the tradition in the light of the gospel and the Shoah. On the surface, to see the resurrection as essentially a reward for faithfulness in crisis fits if the context of the story is the exile which is transferred to the gospel narrative as the tendency to see only a proleptic redemption in present events. These events point our attention to a future resolution but this future orientation can lead to the very dangerous ignoring of present threat, to a kind of acceptance of the inadequacies of interim solutions.

Nevertheless, the mere focus on faithfulness in bare terms leaves us with a rigid position. Indeed, we might, along with Roy Eckardt, operate with a rule that disallows futurism as an appropriate reading of resurrection to the exclusion of concern for the real threats that face us.[23] Still, the one tradition must be tempered with the other lest we sink into a world that sees everything as an ultimate battle between good and evil, and the motivation for righteousness potentially arising from an individualistic desire for a place in the world to come. What brings about the motivation for intercession? What would lead any of us to act in the same way as Phinehas? Surely, the blessing comes after the act not as a motivation for the act.

The Application of this Midrash

The Marcan text (Mark 1 linked with Mark 16) is clearly an interpretation that reads Exodus through the prism of Isaiah 53, even if the tradition of the link with Numbers would have been known. We cannot argue persuasively that the Jesus of Mark was to be fit with this earlier connection. We can argue, however, that the notion of eternal life as blessing for rigteousness so evident in Isaiah, is likely the view implicit in the empty tomb narrative and as such represents a piece of the larger tradition of the resurrection developing in early rabbinic Judaism. Jesus could be perceived as a type of Phinehas in that God rewards Jesus with life and blessing for having interceded on behalf of Israel to protect Israel from apostasy.

Our problem is greater; can we apply this motif more generally as a way of understanding the action of God in relation to the Shoah. That righteousness is rewarded with the blessing of life may be one way of coping with the enormity and finality of the evil of the Shoah. That apostasy in Israel was one problem facing Judaism in modern Europe has been contended by some thinkers. That what was needed was intercession and reform at the point of apostasy might be argued but such arguments seem weak in the face of the actuality of the Shoah. The answer, in Emil Fackenheim's terms, is too small and as such borders on obscenity.[24]

For Christians, the issue is different. The image of the God who rewards the righteous may be quite fitting in the face of enormous evidence of Christian apostasy during the Shoah. The point is not that rescue is the motivation for righteousness (though the image of God as rescuer of Israel and Jesus as means for that rescue might lead more readily to righteous action by Christians); the point is that God is perceived as rescuer of Israel—that to be with God means, even as we stand at the empty tomb, to be at the work of rescuing Israel to be Israel (indeed, to allow Israel to define what that may be). Perhaps the Christian of Nazi Europe could more easily imagine filling the role of Phinehas, the one who slays the apostate in the midst of the people. Whatever our image leads to, the issue for Christians is that of being God's instrument for rescue, not of procuring our own rescue.

That the empty tomb narrative is to be read as a call to the mission of rescue (specifically the rescue of Israel, even though that rescue still awaits completion) is likely a unique way of reading this text for Christians. The guiding rule for us becomes, then, that any use of the image of resurrection not pass over the line to be used solely for the assurance of one's personal salvation for to do that would be to diminish the likelihood of action on the part of the believer. To see the resurrection as simply the affirmation of Christian (Christ) truth would be to divert attention from the God who is already and always busy seeking the rescue of Israel. Indeed, to read the resurrection narrative in that way would seem to be working against God even in spite of ourselves so that we are likely to be left gaping at the empty tomb struck inactive in awe as were the women of Mark's narrative. Is this, in fact, the legacy of Christianity?

Including the Image of Jonah

While the Marcan text clearly associates Jesus with the Servant songs of Isaiah and sets the tone for the narratives in both Matthew and Luke, the Mathean text introduces another image as background for the narrative of the empty tomb. The Jesus of Matthew chooses to associate the event of the tomb and empty tomb with the narrative in the Jonah. That this narrative is so often also associated with Isaiah makes the analogy even more interesting.

The story of Jonah (see Matthew 12:39-41) is a backdrop for Matthew's understanding of the resurrection narrative and specifically for the section on the empty tomb. That Matthew includes this reference to Jonah independently of Mark's version is striking for Jesus is pictured, thereby, as seeing his resurrection in continuity with the prophetic call to witness to the nations. The Jesus of Matthew's pre-resurrection narrative sends the disciples out to witness only to the "lost sheep of the House of Israel." The close of the gospel has Jesus sending the disciples out to "all nations." The resurrection changes the whole scope of the mission of Jesus and his disciples. But why does the resurrection do this or is the close of the gospel simply a reflection of a failed mission to the Jews already evident to the gospel writer near the end of the first century C.E.? That we are led to ask this question and precisely this question is vital for our whole midrash.

A complete answer to the questions posed will require a full interpretation of the resurrection narrative (that is, the narrative of the appearances of Jesus as well). Still, the intentional link that the pre-resurrection Jesus makes with the story of Jonah may serve to fill out our midrash in an important way. Jonah is sent by God to witness to the nations, specifically Ninevah. The point of the Jonah story can be generally captured by a summary like, "the escapades of a reluctant prophet." Jonah ends up in the great fish because he refuses to accept the prophetic challenge and attempts to run from God. That Jonah's efforts are to no avail suggests that God fully intends from the outset to send the prophet to the nations regardless of the response of the prophet. The reluctant prophet is made to go to Ninevah in spite of himself.

That Jesus compares his stay in the tomb with Jonah's time in the great fish (never mind the problematic with number of days) may be simply a vague analogy. Such a conclusion would ignore the way that Matthew especially makes use of midrashic references in a specifically intentional way.[25] In keeping with countless other references, Matthew appears to be linking the resurrection of Jesus not simply with a metaphor but with the "story" of Jonah. That is, the Jonah story is either to be used to help us understand the full meaning of the empty tomb narrative or vice versa (or, perhaps, both). The open ambiguity of this reference makes the reference, itself, richer than we would at first suppose.

On the one hand, the empty tomb narrative can be seen as a reversal of the Jonah narrative. Jesus accepts his prophetic mission willingly, even if he is pictured as having some initial reluctance. Whatever, the outcome is the same; God's intention will be accomplished regardless of the willingness of the prophet. The tomb will not contain Jesus not because Jesus is so powerful or so obedient but because God intends that his purpose be accomplished regardless. The Jonah narrative can be a clue to help us see an alternative meaning for the empty tomb. The empty tomb is not principally an affirmation of Jesus or even of the divine presence but of God's intent.

The issue at stake, however, according to the pre-resurrection Jesus is not the fact of Jonah's entombment in the fish but rather this mysterious sign of Jonah. Thus, on the other hand, the narrative of the resurrection can be seen as a way of understanding the prophetic tradition. What is the sign of Jonah? That sign is not immediately clear nor is it explained by Jesus. Instead, Jesus claims that his generation will be given only the sign of Jonah, that the point of the Jonah narrative will be made clear through the story of Jesus' own resurrection.

The ambiguity of this sort of interpretation—understanding one story with another—is obvious and part of the midrashic tradition of interpretation. We dare not attempt to reduce this ambiguity to a simple formula. However, certain fascinating conclusions can be drawn given the invitation to midrash. First, Jesus' mission is not to the nations but to Israel. The gospel narrative makes this point abundantly clear. Whatever the other implications of the resurrection might be, the central point appears to be aimed at the self-understanding of Israel. That the connection is made with Jonah helps us see that much more clearly than traditional readings have tended to emphasize. Thus, the sign of Jonah has to do with the prophetic mission and not just of Jesus but more specifically of Israel. Israel, and not Jesus, is Jonah called to witness to Ninevah. The resurrection of Jesus is the "sign of Jonah," that is, the sign given to Jonah that the prophetic call to witness to Ninevah cannot be escaped because *that is God's intention.*

Second, the sign of the resurrection is an indication (like the rescue of Jonah from the belly of the great fish) of the beginning of that witness. Two sub-points arise from this realization. On the one hand, this means that the empty tomb cannot place specific attention on Jesus. That attention is not the point. Matthew's version makes the point even more obvious as the messenger at the tomb says that Jesus is not here but has gone on before you. The empty tomb is a sign of the beginning of the mission of Jonah to the nations. That the Jesus at the gospel's end sends the disciples out is then an appropriate conclusion to this whole midrash. At a time when Israel would be tempted to close ranks, this Jesus brings the sign of Jonah, the call to witness to the nations of the God of Israel.

Shall we say that this is the point of the covenant from the beginning, that God leads Israel out of bondage not only to claim Israel for his own but to set them to work at the witness to the nations. Surely, the prophetic witness was precisely this. And just as surely, Jesus expected that this witness would receive the same result as the witness of Jonah. Even in spite of Jonah's expectation (and desire?), Ninevah repents. At Joshua's trumpet blast, the walls of Jericho fall. In response to the witness of Jesus' disciples, every knee shall bow to the lord and father of us all. If this is the sign of Jonah, then the whole narrative of the empty tomb is to be read as an affirmation of God's intent for the nations and of the

The whole ultimate point of the Jonah narrative is that Jonah is also called to a repentance for not expecting God to be one who rescues, for not joining with God in the work of rescuing, for hoping instead for a God who destroys. This point so clear to us now from the pages of Matthew's gospel speaks volumes about Christian treatment of Jews and Christian action during the Shoah. For in this modern day narrative that takes on enormous dimensions for us, Christianity has become Jonah, seeking destruction of Jews rather than trusting a God who intends rescue, even if implicitly and subtly. And what sign does our generation look for? Is it possible even now that our Christian generation still looks for the destruction of the Jews? Is this our sign? How perverse and wicked is our generation. For us, all that we can expect is the sign of Jonah or maybe the sign of the empty tomb that witnesses only to the centrality of God's will to rescue. We are Jonah needing to be snatched up for God's work of rescue. Perhaps this is our modern midrash of the narrative of the empty tomb.

The Full Critique of the Shoah

If we have uncovered an important aspect of the resurrection narrative in this reinterpreted midrash on Jonah, then the empty tomb is a necessary element, particularly post-Shoah, for the Christian narrative. Despite Eckardt's claim that only an unresurrected Jesus can be our narrative now, we must argue that without the empty tomb the Christian narrative has no fundamental affirmation of the God who rescues.[26] Ambiguous as that claim must be even given the gospel narrative, the thread of the story supplied by the empty tomb is an essential, perhaps the central, figure of the whole resurrection narrative. To receive the sign of Jonah is to know that we are called to follow the God who rescues in the work of rescuing. That message is vital in our own generation.

Still, the message is ambiguous for us who live after Auschwitz. Certainly the message rings somewhat empty for Jews who saw little or no sign of the God who rescues. Never mind that the signs they saw then and still might see are the signs of Christian apathy or even hatred. Even in spite of this overwhelming apostasy by the church, the Jewish people must be able to see the God who rescues quite independently of Christianity and the actions of Christians. To say that these people saw or even see any sign from God in the Shoah, let alone the sign of the God who rescues, is more than ambiguous; it is ludicrous, meaningless. And surely we do little to help this trauma of Jewish history by pointing to Christians as modern day Jonahs, even in spite of the metaphorical truth that might be carried by that analogy. Echkardt's argument still holds in this matter. The empty tomb cannot be an answer to the many who died without burial or *Kaddish*.[27] Christians can have no special privilege in claiming a resurrection now unique to Christians or Christian identity.

The question of trust in the God who rescues is crucial for any post-Shoah theology. That we cannot say with full assurance that we know this God who rescues or that we know that this God does rescue is a sign of the ambiguity that is central to our theologies now. We are left with saying that we continue to act as if the trust is true, that God will rescue. No other response can adequately motivate us for living, Jew or Christian, even though this last reading of the empty tomb narrative is yet another invitation to dialogue about the possibility or the necessity to trust in the God who rescues. Perhaps we don't act because God rescues. This lesson from Phinehas is worth preserving. Thus, we are not arguing that we are motivated to act only because or when we see God acting or promising to preserve or reward. The matter is deeper than that, more complex and threatening than that.

The "as if" is our personal re-affirmation of God in spite of all that we see. We do, indeed, stand at the empty tomb ready to say that God has failed, hearing only the word of the messenger that God has already rescued, or has gone before us. There is no evidence but the empty tomb. There is little to see around that has changed. Still, and this is Eckardt's point, only a future hope can adequately allow us to face the terror of the present.[28] We act on the trust that God, in spite of all that we see, is the God who rescues. We act because the alternative is future despair. This is at the heart of our post-Shoah Christian theology. Perhaps, this is a theology that we can share, Jews and Christians. Our dialogue will show us how much we can share. In this choice we, Christians, stand at the threshhold of action or surrender, whether we will be rescuers or bystanders in God's work.

Notes

[1] There is a great deal written to give support to this claim, e.g., Richard Rubenstein and John Roth, *Approaches to Auschwitz* (Atlanta: John Knox Press, 1987), pp.199ff; Franklin Littell and Hubert Locke, ed., *The German Church Struggle and the Holocaust* (Detroit: Wayne State Univ., 1974); Robert Erickson, *Theologians Under Hitler* (New Haven: Yale Univ., 1985).

[2]The literature is expanding on this theme, e.g.: Nechama Tec, *When Light Pierced the Darkness* (New York: Oxford Univ., 1986).

[3]A. Roy Eckardt and Alice Eckardt, *Long Night's Journey Into Day* (Detroit: Wayne State Univ., 1982), pp. 140ff.

[4]Willi Marxsen, *The Resurrection of Jesus of Nazareth* (Philadelphia: Fortress Press, 1970).

[5]A treatment of the Pauline material is an important ingredient in filling out a post-Shoah Christian theology. Still, I have confined my reflections to the passion narratives offering Pauline accents only as they relate directly to the material in the gospels.

[6]Yaffa Eliach's comments at the 1990 Scholar's Conference on the Holocaust (Nashville, March 4-6, 1990) emphasized the need to allow for just this for the second generation as well. This essay is to published in the forthcoming proceedings of the 20th Annual Scholar's Conference from Edwin Mellen Press.

[7]The number and variety of materials that can be included in the revisionist camp is growing.

[8]I know of no commentary on this text that recognizes the act of the women as a Jewish act in this way. Thus, the meaning of the story is impoverished because the narrative is not read as a ritual, liturgical act but rather as a family responsibility.

[9]Willi Marxsen, *The Resurrection of Jesus of Nazareth*, p. 43.

[10]Eckardt. *Long Night's Journey*, p. 150.

[11]Tillich's famous interpretation that Jesus is symbol and the resurrection is a non-historical event that points to the eschaton and God's promise in that is an example of one type of approach to the resurrection narratives. cf. Paul Tillich, *Systematic Theology* - Volume Two (New York: Harper and Row, 1957), pp. 153ff.

[12]cf. John Pawlikowski, *Jesus and the Theology of Israel* (Wilmington, DE: Michael Glazier, 1989).

[13]Paul van Buren, *A Christian Theology of the People of Israel* (New York: Harper and Row, 1987); Rosemary Ruether, "Christian Theology and Antisemitism," in *Auschwitz: Beginning of a New Era?* (New York: KTAV, 1977), pp. 79-81; Eckardt, p. 110.

[14]van Buren, pp. 33ff.

[15]This difficult question about the relation between Judaism and Christianity on this question of the messiah is nicely left ambiguous in van Buren's text.

[16]cf., Rosemary Ruether, *To Change the World* (New York: Crossroad, 1983), pp. 42-43.

[17]John Pawlikowski, *Christ in the Light of Christian-Jewish Dialogue* (New York: Paulist Press, 1982), pp. 136ff.

[18]Cf., my comments in James F. Moore, "The Holocaust and Christian Theology: a Spectrum of Views on the Crucifixion and Resurrection in the Light of the Holocaust" in *Remembering for the Future* (New York: Pergamon Press, 1990), Vol. I, pp. 844ff; also see Clemens Thoma and Michael Wyschogrod, ed., *Das Reden vom Einem Gott bei Juden und Christen* (Bern: Peter Lang, 1984).

[19]Cf., Ellis Rivkin, *What Crucified Jesus?* (Nashville: Abingdon Press, 1984), p. 98.

[20]This among other factors in Ellis Rivkin, *What Crucified Jesus?*, pp. 115ff.

[21]Cf., C. G. Montefiore and H. Loewe, *A Rabbinic Anthology* (New York: Schocken Books, 1974), p. 227.

[22]Cf., Ellis Rivkin, *A Hidden Revolution* (Nashville: Abingdon Press, 1978), pp. 259ff.

[23]Cf., Eckardt's discussion of this in A. Roy Eckardt, "Christian-Jewish Issues Today" in *Jews and Christians*, James Charlesworth, ed. (New York: Crossroad, 1990), pp. 162ff.

[24]Emil Fackenheim, "Holocaust and Weltanschauung: Philosophical Reflections on Why They Did It" *Holocaust and Genocide Studies*, Volume 3, no. 2, 1988, pp. 197ff.

[25]An argument to this effect has been made by, at least, Krister Stendahl, *The School of St. Matthew* (Uppsala: G.W.K. Gleerup, 1954).

[26]Eckardt's argument, nevertheless, has always seemed to me compelling, especially well stated in A. Roy Eckardt and Alice Eckardt, *Long Night's Journey Into Day*, pp. 147ff.

[27]Eckardt, *Long Night's Journey into Day*, pp. 142ff.

[28]Eckardt, *Long Night's Journey Into Day*, p. 150.

CHAPTER 9:
THE NARRATIVE OF THE
RESURRECTION APPEARANCES

With the full development of a midrash on the empty tomb narrative, we have apparently filled out our post-Shoah Christian theology. Indeed, that the gospel of Mark apparently includes no witness to resurrection apearances might tempt us to conclude this theology at this point.[1] Even so, two factors impel us forward to consider the second part of the resurrection narrative in the gospels. First, the two gospels that include extended accounts of the appearances have done so with some purpose. That is, Christian tradition has extended the impact of the gospel story of the resurrection by making specific appeal to these stories of the appearances. Not to consider this tradition would be to ignore the potential impact of these stories on any claims we would make so far. Second, the stories of the appearances principally found in Luke and John with an extension in Acts and by implication in the Pauline corpus do include elements with specific importance for understanding Jewish-Christian relations. To ignore these elements would be to ignore sources of some of the teaching of contempt that we have attempted throughout this book to address.

Still, we cannot assume that our treatment represents any final word on these matters. At best, our accounts have aimed at beginning a discussion with suggestive insights at a new vision of the texts we have treated. Too much is contained in these narratives of the appearances for us to attempt a full exegesis, and such is not our intent at any rate. The point is midrash and not exegesis as it is usually understood. The point is to wonder aloud what a new look at these stories might produce if treated with the sensitive eyes of the post-Shoah Christian thinker. The point is to recognize the broad range of possible meanings in the texts and what these new insights might provide for new understanding and for different Christian living.

We have thus far treated Mark and Matthew. Mark has no stories of witnesses to the resurrected Jesus. Matthew's post-empty tomb witness is confined to material we have already treated in previous chapters, filled out now with this new insight gained in an application of the Jonah analogy. The other two gospels, on the other hand, include extended accounts of appearances of the resurrected Jesus that can enable us to (1) ask what these accounts add to what can be said through the empty tomb narrative, (2) explore the specific issues of the separate gospel traditions of Luke (and with that extended to Acts and Paul) and John, and (3) bring a specific, post-Auschwitz perspective to the theologies implicit in these narratives.

On the Road—Luke's Version

The version in Luke is noteworthy in that Luke is clearly not Jewish and probably writes to a non-Jewish audience (at least in part, cf., Luke 1:1-4)). That this document is a thoroughly gentile writing may be argued quite persuasively.[2] Nevertheless, the form of the story that Luke tells (the method of the risen Jesus) takes the shape of midrashic, perhaps already common before the gospel was written in full. This Jesus is concerned to emphasized "all that the prophets have declared." He challenges the disciples on the road with the question "Was it not necessary that the Messiah should suffer these things and then enter into his glory?" And these challenges serve as a beginning of a discussion of the Torah as it relates to Jesus. The form of this story is midrash even if the reference is general.

Perhaps Luke does not know or is not aware of the midrash that shapes these claims. Where is it written that the Christ must suffer? And what specifically do the prophets have to say about the intended redemption of Israel? We are left to fill in the gaps left vague. Perhaps some of the readers had long since been familiar with these connections. Perhaps the link with Isaiah so pronounced in Mark is simply assumed here. Whatever, the form of the story suggests that the resurrection appearance of Jesus is as with all else to be understood in the light of the Torah and prophets.

The irony of this story is that two significant demonstrations fail to convince the disciples of the truth to be found. Not even the empty tomb story nor the actual midrash on scripture enabled the disciples to recognize the resurrected Jesus. Only the act of breaking bread and eating opened the eyes of the disciples. The ritualizing of this event is fascinating and worth drawing out more. For now we see that the resurrection of Jesus is depicted as a completely unanticipated event, even for those prepared to believe.

Now this element of the Lucan version lends even more ambiguity to the narrative than we have had to this point. The climax of the entire gospel narrative is shrouded in vagueness and ambiguity. The very presence of the risen Jesus does not produce faith. In fact, the thrust of the story suggests that the point is not the production of faith, at least not singularly faith in Jesus. The point is not faith but recognition. The disciples on the road were engaged in a process of recognition—for what purpose?

In fact, the Lucan text (Luke 24:30-33) is somewhat mysterious about this matter. The story reads as if Jesus is the target for recognition except that the disciples do not recognize Jesus until they eat with him. The later encounter with the group of disciples also is shrouded in doubt until Jesus eats. Marxen argues that the point is ultimately the ascension of Jesus and gift of the Spirit.[3] If this is so, then many problems remain with the text. Perhaps the problems arise because the target, despite appearances, is not the recognition of Jesus as risen lord. Perhaps the recognition is of something within the story.

The point might be that Jesus as teacher is what is the aim of recognition, specifically the way that Jesus teaches about Scripture (the disciples share that after Jesus' departure they remember how their hearts burned on the road "while he opened to us the scripture... "). The resurrection appearances are at least a reaffirmation of Jesus' understanding of scripture. Thus, the sharing of the Spirit becomes a literal continuation of that teaching. The target for recognition all along is the teaching, the midrash, and specifically the claim that Jesus' teaching is to be followed (I take it as opposed to other options then available).

The only conclusion that fits this contention is that Luke saw the crucifixion as a disconfirming evidence needing this further reaffirmation.[4] The scene of the crucifixion in Luke is distinct from the comparable scene in Mark and Matthew. While Luke follows Mark in many details otherwise, the crucifixion narrative in Luke is unique in critical ways. Luke alone includes the debate among the criminals on the cross over the justification of Jesus' sentence. Luke alone concludes this with Jesus' claim that paradise (and thus the display of Jesus' power) will not be clearly seen here and now. Luke has the centurion at the cross say that "certainly this man was innocent" (Luke 23:47) not what Mark writes that "Truly this man was the God's Son." (Mark 15:39) For Luke, the crucifixion does not appear to carry the same message. Instead, the crucifixion appears to be disconfirming evidence.

Thus, the resurrection appearances are Luke's way of providing assurance that the specific work (teaching) of Jesus will be continued (emphasized even more strongly in the gift of the Spirit, in contrast to Matthew who has Jesus say he will be with the disciples to the end of the age). That the disciples (those closest to Jesus) had difficulty being convinced, even recognizing, is further evidence that Luke knew the continuation of Jesus' work would be difficult at best. For Luke the resurrection appearances are necessary to counter the negative evidence of the crucifixion.

It seems that Luke must be written in the context of a conflict motif, and, indeed, the book of Acts does develop out of a simple conflict motif that suggests the precarious future of the Jesus cause. Because this motif is so central to Luke's second book, that text bears an inordinate level of anti-Judaism. Perhaps because Luke writes as a gentile, the anti-Judaism of Luke (perhaps no more vitriolic than Matthew in tone) is especially worrisome. The point is a conflict of interpretation that makes the essential issue the conflict between the Jesus party and contemporary Judaism. That the text does little to reflect the potential agreement between Jesus and certain factions of Judaism, except for a minor reference to a conciliatory Gamaliel, makes the picture here one-sided at best and distortive at worst. We cannot know if the conflicts mentioned actually took place or were extensions of Luke's narrative motif.

Our Road

The conflict motif puts extraordinary pressure on the issue of choice and requires that the author clearly set out the alternatives. Thus, the road image of the Emma'us which is repeated in the story of Saul's conversion is a fitting picture literally describing what the point of the whole narrative is. That the book of Acts ultimately sets up the division between Paul and the Jerusalem church as the symbol of the roads to be taken makes this motif all the more likely as a way to understand Luke's purpose. Our question is how do we read Luke's narrative today?

Perhaps one schism is enough. Our rendering of a new midrash does not aim at a new schism, either in Christianity or in our openness to Judaism. Surely the issue of what constitutes the "true" road to follow is no more obvious to us today than to the disciples on the road to Emma'us. The questions thrust upon us by Auschwitz do little to confirm our view and much to disconfirm.[5] And the message cannot be simply that appearances in the flesh of the messenger of God or the resurrected lord are required every time that our convictions are challenged. Much less can we say that our convictions are primary in the face of the loss of lives in mass at Auschwitz. For the post-Shoah generation, the narrative of Emma'us seems almost offensive. The point cannot be just that Jesus appears to settle a dispute between rival people of God. Now that trivializes both Jesus and Auschwitz.

Faced with what we now know, how are we to understand Luke's story? It is clear that Luke saw as ultimate expression of the conflict the central missionary effort to the gentiles. The question is not whether Jews would be excluded or that

Judaism would be rejected but whether a new kind of approach to the gentile world arises from the resurrection of Jesus. That choice by Christians led ultimately to the schism between Jews and Christians. Whatever other key differences remain in terms of belief (and they are significant) the key issue that divides is Christian inclusion of the gentiles.

Twenty centuries later, this is still the issue at hand. The passage of time has not so favorably indicated that the promises of God are rightfully entrusted to the gentiles. Nevertheless, Christianity is Lucan-Pauline Christianity. The road taken, regardless of its compatibility with the gospel image of Jesus, has been to makeover Christianity into a gentile community. The question remains as before whether a gentile community that cannot take with all seriousness the full Torah can effectively witness even to Jesus and his work. The schism is still before us and remains an issue that the presence of Luke's resurrection narrative makes impossible to avoid

But it is Luke's conflict motif that sets the tone of this debate as real as it is. It is the image that one must choose one direction and abandon the other, indeed that one is even on a road that divides, that has pulled us into this schism. If the resurrection of Jesus is essentially a confirmation of the "truth" of Jesus' teaching, then Luke's story that now appears to be the essential story of the history of Jewish-Christian relations is unavoidable. Haim Macoby is correct; the only way to heal the schism is to dispose of the narrative.[6]

Even more critical is that this image works against the essential image of rescue that comes through so clearly in the Marcan and Matthean texts. This schism of unavoidable alternatives is a numbing mechanism that can effectively cover over the instinct to rescue that flows from the resurrection story. Could this be the heart of the indifference that stung the Christian world during the Shoah? Surely many cowered in natural fear that led to seeming indifference. Still, others, perhaps many, were caught in a conflicting tension between the motivation to rescue all people and the motivation for confirming evidence of the "truth" of our position. As blunt as that sounds, the truth may be found in this.

We simply cannot read the Lucan narrative in this way without ultimately destroying the foundation for any future philo-Judaism, any future altruism. As apparantly obvious as this reading of Luke seems, we must find another way of reading the narrative. I cannot say that this alternative holds exegetical primacy for any attempt to uncover what the "true" intent of Luke was would undoubtedly lead to the view thus far offered. Still, we can open the text itself again to discover within the obvious ambiguity of the story another possible reading that has an existential primacy forced on us by dark history and recent apostasy.

The Meal Eaten

The road image does lead rather effectively to a picture of schism and conflict, but that is not the only image in the narrative. Indeed, another image seems to appear not merely as alternative but in stark contrast to the road image. In fact, the structure of the narrative appears to set up a clear comparison between these images as ways of understanding the resurrection. That is to say, that despite tradition the Lucan narrative is not so obvious in meaning as appears at first. The narrative leaves us with an ambiguity even greater than the mysterious lack of recognition by the disciples. This image is the image of the meal eaten.

In addition, the meal image is more specifically midrashic (a running narrative that clearly is intended as a clue for reading the whiole gospel) than any other element of the text. Thus, the image of the meal is a way of interpreting inter-linking elements of the story and may be a way of connecting this narrative with the larger Jewish world—with Torah—not even contemplated by the original author. Why is it that the disciples recognize Jesus only in the eating of the meal? As Marxen argues, something happens in the meal that makes recognition possible.[7] Could it be that the image of the meal is a clue even to the rest of midrashic interpretation, that Jesus opened the Scriptures to them?

Mircea Eliade has argued that the meal is an archetype that accomplishes any one of a number of connections with the sacred.[8] The meal participates in the original divine order (the setting of order) and also signifies the regeneration of time. The meal can also represent the re-sacralization of time, the setting of time off into sacred space. Or the meal can represent a foretaste of the divine age, the end of time, completion of time. Each of these motifs have foundation in Torah for the Jewish community, perhaps most especially linked with the meal of the Passover as a symbol of God's redemption and covenant with Israel. In fact, this image is projected by Jesus as a central way to understand the meaning of the covenant. If this is the case, then the image of the meal is another opportunity for dialogue as both Jews and Christians can speak of the arising importance of Pesach as a central feature of the liturgy of the community.

Thus, the image of meal is not a specific reference to a text of Torah but a general reference to the message of Torah. That all recognition becomes clear in the eating of the meal is again a way of suggesting that Torah is the focal meaning of Jesus rather than that Jesus is the focal meaning of Torah. Only when the disciples are focussed on Torah can they see Jesus. Even more, the focus is put on the sacred meal as the key for understanding Jesus' role and mission. The resurrection appearance of Jesus serves not as a reaffirmation of the truth of Jesus so much as a reaffirmation of the truth of Torah, and here especially that Passover symbolizes the God who rescues Israel. The ancient promise is to be fully trusted even so.

However, since the meal image participates in sacred time, even setting off sacred time, the image leads us beyond the mere message of promise to the call to participation in this hope, in the sacred history that the meal represents. Thus, the disciples not only recognize Jesus in the context of the meal; they also see themselves fully only in the meal (didn't our hearts burn). The point of the meal is not just to reaffirm Torah but to invite us into a process that aims at the redemption of history itself, at the sacred time in which time is restored and filled out, the day of the Lord. What happens in this meal that makes all things, previously fuzzy, clear? Indeed, the meal enables the disciples to see history above history that ultimately enables righteous action. Bound by time, we can only be frustrated by the ambiguity of time. This ambiguity can threaten to destroy the sacred. Even the image of the road that marks off the true way from the false can be lured into the destruction of the sacred for the sake of human vainness. The meal in its conciliatory realness introduces sacred time over our time. And our midrashic voice says, **"In the meal God drew near to them and in the presence of God they were drawn near to each other."** If the nearness of God and the recognition of God is found in the meal of reconciliation, then the meal is also a model of reconciling dialogue between Jews and Christians.

The message can mean then only that hope in the resurrection is not a matter of proving the truth of Jesus but in hoping for the establishing of sacred time over our time, the hope for the day of the Lord. Without this hope, even the joy of resurrection can be shattered in the brutality of our own egos. In the light of our humanness, those who have seen the resurrected lord are privileged. In the light of sacred time, those who simply believe even if they have not seen are even greater. The focus of the resurrection appearances is this belief in the Lord who promises even in spite of ourselves.

For the one driven by a vision of the truth that divides, conversion is necessary. For the one blessed by the meal, invitation is necessary. Thus, we have before us the two dominant images of the resurrection that can decide the very character of the disciples of this Jesus. If the meal pre-dominates, then the image will form an invitation to join the God who rescues in the process of rescuing time for sacred time, claiming history for the God who would rescue. Out of this image is born the righteous gentile who would be so compelled by this God who redeems us and time that rescue and inclusion become second nature to our spiritual selves. This is not a question of whether we can successfully rescue time and history (could Jesus of this narrative rescue his time, his life?) but whether we will enter into the process of God's redemption or be lost in the frailty and potential evil of human time and history.

The Fragility of this Invitation

The recognition of the risen Jesus by the disciples is oddly concluded by the disappearance of Jesus leaving only a fleeting moment of recognition and a question of reflection (didn't our hearts burn when he spoke to us on the road?). The moment of recognition which becomes the moment of invitation is extraordinarily fragile. Certainly the intent is to suggest that Jesus no longer is contained by the limits of our experience and time. Still, the implication is that the disciples are left to make judgments on the basis of little evidence, fleeting moments of recognition. We may wonder how such fragility could spawn an entire and virulent religious movement.

What remains a question mark is whether the movement is a response to the experiences of the road or to the invitation of the meal. The long history of Christianity suggests that Jesus' disciples more often than not shaped their response on the belief that they had witnessed *the* truth. Thus, the mission of Christianity had to be perceived as a fulfillment of Judaism. Resuce on those terms had to be seen as conversion and this perception held true even in some of the altruism of the Shoah period. Because the link to the meal invitation remains fleeting, Christians have seldom seen this sign of connection with the covenant of Sinai that draws us to see Jesus' resurrection as an ultimate affirmation of God's rescue at the Red Sea and then the covenant and revelation at Sinai.

Some Christians, to be sure, have always seen the central message of rescue to be pictured in the meal invitation. Even if the zeal for Christian truth is present among such Christians, the overriding motivation is still the need to rescue all in threat or bondage in spite of what might be the truth. Indeed, the greater truth becomes the righteous deed, the act modelled after the God who brought Israel out of the house of bondage. And so, in the Shoah these Christians, though few in number, acted to rescue quite deliberately even though they still were committed to the truth of Christianity. The decisive moment of action was fleeting. Action had to precede debate.

These two avenues of interpretation will remain options within Christianity and the shape of Christian action in the face of future Shoahs will depend largely on how we read the resurrection appearances of Jesus. The alternatives may both speak important aspects of the narrative but lead in quite different directions in terms of decisive action to rescue or what constitutes rescue. The question is, can we afford not to re- capture the invitation of the meal as a basis for understanding this narrative?

John's Story

We may or may not be reproducing the author's intent in our reading. Indeed, such a task may be next to impossible. Our efforts have been to unfold both the ambiguity in the text and the alternatives for understanding of the each of the narratives. In that vein, we have consistently recognized that the gospel of John has been an alternative understanding from the synoptics in nearly every way. John's treatment of the resurrection is no exception.

Of course, this gospel presents acute problems throughout for any Post-Shoah Christian theology. The gospel appears to contain as virulent an anti-Judaism as any piece of Christian scripture, even though we have offered alternative views already in our previous treatment of this gospel. Again, we should not be surprised to find remnants of anti-Judaism in the resurrection narrative as well. What we find is only a slight mention of the Jewish authorities and almost complete concentration on Jesus' appearance to his followers; and the shape of this narrative is very different from that of any of the synoptics.

Our aim continues to be searching for a possible reading of these narratives that can form the basis for a post-Shoah Christian theology. Among the goals we have set is the need to open up the ambiguity that naturally lives in the narratives. Adding the reading of the gospel of John will help accomplish that goal so long as we can uncover a reading of the text that can effectively address the Shoah. Even more, this gospel is clearly most thoroughly theological in its structure and as Willi Marxsen argues, unconcerned about historical accuracy.[9] Essentially that means that the Johannine narrative intentionally links images of this resurrection story with images throughout the gospel text thus forming a unified theological position. For example, the pharisee, Nicodemus, is mentioned in the story of the burial in John and not in any of the synoptics. The connection with the Nicodemus discussion in John 3:1-15 is an intentional link indicating not an historical detail but a theological point.

Already we recognize that detail in John's resurrection narratives differs strikingly from details in the synoptics. These differences can set up for us potential alternative readings of this narrative. In John, for example, the visitors to the tomb are different than and come in different order to the sequence of the Marcan narrative. Most interesting however is that the tomb is empty but is not really. Jesus is clearly gone from the tomb but he appears already to Mary Magdalene at the tomb entrance. Thus, John links the separate narratives of the empty tomb and the appearances (even though, Jesus is, again not recognized at first). The point is clearly a different theology. John throughout the gospel depicts a Jesus in control of things. For John, the empty tomb cannot be left fully ambiguous with the question of Jesus' resurrection left open. Jesus continues to control the situation after his death as he did during his trial.

This detail of the narrative (John 20:19ff.) is emphasized consistently in the story as Jesus comes and goes as he pleases and directs the actions of the disciples (breathing on them the Holy Spirit he had promised earlier in the gospel text). We are, thereby, given a clearer image of the validity of Jesus' ministry (almost irresistible, beyond the particular decisions or people, friend or foe). The point is unmistakeable. This gospel emphasizes the effectiveness of God's plan in Jesus in spite of whatever other forces might present themselves to thwart that plan. The God of John's Jesus is invincible, beyond the powers of this age.

Many have called this basic characteristic of John's gospel a realized eschatology not so much because the eschaton is actually realized in the present but rather because the full power of God is known, the probability of the rule of God is now assured.[10] Unlike the synoptics who link the Exodus story with the resurrection, a God who works within history to accomplish an ultimate purpose for history, John's God appears to work inspite of history. This is clearly a different reading of the resurrection both as a part of Christian confession and as a theological idea, for the synoptics appear to point us in the direction of a process in which the resurrection (the rescue) that God brings gradually unfolds in history, with Jesus' resurrection only a proleptic sign of what is to come. The Jesus of John welcomes the disciples into a transformation of history that can be fully realized in us now through the Spirit of God. The confidence of this message can hardly be sustained in the face of the events of the Shoah. Irving Greenberg's challenge to the Christian claim that Jesus has changed history can be aimed directly at the apparent confidence of the Johannine narrative.[11]

The Efficacy of Doubt

Indeed, this may be the necessary reading of John's narrative except for the unique stories that fill out the narrative in this gospel. If God's plan is efficacious even in spite of human inadequacy, then why is the mission (the special mission of the disciples) so significant? And, why is the doubt of the disciple Thomas (John 20:24-25) compared so emphatically with the more admired ones who believe even though they do not see? Much in the flow of John's narrative makes the apparently invincible power of God more ambiguous than it seems. The response of the disciples and their participation in the mission is viewed as crucial to the success of God's ultimate plan. Rescue as such cannot be achieved without the commitment of Jesus' followers.

This radical contrast of ideas leaves us with a difficult quandry. On the one hand, the power of God cannot be thwarted by human action; yet on the other, God's plan cannot be finished without human action. This gospel transforms the whole idea of the resurrection, now not seen as an historical event but as a religious idea. Even Mary Magdalene is incapable of taking in the resurrection until Jesus empowers her by calling her by name. The resurrection does not have an automatic impact on human history but always lays in the balance of potential human response. Thus, the resurrection does not remain as an historical event to be affirmed but a human potential to be grasped, received.

The story of Thomas gives much the same lesson. Whether humans are typically "doubting Thomases" is beyond our inquiry. The result of the story is to suggest that the power of the resurrection is released only when Jesus is recognized. The potential of the resurrection remains in balance depending on human response. Thus, Jesus' point that even more praiseworthy are those who believe but have not seen makes sense. The point is not whether Jesus has been raised as such (which we can affirm by seeing) but whether the followers of Jesus can accept the implications of the idea of the resurrection, as proposed by the fourth evangelist through the words of Jesus.

What is implied by this story about Thomas is that the resurrection is an underlying theme for a process (a messianic process) that, on the one hand, affirms the power of God achieving the messianic age but on the other, affirms the centrality of human action as a part of the process to bring about the messianic age—the age of rescue. If the Thomas story is insufficient to make this point, the second ending of the gospel drives the point home. Peter, representing the disciples (a critical passage about the bystander as we saw earlier), is challenged to feed Jesus' sheep (John 21:15-19). Clearly the sheep are, in John, those that the Father has set apart, that is, Israel (the chosen ones). Peter is challenged to take on the task of rescue, loving and caring for the sheep. Jesus suggests in this rich text that Peter's actions are in fact in concert with devotion to Jesus as lord. The caring for the sheep is a messianic deed.

That this gospel more than the others struggles with the central question of the imminent division between the Christians and Jews seems without question. That the images of the gospel suggest that the author aims to provide a basis for reconciliation between Judaism and the Christians also seems likely. Undoubtedly the author saw that healing would require a long-term commitment, process, that aimed for unity among God's people. That the author saw the actions of the Jewish leadership as most destructive for that process also seems likely. Whatever, the lesson for Christians is that the Jesus in this gospel rather explicitly calls for reconciliation between his followers and the Jews in order to assure the success of the messianic process. The point of the gospel is not so much whether God has shown something completely new in Jesus but rather that the people of God be pointed in the right direction joined with God in the process of rescue (redemption).

Among the various possible readings of this gospel, the one offered here is quite plausible. If so, then this gospel becomes fully complementary to the others. The issue of the resurrection is the claim that God will fulfill his promise to rescue and the re-commitment of God's people to a process, messianic, of rescue. The fascinating polarity of a God who is in control with the God who is utterly dependent is a feature worth maintaining for our purposes. In the ambiguity of that polarity is a view that might provide a necessary element of a post-Shoah Christian theology. Maintaining this ambiguity might also provide an opening for dialogue since the confident claim that redemption is accomplished in the resurrection of Jesus is refuted.

The Critique of the Shoah

We are developing a view of theology that produces images of Christian action. The resurrection narratives are clearly an effort to re-affirm the promise of God to rescue (redeem) his people, each narrative providing a different angle to that affirmation. Still, the Shoah represents for Christians and Jews a supreme challenge to just the kind of confidence in God's action, even God's promises, that is depicted in and through the Jesus of John. That God is expected to accomplish his purpose in spite of human evil is a belief not only characteristic of the fourth gospel but also of traditional Christianity and also some of traditional Judaism. The devastation of the Shoah challenges all such orthodox claims. Our question truly is, "Can we expect God to act to bring in his kingdom, and if we do what does that mean for us now that we have seen the horror of Auschwitz?" Hope in an all-powerful God who is in control seems painfully frustrating in the face of the dashed hopes of the prisoners of Auschwitz.

Still, can we (Jews and Christians) talk about future history with hope without some belief beyond belief that God's promises are to be trusted in spite of what has happened. This is a claim that at once cannot be made but also must be made. To argue for such orthodoxy now seems to make us out to be fools. To cast aside such orthodoxy would leave us completely dependent on a weak and devastated humanity that surely is no more a source of hope than dreams of a messianic age. To remain witnesses to God's redemption is the challenge of our age for both Christians and Jews even if we think at times the task to be ludicrous.

Yet, this gospel disclaims an automatic fulfillment of God's messianic age that requires only our naive trust. This gospel so full of images of divine control finally makes God's plan dependent on the response of faithful followers. That Christians have so easily bought the package that we are saved by God without anything that we do may be a travesty of our history that has blinded us to the major thrust of each of these gospel narratives.[12] Certainly the fourth gospel calls for messianic deeds as the implicit meaning of the resurrection of Jesus. We act to become rescuers because we still believe that God is rescuer, or even that we have come to see ourselves as lovers of God and his people. We do this even if we cannot see the end (which lets us recall the odd text of the fate of the beloved disciple in John 21). Our midrashic voice says, **"Blessed are they who believe even though they have not seen." Yet that same voice reminds us that in the meal we do see.** See what? This gospel more than the others calls us to heroic action in assisting God in redemption. **We can see and heed the messianic mission.**

What does it mean for the church to hear and accept this mission now only after Auschwitz? The far more serious question is, "What does it mean for our future if we do not accept this mission?" The call is not selective, but this gospel does make the task clear. This rescue should seek the reconciliation in God's people— Christians and Jews. We are called to be friends, lovers, of God's people, **to share the meal of reconciliation.** Would such an image taught with vigor over centuries have told a different story than our century has heard? Such speculation does little to meet the exegencies of the moment, but the new story, the midrash of the messianic meal does invite a hope for the future, ever so slight and filled with the ambiguity that human integrity and action bear. Still, the mission is there for the one who is called by name as with Mary Magdalene.

A Review of this Interpretation

Richard Vieth, in commenting on Moltmann's position, refers to the resurrection as "God's great protest."[13] He says this in the context of his revision of the Biblical view of God's power, a perspective not unlike the one offered in this book. God's protest is shouted in the midst of God's persuasive power to call us to mission. The resurrection is at least the central image of this call to compassion. Even so, a protest is not actual rescue and a compassionate God no matter how more attractive than a powerful but unattentive God still remains puzzling in the face of such great evil as the Shoah. Despite all our claims, the language of the resurrection remains ambiguous.

If ambiguity even concerning the resurrection is to be a controlling factor in our post-Shoah theologies, then we must be explicit about how that ambiguity affects our theology. Surely, one effect is that certain theologies cannot work anymore. Thus, Roy Eckardt's critique of both Pannenberg and van Buren is more than illustration of a theological debate but rather the strong claim that the way that

Pannenberg and van Buren treat the resurrection cannot be genuine in a post-Shoah christology.[14]

Pannenberg's position is well represented in his christology.[15] Pannenberg holds that the resurrection is an historical event as a prolepsis of the future kingdom of God. In that way, this is not the resurrection of a single person but a breaking into history of the eschatological future. Pannenberg's efforts to explicate this view have never been fully satisfactory, however the view has had enormous impact on other thinkers. Eckardt's critique is two-fold. First, the view is fundamentally an affirmation of the longstanding claim of fulfillment theology, even if proleptic. It is an ontological claim that the resurrection transcends and in that transforms ontic history. Indeed, the claim is difficult to sustain with any analysis of ordinary history but crumbles in the face of Christian complicity in the Shoah. At the very least, we are left with ambiguity, any kind of understanding of what this transformation of history means is beyond us in the face of history so recent in our memory.

In fact, the interpretation we have offered produces both the possibility of a reading like Pannenberg's and an alternative that can escape the trap of an historical, ontic transformation. Perhaps, even the recognition that the passion narratives offer a variety of views and not a single line gives hope for some other Christian theology than what has been offered even in the creativity of Pannenberg.

Eckardt's second critique is more far-reaching. Pannenberg's theory of the resurrection is ultimately tied to his view of the crucifixion. The resurrection is, for Pannenberg, the affirmation of the truth of Jesus over-against the oppressive forces in Judaism of the time. In other words, the resurrection is a tool which serves to sustain the teaching of contempt we have just fully dismissed. I am not sure that Pannenberg's view of the resurrection can be maintained apart from his view of the crucifixion since implicit in the resurrection, in this view, is this theology of conflict and of supercession.[16]

With this critique we face the crux of our task. Indeed, the gospel resurrection narratives are an extension of the prior crucifixion narratives. The point is not whether we can or should connect the two pieces of the gospels. They are a natural extension of one another. Vieth is correct when he notes that a crucified God is no hope at all. Good Friday is nothing without Easter. The point is identifying what Good Friday and Easter are, and deciding how the crucifixion and the resurrection can be joined in a new midrash. The hermeneutic we are working with in this book and illustrated in this chapter is one that can shape a new story for us based on the images of resistance and rescue. The crucifixion, by this reading, is God's great protest that hopefully produces like protest (resistance) in us. Yet, the protest is nothing without redemption. We have argued that the resurrection narratives, despite the obvious possibility of reading them as images of ontic transformation (and therefore as affirmations of the unique truth of Jesus' teaching and life), can be read as images of God's rescue more universally, but particularly, understood. That is, the resurrection narratives are affirmations of God's plan for redemption that is realized in a process that assumes the covenant relationship and commitment to messianic deeds on the part of Jesus' followers, that we, too, become rescuers.

Van Buren's view is no more acceptable for Eckardt.[17] Van Buren's position on the relation between Christianity and Judaism leads directly to his treatment of the resurrection, for van Buren focusses attention on the way of discernment. Jesus is that figure through whom the gentiles are invited onto the way of God. The resurrection is then the advent of this mission to the gentiles. Now, van Buren is certainly to be commended for his effort to challenge us to restore the Jewish roots of Christian faith and theology, but the view makes the resurrection little more than a trumpet call to mission.[18]

The problem with this view, and van Buren is certainly not the only one to espouse the view, is that it fully ignores the way that the resurrection has been at the heart of Christian anti-Judaism throughout history. Indeed, the earliest impact of the resurrection was not to found a mission to the gentiles but rather to the Jews. Even if the ultimate effect of the resurrection has been to create a fully gentile church; the flip-side of that mission has always been a claim of antipathy toward the Jews who have obstinately refused to join the mission. It seems more than idealistic to me that we can write off history by saying that genuine Christianity is and always has been Judaism for the gentiles.

No matter how we devise this theology we are ultimately left with the fact that Christianity is in no way Judaism for anyone. The two are separate traditions, faiths, ways of life. It is this factor more than any other that enables us to bring the necessary ambiguity to bear upon our theologizing. If Christianity is not Judaism, then the resurrection serves to emphasize not our relation with Jesus but the gulf between our gentile world and the Jew, Jesus. Surely any theology of mission can make sense only when we can speak of mission carried out in dialogue with Jews, when we are led to dialogue and mutual respect.

And this is precisely our point on another level as we have unfolded this new midrash. Understanding this mission as only a Christian mission of hope seems vacuous after the Shoah. A completely gentile church so enamored with mission can easily turn its back on the Jewish people in need of rescue. We can refuse the call in more ways than one. How can we read the resurrection narrative in such a way so as to refuse the exclusive implication that Christians have the unique role of bringing hope to the world, especially when Christians have often turned from this mission and become the world's bane? Undoubtedly we can resolve this matter only by a return to the text of the resurrection narratives and to our interpretation in which the resurrection is seen not as an initiation (at least not only) of a new mission but ultimately an affirmation of Torah and Sinai. This point can be illustrated by a brief analysis of another passage in the gospel of Matthew, Matthew 28:16-20:

> Now the eleven disciples went to Galilee, to the mountain to which Jesus had directed them. When they saw him, they worshiped him; but some doubted. And Jesus came and said to them, "All authority in heaven and on earth has been given to me. Go therefore and make disciples of all nations, baptizing them in the name of the Father and of the Son and of the Holy Spirit, and teaching them to obey everything that I have commanded you. And remember, I am with you always, to the end of the age."

This passage is filled with twists that would require much more space than we can make available to unravel. Thus, I will focus on a couple of critical matters. First, this is a record of a resurrection appearance. It is the only appearance to the eleven recorded in Matthew's gospel; thus this passage has the duel purpose of describing the impact of the resurrection on the disciples and the intent of the resurrected Lord. In the context of the first matter, we are confronted by the strange counterposing of two responses—some worshiped him but some doubted. We are not told either what led to the act of worship and what that means or why some doubted or even what they doubted. The first point seems odd given the Jewish setting of this encounter (the disciples and Jesus) and especially the matter of worship as it was treated earlier in Matthew's gospel at the point of the temptations of Jesus (4:10, "Worship the Lord your God and serve only Him.") This odd counterposing is further enhanced by the way Jesus is said to respond. He acknowledges neither response as if to say that neither is an acceptable response to the resurrection. Now that leaves us with an ambiguity that the text only partially resolves—how then shall we respond?

In fact, the ambiguity that is displayed in this text gives reason to argue that the resurrection of Jesus is not an event that has meaning in and of itself. We have surely seen at least this in every part of our treatment of the resurrection narratives. The resurrection has meaning only in the words that Jesus shares (which we cannot be certain are Jesus' words). Jesus first calls the disciples to mission (to go and make disciples in every nation). The baptism to be performed is the baptism of discipleship. Whatever else Christians have made baptism to mean, Matthew fully intends to connect baptism with discipleship. The disciples are to observe all that Jesus has commanded (which in Matthew is the whole Law and the prophets). Observance is the appropriate response to the resurrection. Again, we hear a note that opens us to dialogue for this connection reminds us of the Exodus account in which the call to observance also is seen as the appropriate response to God's rescue at the Red Sea.

But to say this is as much as to say that the resurrection changes nothing. Would the disciples not have taught observance anyway? Indeed, the resurrection seems to be an affirmation of one thing alone—the lifestyle of faithful obedience to Torah. If there is no word of completion, no indication of victory or vindication, then this faithful obedience becomes the center of our response. The last words of the text serve to reinforce this claim—Jesus remains with the disciples until the end of time. **The resurrection is not the consummation of history.** There is no full kingdom of God, no ultimate victory over evil. If our response must be faithful obedience regardless, then our attention is naturally directed away from the risen Jesus to God, to the end of time.

This text has, of course, been used to verify the new Christian mission that separates Christian from Jew. Even the command to go into every nation has been used to prove the foundation for the mission to the gentiles. Indeed, we are the fruit of that mission, we are those gentiles. But can we say that the mission has been fulfilled if we are not prepared to observe all that Jesus commanded? Surely now is the time to recognize that we can no longer spiritualize this text or play games like gospel and law in our interpretations. Now, post-Shoah, we are commanded by this very same Lord to, at the very least, honor those who have observed, those who strive to be faithful, and in that honoring can we learn what Christian observance might be? Now is the time to make of the resurrection a potential link between Christian and Jew forever breaking the back of fulfillment theologies that would make the resurrection a triumphalism that is always a slap at the Jew.

But also, post-Shaoh, the language of resurrection is brought into question. What possible hope is there in one man's resurrection even if ordained by God over against the lives of all those children whose names are even forgotten by most, some not even known. The language of resurrection is now broken as the heart of the resurrected Lord must certainly be. Even using the term leaves us empty when we walk through the gates of Auschwitz as I have. What hope dare we speak there? Eckardt's view that only a future hope can possibly be genuine is a bold attempt to liven the word "resurrection" again.[18] But future hope is ambiguous, full of waiting and anticipation. Never certain. Even Jesus waits with us. Our question is, "Can we gentiles possibly learn to use the word in this way?" We must try.

We can also see the final critique of van Buren's view rise out of this analysis.[19] If Christianity is Judaism for the gentiles, and there is no indication that the disciples mission is simply that, then that mission is a Jewish mission. That is to say, it is a mission to the world to heal the world, to call the world to observance, to teach the world faithful obedience and loving kindness. Perhaps as Christians learn to listen to their Jewish partners in dialogue, they will again learn the meaning of this resurrection narrative that is so vital to our faith.

The kind of theological response that emphasizes ambiguity means not so much rejection of theological claims as the full recognition of the uncertainty that all Christian claims bear, most especially the central narratives of the crucifixion and the resurrection. Such an uncertainty drives us to listen more fully with openness to our Jewish brothers and sisters who not only teach us about our theological heritage but also represent for us a continuing symbol of our own need for theological redemption. A fully open Jewish-Christian dialogue given this sort of theological response to the Shoah would provide the optimum context for maintaining the necessary ambiguity in our theologizing.

A Return to Eckardt

The position I have outlined above is sketchy and requires a more thorough treatment of the Biblical narratives as well as the history of Christian theological thinking in order to shape a more complete post-Shaoh theology of the crucifixion and resurrection. Nevertheless, these rudimentary sketches do provide a framework for projecting an adequate theological response to the Shoah and its victims. In that way, we would produce an adequate theology for the post-Shaoh dialogues between Christians and Jews.

The unsettling claim of uncertainty merged with hope is, however, forcefully and brilliantly developed by A. Roy Eckardt as noted above. While his position differs from mine in some particulars, Eckardt does represent how such a theology of ambiguity might look more fully developed.[20] His position is volatile as might be expected verging on full denial of central Christian confessions on the one hand and retreating back into fragments of traditional Christian language on the other.Eckardt holds those extremes together through a continuing mode of irony that sharply emphasizes the brokeness of our theological language. Thus, Eckardt stands alone as one who leads, beckoning others to follow with insight and further challenges.

Eckardt's use of the term "resurrection" as the way to point to future hope may still be troubling to many. Despite the fact that we, Jews and Christians, both can claim this term as our own, there is little doubt that the word has been too completely Christian in the past for it to be a term easily used by us both. While we do not mean that the hope is simply the Christian hope for resurrection to which Jews must assent, just the use of the term creates that impression. I wonder if there is an alternative.

There is a far greater concern, however, in the use of this term. I am constantly confronted with the challenge that Irving Greenberg long ago gave us, that we must not say anything that could not be said in the presence of the one million children who died. Can we speak of resurrection in front of these children? Perhaps Eckardt is correct, that we are at that point when we must speak of resurrection. I am not sure. We are still not yet a full generation beyond this horror. Are we too impatient? Indeed, we might also take heed of Elie Wiesel wondering what meaning such hope has in the face of what we have now experienced.[21] We cannot know God's mind, but we can know that there will always be some emptiness in our talk of hope, even future hope.

We can overcome this dilemma only through dialogue. Christians cannot be confident judges about this matter. I suspect that we must speak of hope and do so with as much confidence as we can muster. We must do so not to allow the voice of darkness to be heard so loudly. Over against the Kingdom of the Night we must proclaim at least a dawn. But we do so with ambiguity as with all of our talk now. We do not know hope as future hope. We know hope as the child in one of the marvelous tales related by Yaffa Eliach, in our mother's arms, the safest place in the world.[22] Can we know with the kind of certainty that makes us persevere that a future hope can suffice? We do find in those who are faithful, those who are loving, those who are courageous, faithfulness, love and courage. Perhaps we will also find hope in and through those who are hopeful. Or even more, perhaps we will find hope in those things and through those people who give reason for hope, who heal, who are noble, who are gracious. Such victory is won ever so slowly and with little assurance. But in these things, we will learn how to use our language once again.

Eckardt does not stand alone in terms of the desire to find a language that adequately serves the post-Shoah dialogue. Others, even those holding such differing views as Moltmann, van Buren and Ruether, are also shaping and re-shaping theologies that can give ground for both full recognition of the evil of Auschwitz as well as the reality of a new openness between Christians and Jews. There is hope in that fact alone that progress can be made to a new world of inter-faith respect, particularly if that concern lays open the possibility for Christians to re-think, even re-shape, their theologies of the crucifixion and resurrection.

Epilogue

What I have written thus far is, as it were, a message for my Christian colleagues in terms of a reminder of what we have said and a suggestion about what might be otherwise said in response to the Shoah. I have always had in mind our partners in dialogue as I have written these reflections, but there is little in these words that reflect the voice of our Jewish partners. I cannot as proxy speak for them but I must add one more important word from the prominent Jewish scholar, Emil Fackenheim, as a necessary element in our post-Shaoh reflections on the crucifixion and the resurrection. Fackenheim argues, in *God's Presence in History*, that one command must be heard by all Jews after Auschwitz. "In ancient times, the unthinkable Jewish sin was idolatry. Today, it is to respond to Hitler by doing his work."[23] Indeed, we Christians must hear that word. We too cannot respond to Hitler by doing his work. If Hitler's work was to annihilate Judaism as well as all Jews, then we cannot promote a Christianity that in any way aims to do away with Judaism. We cannot ask Jews to turn from their Judaism.

Now, even if we have long ago put away Christian exclusivism and trium-phalism often associated with the crucifixion and the resurrection narratives (as I have shown in these chapters), we might still be subtly expecting that Jews will see in the Christian story an attempt to speak about a source of hope that combats Auschwitz. The position I have argued for, the position of ambiguity, aims to put to rest this kind of theologizing. And we must ask whether the naive hope of the resurrection can even be a satisfactory Christian hope after Auschwitz. That is to say, the spectrum of views presented in this essay represent views put forth by scholars seriously concerned about the progress of dialogue. We must ask whether some of these views must be rejected as inadequate responses to the Shoah even if they are presented in good faith. We must act to announce this so that those who do teach and preach in the name of Christ are, at least, challenged to hear the commanding voice of Auschwitz. Our task is certainly not finished with theological debate but continues in an effort to resolve the matter of how Christianity is going to be presented by teachers and preachers today and in the future. That is our present task.

Notes

[1]Of course, the problem of the ending of Mark's gospel has been a matter of debate for some time. One treatment of the gospel that gives some support to the direction of my reading is Norman Peterson, "When is the End Not the End?" *Interpretation*, Vol. 34:2, April 1980, pp. 151ff.

[2]Again, the matter of the author's identity and the nature of the community of the gospel is open to debate. A discussion of this can be found, among other places, in Norman Perrin, *The New Testament: an Introduction* (New York: Harcourt, Brace and Jovanovich, 1974), p. 195ff.

[3]Willi Marxsen, *The Resurrection of Jesus of Nazareth* (Philadelphia: Fortress Press, 1970), p. 54.

[4]Marxsen, pp. 49-50.

[5]I say "our" view here not to suggest the appropriate reading of Luke but to suggest what has often been the perspective of Christian interpretation. For example, a recent interpretation of the Lucan treatment of the religious leaders argues, again, for the centrality of this conflict motif: Mark

Powell, "The Religious Leaders in Luke: A Literary- Critical Study," *Journal of Biblical Literature*, Vol. 109:1, Spring 1990, pp. 93ff.

[6]Haim Maccoby, "Antisemitism and the Christian Myth," *Remembering for the Future* (New York: Pergamon Press, 1988), pp. 842-843.

[7]Marxsen, p. 51.

[8]Mircea Eliade, *The Myth of the Eternal Return* (Princeton, NJ: Princeton University Press, 1974), pp. 60-61.

[9]Marxsen, p. 55.

[10]As for example, in Hans Conzelmann, *Outline of the Theology of the New Testament* (New York: Harper and Row, 1968), pp. 356-357.

[11]Irving Greenberg, "Cloud of Smoke, Pillar of Fire: Judaism, Christianity, and Modernity after the Holocaust," in *Auschwitz: Beginning of a New Era?* (New York: KTAV, 1977), p. 13.

[12]Clearly the theme of justification found in Pauline literature that has so affected Western Christian theology has also been used as a central hermeneutic for interpreting the gospel texts. We will need to pursue later the problem of the relation between Pauline themes and gospel perspectives.

[13]Richard Vieth, *Holy Power, Human Pain* (Bloomington, IN: Meyer/Stone Books, 1988), p. 103.

[14]A. Roy Eckardt and Alice Eckardt, *Long Night's Journey into Day* (Detroit: Wayne State University, 1982), pp. 125ff.

[15]The point here is not just the theology but the resultant teaching about Judaism that is intolerable for Eckardt. Thus, our aim is reiterated in its twofold nature. We hope for both a midrash that escapes "bad theology" and counteracts the teaching of contempt.

[16]Wolfhart Pannenberg, *Jesus–God and Man* (Philadelphia: Westminster Press, 1977), pp. 53ff.

[17]Eckardt, p. 130ff.

[18]Eckardt, p. 150.

[19]I believe that Van Buren has made an effort to alter this direction of his thought in his more recent volumes of his theological trilogy with some but not complete success. The pattern of looking at the resurrection in this way is similar to the conclusions of Willi Marxsen as well. Thus, despite the valuable assistance that Marxsen has provided us, his conclusions must also be challenged.

[20]See especially James F. Moore, "A Spectrum of Views: Traditional Christian Responses to the Holocaust," *Journal of Ecumenical Studies*, Volume 25:2, Spring 1988, pp. 217-218.

[21]Robert McAfee Brown's discussion of the Messianic includes reflections on Wiesel's caution: Robert McAfee Brown, "The Coming of Messiah: Divergence or Convergence?" in *Human*

Response to the Holocaust, Michael Ryan, ed. (New York: Edwin Mellen Press, 1981), especially, p. 210ff.

[22]Yaffa Eliach, *Hasidic Tales of the Holocaust* (New York: Avon Books, 1982), pp. 32, 79.

[23]Emil Fackenheim, *God's Presence in History* (New York: Harper and Row, 1970), p. 84.

CHAPTER 10:
CONCLUSION

We have only made a beginning in this book, but to make a beginning is a significant step forward in understanding the shape of Christian theology after the Shoah. We have imposed a method consistently in this book that can be seen even more clearly now as we look back on what we have said. In the final chapter of this book, then, I will summarize key points of this approach, we have identified as a midrashic process of interpretation, as well as the important "rules for our theology" that have emerged from our reading of the passion narratives. While these latter discoveries are also merely a beginning, they represent what can be applied to the subsequent reading of any Christian text for the sake of forming Christian theology for preaching and teaching.

Summarizing the Key Features of Our Method

The method employed in this book is not like standard approaches to Christian theology or interpretation of Christian scripture, for that matter. Our argument has been that despite the value of the various approaches that have been used, the Shoah has rendered those approaches broken, unable to give account for the radical nature of the Shoah and the radical challenge of that event to all Christian theology and theological language. I follow in this claim the advice of thinkers such as David Tracy and Johannes Metz from the Christian perspective[1] and Emil Fackenheim and Irving Greenberg from the Jewish point of view.[2] I do not contend that such a radical revision of Christian theology is accepted by all or even understood by all either Christians or Jews.[3] But one conclusion is certainly true given the beginning point of the theology I am proposing. The approach to Christian thought in this text must be understood on its own terms and not as some variation of standard theological approaches.

Thus, this theology is not to be understood as exegesis in the standard ways (historical-critical methods) that exegesis is understood. To regard this approach as exegesis is to confuse and even contradict the primary theses of my proposal. I will return to this matter below. This theology is also not to be understood as a dogmatics. While I must of necessity consider the impact of Christian dogmatics at various points of the discussion of the passion narratives, the interpretation offered is not an effort to suggest a new dogmatics (new christologies or theologies or ecclesiologies). Finally, this approach to theology that I propose is not an historical analysis. I am not considering the various alternative views that have arisen about each text through the history of Christian thought, even though such approaches are immensely helpful and some consideration of various positions of leading contemporary thinkers must of necessity be presented as part of the interpretation of the passion narratives offered in this book.

The principles that govern the approach in this book are, nevertheless, clearly presented and now may be even more clearly set forth in the context of the review of the passion narratives in the second half of the book and in contrast to the three alternative approaches that I have just noted. First, this theology must be a theology "in dialogue" beginning with the first principles and arguments offered. Every approach and conclusion must be judged on the basis of how that would be received by our Jewish partners in dialogue. Second, this theology must account for the radical critique of the Shoah that is directed toward all theological claims and all theological language. Thus, meaning itself is placed under radical critique. For this reason, the twin principles of ambiguity and pluralism are basic to every theology that is post-Shoah theology. Third, this theology is midrashic, that is, the theology is fundamentally aimed at disclosing basic principles for understanding and teaching of Christian texts which form the basis of Christian thinking. The fundamental aim is two-fold as we undertake this interpretive process: (1) we attempt to locate and undo the "teaching of contempt" that has been implicit in much of Christian thinking from the earliest era of Christian theology,[4] and (2) we aim at developing the context for a teaching of respect that attempts to move beyond mere tolerance of Judaism toward a Christianity that is obligated to safeguard the legitimacy of Judaism.[5] The reader might rightfully ask whether judgments can be made with these criteria about what are appropriate and what are inappropriate Christian understandings of Christian texts. Surely, these criteria, even if different from the criteria of, say, standard exegesis, do make judgments possible (even those that might contradict the instincts of historical-critical analysis). Still, we make these judgments cautiously since the temptation to dogmatism is also under severe critique after the Shoah despite what appears to us to be fitting given our instincts. We can be clearer about this caution and the judgments we can make by using the interpretations found in this book as examples for each of these criteria.

Dialogue as the Context for all Theology

The central criteria for any post-Shoah Christian theology is that such theologies must be dialogical. The point may be easily trivialized in any number of ways not the least of which is the recognition that any theology is hermeneutical (always characterized by a dialogue with a text). In fact, the long history of Christian interpretation is proof of the open-ended nature of even this enterprise. Any interpretive process produces readings of texts that not only differ but even contradict one another. Not only that, the hermeneutics applied to a text must always account for the various historical eras of Christians that both produced the texts of Christian scripture and also the various possible interpretations.

Understanding dialogue in this way makes any era, perhaps especially our own, merely one among many in a long chain of interpretations. There is little way to judge which period is authoritative or even whether the results of contemporary dialogue should have greater sway than other factors in determining which interpretations are fitting. This plurality of possible interpretations has nearly always been resolved in Christian history by one of two means—consensus of the church and/or the assumption of the absolute norm of the objective text. Aside from the many debates about whether the norm of the text can actually be established outside of specific theological presumptions, an argument that presumes resolution by consensus in the church is already ruled out by the post-Shoah demand for a community of dialogue between Christians and Jews. Christian interpretation of Christian texts can no longer be the exclusive domain of Christians (even those quite sensitive to Judaism and Jewish concerns).

This first implication of the criteria of dialogue (posed earlier in this book as a re-application of Irving Greenberg's dictum about theological language after the Shoah) becomes a rule of interpretation, then, for post-Shoah theology.[6] All Christian theology is to be done in the context of a community of Jewish-Christian dialogue. Any reading of a Christian text, then, becomes a tentative reading subject to examination by this expanded community of interpretation. Whether or not this community actually exists for a theologian (there is reason to hope that a community is developing and certainly several small but long-standing groups of dialogue partners are good candidates for such a community), any theology is done as if it were being done in the context of that community.[7] The rule effects certain judgments then about possible readings of Christian texts—any possible interpretation that would serve to close off dialogue between Christians and Jews (specifically those readings that sustain the Christian "Teaching of Contempt" for Jews) would be of necessity rejected no matter how reasonably the interpretation could be defended on exegetical, textual grounds. In a book written by a Christian theologian (such as this one) the rule can be applied and must be applied in a way that invites conversation.

There are actually two ways that a Christian theology can invite conversation with Jewish partners. The first is most common among post-Shoah theologians, to assume that Christianity can be known fully only by recognizing the Jewish roots of Christianity. That assumption has been consistently applied in this book and an example can easily illustrate the point. Most especially, the reading of Christian scripture is constantly being set into the wider context of the Hebrew scripture in this book. The section in chapter nine on the empty tomb narrative (and Willi Marxsen's work is used in order to develop a traditional understanding of this portion of the resurrection narratives[8]) is enriched by reference to several companion narratives in the Hebrew scripture, most particularly the narrative of Jonah. The point is that a reference in the Christian scripture to a Hebrew text requires not merely a Christian reading of the reference but a return to the Hebrew scripture in order to set the context of the reference. The assumption in this book has been that Christian scripture is, itself, a type of midrashic interpretation that appeals not merely to stereotypical patterns or uses but to an audience who must know the full implication of the text from the Hebrew scripture. The Christian text points to a truth found in the Hebrew text.

This path for developing post-Shoah Christian theology is almost self-evident for theologians working to be truly post-Shoah. Yet a second implication of inviting conversation is necessary for post-Shoah theology and this intention is also evident in this book even if the task is a bit more difficult. A post-Shoah Christian theology is also an open-ended discussion and several references, particularly in interpretation of texts, expose points of genuine mutual interest between Christians and Jews today. Those points of possible contemporary conversation are also highlighted in this book by special reference to the need for dialogue on those points.

An example of this invitation to dialogue can be found in the section of the images of Jesus in the trial narratives discussed in chapter seven of this book. The conclusion of that discussion is that Jesus becomes, in the narratives, the resistor par excellence, particularly in the context of Roman occupation and domination. The issue of that narrative seems to be how one defines what it means to be a real Jew. That Jesus is taken to be a model in response to that question is not viewed in our book as settling the question but rather inviting dialogue. Indeed, our presumption is that an adequate reading of such texts can be achieved only by considering the question a matter for contemporary dialogue, letting our Jewish partners define for themselves what it means to be a Jew. Thus, our theologies should incorporate this implicit or explicit invitation whenever we render an interpretation of texts such as the trial narratives of the gospels.

Actually, there is a running tension between these two aspects of our invitation to dialogue. On the one hand, we narrow the field of possible interpretations by locating the Christian texts in a Jewish context. Some readings are, thereby, discounted. On the other hand, we also broaden the field of possible interpretations (more accurately, we open up the process) by suggesting that interpretations cannot be treated as settled outside of the contemporary dialogue and with the active contribution of Jewish self-definition. This tension is a necessary component of all post-Shoah Christian theology. Any attempt to dissolve or resolve the tension will produce a theology that is inadequate for our time.

The Shoah as an Hermeneutic of Suspicion

The first two fundamental criteria for post-Shoah Christian theology are inextricably linked together. The dialogue as we know it would not be what it is if it were not for the events of the Shoah. That disheartening fact is unavoidable even as the results have been a relationship between Christians and Jews that is unparalleled in history. Also, the Shoah would not be possible to grasp in anyway adequate to the event without the possibility and actuality of contemporary Jewish-Christian dialogue. These points are accepted without question among those who strive for a post-Shoah Christian theology. Still, few have managed to incorporate successfully a methodology that makes the critique arising from the Shoah an integral part of Christian theology. Metz' challenge to Christian theologians remains as an important, not yet fulfilled task.[9]

The proposal in this book is methodological, suggesting a means by which that criteria can become a working part of doing Christian theology. First, we press Irving Greenberg's charge forward even more fully and in a way characterized by the approach of Elie Wiesel.[10] That is, we ask whether any interpretation of Christian scripture holds up in the face of the questions shaped by the events of the Shoah. Interpretations that are unable to hold in the light of that challenge must be considered suspect, impossible to retrieve at least in the way presented. The theological understanding of forgiveness in Christian thought is an important example of this difficulty, and the issue is hardly more striking than in the narrative sequence about Peter in the passion narratives. The ambiguity of Peter's role in the Christian narrative makes the issue of forgiveness especially striking. What is clear is that Peter cannot be forgiven by anyone except by the one he has denied (Jesus), but the narrative does not present an obvious answer to our expectations. Jesus does not forgive Peter in any of the versions of the resurrection narratives. At least, forgiveness is not treated in the narratives as a completed act. The Johannine text simply has Jesus inviting Peter to show his love by taking care of God's people.

The story of the denial of Jesus by Peter is unique as is the story of Christian denial of the Jews during the Shoah. We must not merely associate directly forgiveness as applied to these occasions with forgiveness in normal relationships anymore than we can readily compare the bystander Peter with Christian bystanders during the Shoah. But that is the point in a way. The Shoah has challenged normal understandings of forgiveness. The question becomes for Christians, can we talk about forgiveness in the same way even in everyday situations now that we see how forgiveness can crumble in the face of enormous atrocity and apostasy. At least, the shadow of Auschwitz looms over this central Christian theological category making any trivializing and banalizing of the act of forgiveness not only theologically vacuous but obscene.

Peter's story leaves the issue open because the event of the crucifixion challenges the application of forgiveness in that case. How much more are we challenged when those who could forgive are left nameless, without even the dignity of burial and mourning?[11] How we talk about forgiveness, even about God's grace must be an open question both for the future of the Christian community and for the community of dialogue. Of course, we are able to (fortunately) point to the rescuers as some balance to the image of the bystander that we find in Peter, but we must not allow the full critique of the Shoah to slip away. The only way to hold the Shoah fast as a part of the way we do theology is to maintain this sort of open-ended tension.

A second approach is used in this book that aims to fulfill Metz' vision of all contemporary Christian theology. The structure of this book assumes a critical shaping feature of post-Shoah Christian theology. We assume that all theology must fit into the structure of possible Christian responses to the Shoah insofar as the Shoah is the ultimate test of the meaningfulness of any Christian thought and action. Of course, that assumption is not universally accepted, even by all those who take dialogue seriously. The position taken in this book is one of many along a spectrum of possible responses, ours is a re-visionist position.[12] Thus, we sought a way that we could retrieve the meaningfulness of Christian theology within the posture of a revisionist theology. The methodological mechanism used in this book is to identify a related set of ideal models of response that correspond to the actual Christian responses during the Shoah and also find root in Christian scripture. The passion narratives lend themselves well to this approach actually offering up clear and distinct examples of each ideal type (see my argument below concerning the decision not to include other portions of Christian scripture, most especially, the Pauline literature). The approach is not flawless and of course would completely distort actuality if we assumed that the types were rigid (even though, we might be prepared to argue that some types are mutually exclusive).

The point is, however, to establish criteria for possible interpretations, and again, the Shoah acts as a hermeneutic of suspicion with regard to interpretations. That negative criteria is never more obvious in this book than in chapter six—the examination of the collaborator. In fact, the biblical narratives relating the story of Judas already create a confused mix of detail even before we bring the critical questions arising from the Shoah regarding the collaborators. Add to this unsettling ambiguity the history of Christian treatment of Judas (especially, in relation to Christian images of the Jews) and we create a narrative that makes firm judgments about collaborators nearly impossible to make. Indeed, our treatment of the Judas narrative (together with our interlude on the Jewish leaders and Pilate) discloses this ambiguity as a key conclusion of this section.

We might ask for what purpose do we travel a complex road to end with confusion? The narrative clearly stands as a suspicion of any form of theological, ideological or moral arrogance. Above all, we cannot adequately arrive at a judgment about the collaborators since, as the biblical narrative masterfully shows, the story of the collaborator is potentially mixed with competing motivations and pressures. Such is especially the case with stories of collaboration during the Shoah, even though we contend that Christian collaboration is a different case than Jewish collaboration (thus, our treatment of the Jewish leaders). If ideological or moral arrogance has led to collaboration especially during the Shoah, we still cannot simply respond in kind and produce an adequate post-Shoah theology.

This point about moral arrogance, however, does not leave us without direction and the discussion regarding collaboration is an important model for working through the related question of Christian complicity in the Shoah. As complex as the gospel narratives are in speaking to the fate of the collaborator, they provide a spectrum of possible ways to think about and respond to the question of Christian complicity not only on the level of Christian support for or defense of Nazism but also in the fuzzier and more difficult question of Christian historical precedence for Nazism. The negative criteria that arise from the Shoah can, in this way, produce models for theologies that truly respond to the Shoah.

A Midrashic Interpretation

Aside from the fundamental criteria that arise from taking both dialogue and the Shoah seriously in our theologies, this book introduces a midrashic approach to interpretation. Making such an approach clear is difficult since a Christian midrash will not likely reproduce Rabbinic midrash, which has a well-developed pattern and set of interpretive techniques. Neither does this book aim to produce discreet midrash as such, although a couple of examples do arise from the interpretations offered in this book. What we aim to do, instead, is to incorporate the features of midrash into our theologies: the notion of oral torah which creates an open-ended approach to interpretations and the principle of application that makes necessary creative and imaginative treatment of texts.[13]

The notion of oral torah is a likely backdrop for the Christian scripture. We have used Schooneveld's notion of Jesus as oral torah as a way to incorporate the midrashic character of Christian scripture into our theologies and as a means for understanding how we move from text to interpretation.[14] Thus, not only do we, like a number of other scholars, assume that the Christian scriptures are themselves midrash, but we also suggest that the focus of Christian scripture cannot be Jesus, but rather must be Torah. This shift in Christian theology from a Jesus/Christic centered approach to a scripture centered approach is not only a striking re-thinking of Christian theology, but also provides a different way to evaluate various interpretations. Above all, our intention has been to open the Christian text to the full interpretive tradition that forms the context for Christian thought and theology.

This open-enedness of meaning may be especially evident in the trial narrative sequences we have labelled "Jesus of the Trial Narratives" in chapter seven. In fact, we have argued, the Jesus of these narratives seems intent to steer the whole attention of understanding his identity and ministry away from himself. One of the most striking sections of that narrative sequence can be found, surprisingly, in the Johannine text of this narrative. Jesus' simple response to Pilate, the Roman governor, is to say that his entire purpose is to bear witness to the truth. This is not an abstract truth we confront here but the truth of God, the Torah. One of the key interpretations of this complex narrative sequence surely is that the whole of Christian confession finds its root not in an independent Jesus faith but in the Torah.

Of course, the trial narratives are also an excellent example of the second feature of interpretive openness, the conflict of interpretations. Thus, the reading offered above of Jesus' purpose is also just one among many possible interpretations. The intent of this book has been to maintain the ambiguity by exposing the various possible interpretations. From the outset, we have regarded this theological principle to be especially difficult, contrary to ordinary theological thinking. Perhaps we can resolve the ambiguity (the conflict of interpretations) by selecting a single interpretation that appears to be most adequate. But, we have chosen, instead, to heighten the tension by maintaining the ambiguity.

Again the trial sequence can be an important example of this heightened ambiguity. We have suggested, in fact, that several approaches to understanding the trial narrative provide important theological clues, pockets of meaning. We move forward not by resolving the conflict of interpretations but by maintaining the conflict. Much like the innovative approach of Paul Ricoeur, we have presupposed that meaning arises from the conflict itself producing tensions in meaning because, with Ricoeur, we accept the notion that there is a surplus of meaning in the text.[15] Thus, the trial sequence can be seen as staged farce and if that an important theme arises, noting that this narrative is not historically or thematically significant for the whole Jesus narrative. On the other hand, we argue that the trial sequence is historically and thematically significant fitting the important undercurrent of resistance that characterizes the whole of the Jesus passion narrative.

Once the text has been freed from the captivity of reductionism (reducing the text to the most adequate interpretation), the text can become, in its ambiguity, a rich theological source (we can retrieve the text) that can now be tested by the duel criteria of dialogue and the Shoah. The trial narrative produces two models for resistance, each arising from the two, seemingly conflicting, interpretations. On the one hand, Jesus' resistance is rooted in the message that his ministry is not deterred or influenced by the political manipulations of Pilate. Resistance requires foundation in the "truth" that transcends the politics. That claim clearly now becomes a point of dialogue for Jews and Christians not only in our separate understandings of the torah but also in coming to terms with what is the truth about ourselves post-Shoah. What does it mean for each of us individually to bear witness to the truth? But on the other hand, resistance does require involvement in the political arena and that, too, is a point of dialogue.

The notion of resistance, maybe especially in the form of bearing witness, also finds the central and most difficult test within the context of the Shoah. Perhaps we can de-politicize Jesus as we have often done in our theologies in "normal" circumstances, but to de-politicize Jesus in the context of the Shoah is to completely drain the Jesus narrative of its contemporary meaning. Spiritualized, other-worldly visions of resistance and witness are challenged by the historical reality of radical evil which is indiscriminate, destroying at will the lives of children who could not have had the resources to resist. To talk of a Christianity without the necessity for political action after Auschwitz is to discredit our witness. No matter how successfully we can justify a spiritualized reading of the trial narrative, those justifications lose their credibility when heard by the million or so children who died without choice or someone to give comfort and help. Some readings of texts verge on the obscene.

If this style of doing theology is consistently applied to Christian scripture, then eventually discreet midrash will arise. That is, novel interpretive ideas will emerge that become necessary addendum to the scriptural text (the text cannot be read with understanding apart from these innovation notions). Midrash may appear as extended stories but most often flash forward as unique and pointed comments of understanding. We have identified only two discreet midrash,[16] one of which emerges from a point of ambiguity in the narrative of the resurrection appearances in the gospel of Luke (see chapter nine). The meal is so central to the whole flow of the passion narratives that the appearance of this image in the Lucan narrative strikes the reader as a sign of a critical turning point in the meaning of the narrative.

In fact, we have left this novel insight undeveloped in our treatment of Luke's narrative of the resurrection appearances, giving only some clues about how the point can and should be developed further. The meal as the point of recognition means that the fundamental means by which God can approach us with hope is through the inclusive act of eating together. This image stands in direct tension with the image of the road that also flows through the text. Since two striking pictures of Christian response to God are evident from the structure of this text, ultimately the meal must be offered as one way to understand the "truth" of the text in order to resolve the tension. In the case of this tension, however, the ambiguity, the conflict, cannot be allowed to stand because the choice has to do with how Christian theology is done, that is, with the critical criteria of dialogue.

Of course, the point of the meal image is not merely a door into understanding one text but a ruling image for all of Christian theology. Once the image emerges in such a consistent way in the passion narratives, the meal as a way of understanding Christianity, Christian discipleship, takes over all of what we say. The image becomes a way to retrieve Christian scripture in a post-Shoah world and theology. Since the image has not been developed fully in our efforts here, then our beginning begs further effort to build on this important insight.

Now this posing of the two images of the road and the meal is a good example of the difference between ordinary exegesis and the midrashic approach in this book. In fact, the whole theology of the gospel of Luke appears to suggest that the image of the road is an apt way to describe Luke's theology. If we were inclined to be true to the apparent thrust of the text, to Luke's intention, we might conclude that Christianity stands on the road with the choice of who to follow as the central measure of Christianity. But, such a reading that leads to theological exclusivism cannot be the character of Christianity in a post-Shoah world. In the face of Luke's apparent intention we are led by our own *Sitz-im-Leben* and by our underlying criteria to turn to a secondary image, that of the meal as the necessary interpretation of Luke, Luke's own image used in spite of Luke's apparent intention. Otherwise, we are left with dismissing Luke's gospel, as such, as a resource for post-Shoah Christian theology, an approach that is all too easily the direction suggested by many.

Summarizing Our Basic Claims

Aside from the methodological basics of our approach to post-Shoah Christian theology, some key conclusions are evident from our treatment of the passion narratives:

1. We are led to conclude that genuine Christianity, genuine discipleship, is marked by the two themes of resistance and rescue. This conclusion arises not only because we find these two responses the only viable Christian stance during the cataclysm of the Shoah but also because the texts of the passion narratives lead us to that conclusion. Perhaps this claim arises in part because the narratives are, themselves, developed in a context of conflict and challenge to the legitimacy of Christian discipleship.

2. In so far as resistance and rescue are clearly the only models for genuine Christian response, the alternative responses of the bystander and the collaborator are clearly shown as inappropriate responses, failing to mark genuine Christianity. Far from simply dismissing the bystander and the collaborator, however, as outside the reach of God's mercy or Christian compassion, the narratives lead us to an appropriate ambiguity that defies dogmatic ways of dealing with the one who collaborates with the enemy or the one who is driven to deny responsibility for the other.

3. This structure of the passion narratives that can be represented by the models of bystander, collaborator, resistor, and rescuer can be clearly identified in the texts with individuals and separate narrative sequences. These narrative sequences can become an effective way to retrieve these narratives with meaning for a post-Shoah Christian theology. Whether that meaning follows what is implied in our treatment of these texts will surely be a matter for conversation in dialogue on these themes. Still, our contention is that all post-Shoah Christian theology must fit somewhere within the spectrum of these four response models when the focus becomes the validity of Christian discipleship.

4. Nevertheless, our approach also lays the groundwork for a post-Shoah Christian treatment of both theology proper and christology. The narrative sequences surrounding the figure of Jesus compel us to see that resistance is a central determinative theme for any christology, especially post-Shoah christology. The complexity of the narratives, though, challenge simplistic treatment of these themes that ignore other strands of the narratives that connect with the central theme of resistance. In addition, theology proper finds a root in the model of the rescuer. In the same way, this theme takes a different shape in a post-Shoah Christian thought world. We clearly have contemporary models of rescue and without these living

images we will be hard-pressed to give authenticity to our claims about the God who rescues. That is, claims about God and God's redemption now must be tied to the historical reality of any point in time, dismissing all efforts to thoroughly spiritualize the notion of redemption. We might legitimately argue that this dimension of Christian confession has always been present in the text of Christian scripture, and surely a radical historical context is present in the passion narratives. Still, we must fight regular and persistent tendencies to reify the Christian claims.

These points are among the most central themes that emerge from our treatment of the passion narratives. When we match these basic claims with our commitment to the three prongs of our method, we have the framework for a post-Shoah Christian theology. But we have said at the outset of this chapter that we have made only a beginning. Much more is needed than what we have begun to do here. The invitation to join the process is quite clear.

Where From Here, or What About Paul?

The much more that we speak of includes not only building on what we have done with the passion narratives, but also recognizing that Christian scripture and belief is more than what can be found in the passion narratives. Our belief is that the basic structure presented in this book can be an effective basis for all post-Shoah Christian theology. What has been exemplified in our treatment of the passion narratives (our choice to focus on these narratives is defended earlier in this book) should apply to the rest of the gospel texts, indeed, to all of Christian scripture. That belief now remains to be tested and we are committed to carrying that work forward in future books.

The claims we assume here are especially significant with respect to the Pauline literature, which we have chosen to set aside for the most part in this book. Still, the basic consistency of Christian theology as conceived in our work should also work as well in the treatment of the Pauline material as it has for the passion narratives. Again, the specifics of that application lie ahead of us in yet another book (one that is clearly already taking shape). What we have done here can be applied to the Pauline texts if the basic principles of our approach are kept consistent - that theology is genuine only if done in dialogue, that Christian theology must now be post-Shoah theology, and that the method of doing theology is midrashic. If we see that theology must as post-Shoah theology focus on the issue of the nature of Christian discipleship (Christian response), then the Pauline texts can be tested in terms of whether they are consistent with the emerging picture we have seen in the passion narratives. A specific treatment of the Pauline texts is not necessary for us to recognize that basic point, even as a treatment of those texts will be important for a completion of our midrashic approach.

Even so, we do recognize that the Pauline material is distinct and unique in many ways. Most significantly, the Pauline material when viewed from the perspective of our vision of post-Shoah Christian theology appears to be an attempt to do theology in precisely the same way as we have suggested. Paul's work is, in some ways, a completely developed alternative to the theology we have worked out in this book. Our question becomes whether Paul's fully developed theology (that seems so completely christo-centric) is possible to retrieve intact in a post-Shoah climate. The question is not different from the one posed already in this book concerning the passion narratives. The difference lies, perhaps, in the different nature of Paul's material. Thus, we have concluded that the challenge of dealing with the Pauline material as a unique type of text is best left to a separate volume.

Of course, we recognize that the Pauline material is historically central to the shaping of Western Christian theology and, for that matter, to Christian views of Jews and Judaism in the West. The whole issue of the religion of Paul as distinct from the religion of the gospels (of Jesus in particular) deserves a thorough treatment even if we believe that the Pauline material will ultimately fit within the pattern of doing theology that is presented in this text. Thus, we have also offered a beginning in this book that forms the starting point for doing post-Shoah Pauline theology as well even as we argue that specifically working through the Pauline material is one of the tasks that lies on the immediate horizon of our next work.

There is an enormous task of re-visioning Christian scripture and theology that remains to be finished. This book is a beginning, an invitation to join in the conversation. Even so, Christian theology is clearly on a new path, a path that can be understood on the one hand without much confusion but is also open to complexities that create unresolvable ambiguities and conflicts. The tensions that emerge are creative tensions. Post-Shoah Christian theologians have the opportunity to incorporate the full richness of this creative tension, and the approach we have suggested allows for that to happen. Let the work continue.

NOTES

[1]Surely many have spoken in these terms, but I was first led to think in this way by David Tracy, "Religious Values After the Holocaust: A Catholic View" in *Jews and Christians After the Holocaust*, Abraham Peck, ed. (Philadelphia: Fortress Press, 1982), p. 92. and Johann Baptist Metz, *The Emerging Church* (New York: Crossroad, 1986), pp. 20ff.

[2]My first encounter with this theological challenge came through Irving Greenberg, "Cloud of Smoke, Pillar of Fire: Judaism, Christianity, and Modernity after the Holocaust," in *Auschwitz: Beginning of a New Era?*, Eva Fleischner, ed. (New York: KTAV, 1977), pp. 8-13. See also, Emil Fackenheim, *To Mend the World*, (New York: Schocken Books, 1982), p. 280.

[3]In fact, I have offered a survey of various Christian positions in an essay that appeared several years ago. The argument supporting this claim is given in the earlier chapters of this book, cf. James F. Moore, "A Spectrum of Views: Traditional Christian Responses to the Holocaust," *Journal of Ecumenical Studies*, 25:2, Spring 1988, pp. 212-224.

[4]Cf., Jules Isaac, *The Teaching of Contempt: Christian Roots of Anti-Semitism*, (New York: Holt, Rinehart and Winston, 1964).

[5]Cf., Clark Williamson, *When Jews and Christians Meet*, (St. Louis: CBP Press, 1988).

[6]Irving Greenberg, pp. 8-13.

[7]Though no community could actually function as an adjudicating body at present, some communities of discussion do represent models for what we are talking about in this book; e.g., The Annual Scholar's Conference on the Holocaust and the German Church Struggle.

[8]Willi Marxsen, *The Resurrection of Jesus of Nazareth* (Philadelphia: Fortress Press, 1970).

[9]Johann Baptist Metz, pp. 20ff.

[10]Elie Wiesel, "Art and Culture After the Holocaust" in *Auschwitz: Beginning of a New Era?*, Eva Fleischner, ed. (New York: KTAV, 1977), pp. 403ff.

[11]This point about *kaddish* is an example of a discreet midrash that is part of our discussion of the resurrection narratives in chapter 8. In fact, the appearance of this motif is the reason for the abrupt appearance of bold print as well.

[12]Our choice to use David Tracy's label, "revisionist theology," is not to be confused with the revisionist historians whose aim is to re-describe history for the purpose of minimizing or denying the Shoah. For a more complete description of Tracy's conception of theology, cf., David Tracy, *Blessed Rage for Order* (New York: Crossroad, 1975), pp. 43ff.

[13]As Indicated in Chapter 3 above I have used the following in attempting adapt the notions of midrash to Christian theology: Barry Holtz, "Midrash," in *Back to the Sources*, (New York: Simon and Schuster, 1986), pp. 177-211, and the related work of Gerald Bruns, Midrash and Allegory: the Beginnings of Scriptural Interpretation," in Robert Alter and Frank Kermode, ed., *The Literary Guide to the Bible*, (Cambridge: Harvard University Press, 1987), pp. 625-646.

[14]Jacobus Schoneveld, "Torah in the Flesh: A New Reading of the Prologue of the Gospel of John as a Contribution to a Christology Without Anti-Judaism," in *Remembering for the Future: Jews and Christians During and After the Holocaust*, (New York: Pergamon Press, 1988), pp. 867-878, Vol. I.

[15]Ricoeur has spent a lifetime detailing his interpretation theory, but two resources quite helpful in grasping the points related here are: Paul Ricoeur, *The Conflict of Interpretations* (Evanston: Northwestern University Press, 1974), and Paul Ricoeur, *Interpretation Theory* (Fort Worth: Texas Christian University Press, 1976).

[16]Since we have done so little to follow up on possible discreet midrash in this book, we have chosen to highlight the two candidates by marking relevant text, which is the reason for the sudden appearance of bold print in the latter chapters.

APPENDIX:
THE PASSION NARRATIVE TEXTS

MATTHEW 26:14-28:20

CHAPTER 26

14 Then one of the twelve, who was called Judas Iscariot, went to the chief priests 15 and said, "What will you give me if I betray him to you?" They paid him thirty pieces of silver. 16 And from that moment he began to look for an opportunity to betray him.

17 On the first day of Unleavened Bread the disciples came to Jesus, saying, "Where do you want us to make the preparations for you to eat the Passover?" 18 He said, "Go into the city to a certain man, and say to him, 'The Teacher says, My time is near; I will keep the Passover at your house with my disciples.'" 19 So the disciples did as Jesus had directed them, and they prepared the Passover meal.

20 When it was evening, he took his place with the twelve; 21 and while they were eating, he said, "Truly I tell you, one of you will betray me." 22 And they became greatly distressed and began to say to him one after another, "Surely not I, Lord?" 23 He answered, "The one who has dipped his hand into the bowl with me will betray me. 24 The Son of Man goes as it is written of him, but woe to that one by whom the Son of Man is betrayed! It would have been better for that one not to have been born." 25 Judas, who betrayed him, said, "Surely not I, Rabbi?" He replied, "You have said so."

26 While they were eating, Jesus took a loaf of bread, and after blessing it he broke it, gave it to the disciples, and said, "Take, eat; this is my body." 27 Then he took a cup, and after giving thanks he gave it to them, saying, "Drink from it, all of you; 28 for this is my blood of the covenant, which is poured out for many for the forgiveness of sins. 29 I tell you, I will never again drink of this fruit of the vine until that day when I drink it new with you in my Father's kingdom."

30 When they had sung the hymn, they went out to the Mount of Olives. 31 Then Jesus said to them, "You will all become deserters because of me this night; for it is written, 'I will strike the shepherd, and the sheep of the flock will be scattered.' 32 But after I am raised up, I will go ahead of you to Galilee." 33 Peter said to him, "Though all become deserters because of you, I will never desert you." 34 Jesus said to him, "Truly I tell you, this very night, before the cock crows, you will deny me three times." 35 Peter said to him, "Even though I must die with you, I will not deny you." And so said all the disciples.

36 Then Jesus went with them to a place called Gethsemane; and he said to his disciples, "Sit here while I go over there and pray." 37 He took with him Peter and the two sons of Zebedee, and began to be grieved and agitated. 38 Then he said to them, "I am deeply grieved, even to death; remain here, and stay awake with me." 39 And going a little farther, he threw himself on the ground and prayed, "My Father, if it is possible, let this cup pass from me; yet not what I want but what you want." 40 Then he came to the disciples and found them sleeping; and he said to Peter, "So, could you not stay awake with me one hour? 41 Stay awake and pray that you may not come into the time of trial; the spirit indeed is willing, but the flesh is weak." 42 Again he went away for the second time and prayed, "My Father, if this cannot pass unless I drink it, your will be done." 43 Again he came and found them sleeping, for their eyes were heavy. 44 So leaving them again, he went away and prayed for the third time, saying the same words. 45 Then he came to the disciples and said to them, "Are you still sleeping and taking your rest? See, the hour is at hand, and the Son of Man is betrayed into the hands of sinners. 46 Get up, let us be going. See, my betrayer is at hand."

47 While he was still speaking, Judas, one of the twelve, arrived; with him was a large crowd with swords and clubs, from the chief priests and the elders of the people. 48 Now the betrayer had given them a sign, saying, "The one I will kiss is the man; arrest him." 49 At once he came up to Jesus and said, "Greetings, Rabbi!" and kissed him. 50 Jesus said to him, "Friend , do what you are here to do." Then they came and laid hands on Jesus and arrested him. 51 Suddenly, one of those with Jesus put his hand on his sword, drew it, and struck the slave of the high priest, cutting off his ear. 52 Then Jesus said to him, "Put your sword back into its place; for all who take the sword will perish by the sword. 53 Do you think that I cannot

appeal to my Father, and he will at once send me more than twelve legions of angels? 54 But how then would the scriptures be fulfilled, which say it must happen in this way?" 55 At that hour Jesus said to the crowds, "Have you come out with swords and clubs to arrest me as though I were a bandit? Day after day I sat in the temple teaching, and you did not arrest me. 56 But all this has taken place, so that the scriptures of the prophets may be fulfilled." Then all the disciples deserted him and fled.

57 Those who had arrested Jesus took him to Caiaphas the high priest, in whose house the scribes and the elders had gathered. 58 But Peter was following him at a distance, as far as the courtyard of the high priest; and going inside, he sat with the guards in order to see how this would end. 59 Now the chief priests and the whole council were looking for false testimony against Jesus so that they might put him to death, 60 but they found none, though many false witnesses came forward. At last two came forward 61 and said, "This fellow said, 'I am able to destroy the temple of God and to build it in three days.'" 62 The high priest stood up and said, "Have you no answer? What is it that they testify against you?" 63 But Jesus was silent. Then the high priest said to him, "I put you under oath before the living God, tell us if you are the Messiah, the Son of God." 64 Jesus said to him, "You have said so. But I tell you, From now on you will see the Son of Man seated at the right hand of Power and coming on the clouds of heaven." 65 Then the high priest tore his clothes and said, "He has blasphemed! Why do we still need witnesses? You have now heard his blasphemy. 66 What is your verdict?" They answered, "He deserves death." 67 Then they spat in his face and struck him; and some slapped him, 68 saying, "Prophesy to us, you Messiah! Who is it that struck you?"

69 Now Peter was sitting outside in the courtyard. A servant-girl came to him and said, "You also were with Jesus the Galilean." 70 But he denied it before all of them, saying, "I do not know what you are talking about." 71 When he went out to the porch, another servant-girl saw him, and she said to the bystanders, "This man was with Jesus of Nazareth." 72 Again he denied it with an oath, "I do not know the man." 73 After a little while the bystanders came up and said to Peter, "Certainly you are also one of them, for your accent betrays you." 74 Then he began to curse, and he swore an oath, "I do not know the man!" At that moment the cock crowed. 75 Then Peter remembered what Jesus had said: "Before the cock crows, you will deny me three times." And he went out and wept bitterly.

CHAPTER 27

When morning came, all the chief priests and the elders of the people conferred together against Jesus in order to bring about his death. 2 They bound him, led him away, and handed him over to Pilate the governor.

3 When Judas, his betrayer, saw that Jesus was condemned, he repented and brought back the thirty pieces of silver to the chief priests and the elders. 4 He said, "I have sinned by betraying innocent blood." But they said, "What is that to us? See to it yourself." 5 Throwing down the pieces of silver in the temple, he departed; and he went and hanged himself. 6 But the chief priests, taking the pieces of silver, said, "It is not lawful to put them into the treasury, since they are blood money." 7 After conferring together, they used them to buy the potter's field as a place to bury foreigners. 8 For this reason that field has been called the Field of Blood to this day. 9 Then was fulfilled what had been spoken through the prophet Jeremiah, "And they took the thirty pieces of silver, the price of the one on whom a price had been set, on whom some of the people of Israel had set a price, 10 and they gave them for the potter's field, as the Lord commanded me."

11 Now Jesus stood before the governor; and the governor asked him, "Are you the King of the Jews?" Jesus said, "You say so." 12 But when he was accused by the chief priests and elders, he did not answer. 13 Then Pilate said to him, "Do you not hear how many accusations they make against you?" 14 But he gave him no answer, not even to a single charge, so that the governor was greatly amazed.

15 Now at the festival the governor was accustomed to release a prisoner for the crowd, anyone whom they wanted. 16 At that time they had a notorious prisoner, called Jesus Barabbas. 17 So after they had gathered, Pilate said to them, "Whom do you want me to release for you, Jesus Barabbas or Jesus who is called the Messiah?" 18 For he realized that it was out of jealousy that they had handed him over. 19 While he was sitting on the judgment seat, his wife sent word to him, "Have nothing to do with that innocent man, for today I have suffered a great deal because of a dream about him." 20 Now the chief priests and the elders persuaded the crowds to ask for Barabbas and to have Jesus killed. 21 The governor again said to them, "Which of the two do you want me to release for you?" And they said, "Barabbas." 22 Pilate said to them, "Then what should I do with Jesus who is called the Messiah?" All of them said, "Let him be crucified!" 23 Then he asked, "Why, what evil has he done?" But they shouted all the more, "Let him be crucified!"

24 So when Pilate saw that he could do nothing, but rather that a riot was beginning, he took some water and washed his hands before the crowd, saying, "I am innocent of this man's blood; see to it yourselves." 25 Then the people as a whole answered, "His blood be on us and on our children!" 26 So he released Barabbas for them; and after flogging Jesus, he handed him over to be crucified.

27 Then the soldiers of the governor took Jesus into the governor's head-quarters, and they gathered the whole cohort around him. 28 They stripped him and put a scarlet robe on him, 29 and after twisting some thorns into a crown, they put

it on his head. They put a reed in his right hand and knelt before him and mocked him, saying, "Hail, King of the Jews!" 30 They spat on him, and took the reed and struck him on the head. 31 After mocking him, they stripped him of the robe and put his own clothes on him. Then they led him away to crucify him.

32 As they went out, they came upon a man from Cyrene named Simon; they compelled this man to carry his cross. 33 And when they came to a place called Golgotha (which means Place of a Skull), 34 they offered him wine to drink, mixed with gall; but when he tasted it, he would not drink it. 35 And when they had crucified him, they divided his clothes among themselves by casting lots; 36 then they sat down there and kept watch over him. 37 Over his head they put the charge against him, which read, "This is Jesus, the King of the Jews." 38 Then two bandits were crucified with him, one on his right and one on his left. 39 Those who passed by derided him, shaking their heads 40 and saying, "You who would destroy the temple and build it in three days, save yourself! If you are the Son of God, come down from the cross."

41 In the same way the chief priests also, along with the scribes and elders, were mocking him, saying, 42 "He saved others; he cannot save himself. He is the King of Israel; let him come down from the cross now, and we will believe in him. 43 He trusts in God; let God deliver him now, if he wants to; for he said, 'I am God's Son.'" 44 The bandits who were crucified with him also taunted him in the same way.

45 From noon on, darkness came over the whole land until three in the afternoon. 46 And about three o'clock Jesus cried with a loud voice, "Eli, Eli, lema sabachthani?" that is, "My God, my God, why have you forsaken me?" 47 When some of the bystanders heard it, they said, "This man is calling for Elijah." 48 At once one of them ran and got a sponge, filled it with sour wine, put it on a stick, and gave it to him to drink. 49 But the others said, "Wait, let us see whether Elijah will come to save him." 50 Then Jesus cried again with a loud voice and breathed his last.

51 At that moment the curtain of the temple was torn in two, from top to bottom. The earth shook, and the rocks were split. 52 The tombs also were opened, and many bodies of the saints who had fallen asleep were raised. 53 After his resurrection they came out of the tombs and entered the holy city and appeared to many. 54 Now when the centurion and those with him, who were keeping watch over Jesus, saw the earthquake and what took place, they were terrified and said, "Truly this man was God's Son!"

55 Many women were also there, looking on from a distance; they had followed Jesus from Galilee and had provided for him. 56 Among them were Mary Magdalene, and Mary the mother of James and Joseph, and the mother of the sons of Zebedee.

57 When it was evening, there came a rich man from Arimathea, named Joseph, who was also a disciple of Jesus. 58 He went to Pilate and asked for the body of Jesus; then Pilate ordered it to be given to him. 59 So Joseph took the body and wrapped it in a clean linen cloth 60 and laid it in his own new tomb, which he had hewn in the rock. He then rolled a great stone to the door of the tomb and went away. 61 Mary Magdalene and the other Mary were there, sitting opposite the tomb.

62 The next day, that is, after the day of Preparation, the chief priests and the Pharisees gathered before Pilate 63 and said, "Sir, we remember what that impostor said while he was still alive, 'After three days I will rise again.' 64 Therefore command the tomb to be made secure until the third day; otherwise his disciples may go and steal him away, and tell the people, 'He has been raised from the dead,' and the last deception would be worse than the first." 65 Pilate said to them, "You have a guard of soldiers; go, make it as secure as you can." 66 So they went with the guard and made the tomb secure by sealing the stone.

CHAPTER 28

After the sabbath, as the first day of the week was dawning, Mary Magdalene and the other Mary went to see the tomb. 2 And suddenly there was a great earthquake; for an angel of the Lord, descending from heaven, came and rolled back the stone and sat on it. 3 His appearance was like lightning, and his clothing white as snow. 4 For fear of him the guards shook and became like dead men. 5 But the angel said to the women, "Do not be afraid; I know that you are looking for Jesus who was crucified. 6 He is not here; for he has been raised, as he said. Come, see the place where he lay. 7 Then go quickly and tell his disciples, 'He has been raised from the dead, and indeed he is going ahead of you to Galilee; there you will see him.' This is my message for you." 8 So they left the tomb quickly with fear and great joy, and ran to tell his disciples. 9 Suddenly Jesus met them and said, "Greetings!" And they came to him, took hold of his feet, and worshiped him. 10 Then Jesus said to them, "Do not be afraid; go and tell my brothers to go to Galilee; there they will see me."

11 While they were going, some of the guard went into the city and told the chief priests everything that had happened. 12 After the priests had assembled with the elders, they devised a plan to give a large sum of money to the soldiers, 13 telling

them, "You must say, 'His disciples came by night and stole him away while we were asleep.' 14 If this comes to the governor's ears, we will satisfy him and keep you out of trouble." 15 So they took the money and did as they were directed. And this story is still told among the Jews to this day.

16 Now the eleven disciples went to Galilee, to the mountain to which Jesus had directed them. 17 When they saw him, they worshiped him; but some doubted. 18 And Jesus came and said to them, "All authority in heaven and on earth has been given to me. 19 Go therefore and make disciples of all nations, baptizing them in the name of the Father and of the Son and of the Holy Spirit, 20 and teaching them to obey everything that I have commanded you. And remember, I am with you always, to the end of the age."

MARK 14:10-16:8

CHAPTER 14

10 Then Judas Iscariot, who was one of the twelve, went to the chief priests in order to betray him to them. 11 When they heard it, they were greatly pleased, and promised to give him money. So he began to look for an opportunity to betray him.

12 On the first day of Unleavened Bread, when the Passover lamb is sacrificed, his disciples said to him, "Where do you want us to go and make the preparations for you to eat the Passover?" 13 So he sent two of his disciples, saying to them, "Go into the city, and a man carrying a jar of water will meet you; follow him, 14 and wherever he enters, say to the owner of the house, 'The Teacher asks, Where is my guest room where I may eat the Passover with my disciples?' 15 He will show you a large room upstairs, furnished and ready. Make preparations for us there." 16 So the disciples set out and went to the city, and found everything as he had told them; and they prepared the Passover meal.

17 When it was evening, he came with the twelve. 18 And when they had taken their places and were eating, Jesus said, "Truly I tell you, one of you will betray me, one who is eating with me." 19 They began to be distressed and to say to him one after another, "Surely, not I?" 20 He said to them, "It is one of the twelve, one who is dipping bread into the bowl with me. 21 For the Son of Man goes as it is written of him, but woe to that one by whom the Son of Man is betrayed! It would have been better for that one not to have been born."

22 While they were eating, he took a loaf of bread, and after blessing it he broke it, gave it to them, and said, "Take ; this is my body." 23 Then he took a cup,

and after giving thanks he gave it to them, and all of them drank from it. 24 He said to them, "This is my blood of the covenant, which is poured out for many. 25 Truly I tell you, I will never again drink of the fruit of the vine until that day when I drink it new in the kingdom of God."

26 When they had sung the hymn, they went out to the Mount of Olives. 27 And Jesus said to them, "You will all become deserters; for it is written, 'I will strike the shepherd, and the sheep will be scattered.' 28 But after I am raised up, I will go before you to Galilee." 29 Peter said to him, "Even though all become deserters, I will not." 30 Jesus said to him, "Truly I tell you, this day, this very night, before the cock crows twice, you will deny me three times." 31 But he said vehemently, "Even though I must die with you, I will not deny you." And all of them said the same.

32 They went to a place called Gethsemane; and he said to his disciples, "Sit here while I pray." 33 He took with him Peter and James and John, and began to be distressed and agitated. 34 And said to them, "I am deeply grieved, even to death; remain here, and keep awake." 35 And going a little farther, he threw himself on the ground and prayed that, if it were possible, the hour might pass from him. 36 He said, "Abba, Father, for you all things are possible; remove this cup from me; yet, not what I want, but what you want." 37 He came and found them sleeping; and he said to Peter, "Simon, are you asleep? Could you not keep awake one hour? 38 Keep awake and pray that you may not come into the time of trial; the spirit indeed is willing, but the flesh is weak."

39 And again he went away and prayed, saying the same words. 40 And once more he came and found them sleeping, for their eyes were very heavy; and they did not know what to say to him. 41 He came a third time and said to them, "Are you still sleeping and taking your rest? Enough! The hour has come; the Son of Man is betrayed into the hands of sinners. 42 Get up, let us be going. See, my betrayer is at hand."

43 Immediately, while he was still speaking, Judas, one of the twelve, arrived; and with him there was a crowd with swords and clubs, from the chief priests, the scribes, and the elders. 44 Now the betrayer had given them a sign, saying, "The one I will kiss is the man; arrest him and lead him away under guard." 45 So when he came, he went up to him at once and said, "Rabbi!" and kissed him. 46 Then they laid hands on him and arrested him.

47 But one of those who stood near drew his sword and struck the slave of the high priest, cutting off his ear. 48 Then Jesus said to them, "Have you come out with swords and clubs to arrest me as though I were a bandit? 49 Day after day I

was with you in the temple teaching, and you did not arrest me. But let the scriptures be fulfilled." 50 All of them deserted him and fled.

51 A certain young man was following him, wearing nothing but a linen cloth. They caught hold of him, 52 but he left the linen cloth and ran off naked.

53 They took Jesus to the high priest; and all the chief priests, the elders, and the scribes were assembled. 54 Peter had followed him at a distance, right into the courtyard of the high priest; and he was sitting with the guards, warming himself at the fire. 55 Now the chief priests and the whole council were looking for testimony against Jesus to put him to death; but they found none. 56 For many gave false testimony against him, and their testimony did not agree. 57 Some stood up and gave false testimony against him, saying, 58 "We heard him say, 'I will destroy this temple that is made with hands, and in three days I will build another, not made with hands.'" 59 But even on this point their testimony did not agree. 60 Then the high priest stood up before them and asked Jesus, "Have you no answer? What is it that they testify against you?" 61 But he was silent and did not answer. Again the high priest asked him, "Are you the Messiah, the Son of the Blessed One?" 62 Jesus said, "I am; and 'you will see the Son of Man seated at the right hand of the Power,' and 'coming with the clouds of heaven.'" 63 Then the high priest tore his clothes and said, "Why do we still need witnesses? 64 You have heard his blasphemy! What is your decision?" All of them condemned him as deserving death. 65 Some began to spit on him, to blindfold him, and to strike him, saying to him, "Prophesy!" The guards also took him over and beat him.

66 While Peter was below in the courtyard, one of the servant-girls of the high priest came by. 67 When she saw Peter warming himself, she stared at him and said, "You also were with Jesus, the man from Nazareth." 68 But he denied it, saying, "I do not know or understand what you are talking about." And he went out into the forecourt. Then the cock crowed. 69 And the servant-girl, on seeing him, began again to say to the bystanders, "This man is one of them." 70 But again he denied it. Then after a little while the bystanders again said to Peter, "Certainly you are one of them; for you are a Galilean." 71 But he began to curse, and he swore an oath, "I do not know this man you are talking about." 72 At that moment the cock crowed for the second time. Then Peter remembered that Jesus had said to him, "Before the cock crows twice, you will deny me three times." And he broke down and wept.

CHAPTER 15

As soon as it was morning, the chief priests held a consultation with the elders and scribes and the whole council. They bound Jesus, led him away, and handed him over to Pilate. 2 Pilate asked him, "Are you the King of the Jews?" He answered him, "You say so." 3 Then the chief priests accused him of many things. 4 Pilate asked him again, "Have you no answer? See how many charges they bring against you." 5 But Jesus made no further reply, so that Pilate was amazed.

6 Now at the festival he used to release a prisoner for them, anyone for whom they asked. 7 Now a man called Barabbas was in prison with the rebels who had committed murder during the insurrection. 8 So the crowd came and began to ask Pilate to do for them according to his custom. 9 Then he answered them, "Do you want me to release for you the King of the Jews?" 10 For he realized that it was out of jealousy that the chief priests had handed him over. 11 But the chief priests stirred up the crowd to have him release Barabbas for them instead. 12 Pilate spoke to them again, "Then what do you wish me to do with the man you call the King of the Jews?" 13 They shouted back, "Crucify him!" 14 Pilate asked them, "Why, what evil has he done?" But they shouted all the more, "Crucify him!" 15 So Pilate, wishing to satisfy the crowd, released Barabbas for them; and after flogging Jesus, he handed him over to be crucified.

16 Then the soldiers led him into the courtyard of the palace (that is, the governor's headquarters); and they called together the whole cohort. 17 And they clothed him in a purple cloak; and after twisting some thorns into a crown, they put it on him. 18 And they began saluting him, "Hail, King of the Jews!" 19 They struck his head with a reed, spat upon him, and knelt down in homage to him. 20 After mocking him, they stripped him of the purple cloak and put his own clothes on him. Then they led him out to crucify him.

21 They compelled a passer-by, who was coming in from the country, to carry his cross; it was Simon of Cyrene, the father of Alexander and Rufus. 22 Then they brought Jesus to the place called Golgotha (which means the place of a skull). 23 And they offered him wine mixed with myrrh; but he did not take it. 24 And they crucified him, and divided his clothes among them, casting lots to decide what each should take. 25 It was nine o'clock in the morning when they crucified him. 26 The inscription of the charge against him read, "The King of the Jews." 27 And with him they crucified two bandits, one on his right and one on his left. 29 Those who passed by derided him, shaking their heads and saying, "Aha! You who would destroy the temple and build it in three days, 30 save yourself, and come down from the cross!" 31 In the same way the chief priests, along with the scribes, were also mocking him among themselves and saying, "He saved others; he cannot save himself. 32 Let the Messiah, the King of Israel, come down from the cross now, so that we may see and believe." Those who were crucified with him also taunted him.

33 When it was noon, darkness came over the whole land until three in the afternoon. 34 At three o'clock Jesus cried out with a loud voice, "Eloi , Eloi, lema sabachthani?" which means, "My God, my God, why have you forsaken me?" 35 When some of the bystanders heard it, they said, "Listen, he is calling for Elijah." 36 And someone ran, filled a sponge with sour wine, put it on a stick, and gave it to him to drink, saying, "Wait, let us see whether Elijah will come to take him down." 37 Then Jesus gave a loud cry and breathed his last. 38 And the curtain of the temple was torn in two, from top to bottom. 39 Now when the centurion, who stood facing him, saw that in this way he breathed his last, he said, "Truly this man was God's Son!"

40 There were also women looking on from a distance; among them were Mary Magdalene, and Mary the mother of James the younger and of Joses, and Salome. 41 These used to follow him and provided for him when he was in Galilee; and there were many other women who had come up with him to Jerusalem.

42 When evening had come, and since it was the day of Preparation, that is, the day before the sabbath, 43 Joseph of Arimathea, a respected member of the council, who was also himself waiting expectantly for the kingdom of God, went boldly to Pilate and asked for the body of Jesus. 44 Then Pilate wondered if he were already dead; and summoning the centurion, he asked him whether he had been dead for some time. 45 When he learned from the centurion that he was dead, he granted the body to Joseph. 46 Then Joseph bought a linen cloth, and taking down the body, wrapped it in the linen cloth, and laid it in a tomb that had been hewn out of the rock. He then rolled a stone against the door of the tomb. 47 Mary Magdalene and Mary the mother of Joses saw where the body was laid.

CHAPTER 16

When the sabbath was over, Mary Magdalene, and Mary the mother of James, and Salome bought spices, so that they might go and anoint him. 2 And very early on the first day of the week, when the sun had risen, they went to the tomb. 3 They had been saying to one another, "Who will roll away the stone for us from the entrance to the tomb?" 4 When they looked up, they saw that the stone, which was very large, had already been rolled back. 5 As they entered the tomb, they saw a young man, dressed in a white robe, sitting on the right side; and they were alarmed.

6 But he said to them, "Do not be alarmed; you are looking for Jesus of Nazareth, who was crucified. He has been raised; he is not here. Look, there is the place they laid him. 7 But go, tell his disciples and Peter that he is going ahead of you to Galilee; there you will see him, just as he told you." 8 So they went out and

fled from the tomb, for terror and amazement had seized them; and they said nothing to anyone, for they were afraid.

LUKE 22:1-24:53

CHAPTER 22

Now the festival of Unleavened Bread, which is called the Passover, was near. 2 The chief priests and the scribes were looking for a way to put Jesus to death, for they were afraid of the people.

3 Then Satan entered into Judas called Iscariot, who was one of the twelve; 4 he went away and conferred with the chief priests and officers of the temple police about how he might betray him to them. 5 They were greatly pleased and agreed to give him money. 6 So he consented and began to look for an opportunity to betray him to them when no crowd was present.

7 Then came the day of Unleavened Bread, on which the Passover lamb had to be sacrificed. 8 So Jesus sent Peter and John, saying, "Go and prepare the Passover meal for us that we may eat it." 9 They asked him, "Where do you want us to make preparations for it?" 10 "Listen ," he said to them, "when you have entered the city, a man carrying a jar of water will meet you; follow him into the house he enters 11 and say to the owner of the house, 'The teacher asks you, "Where is the guest room, where I may eat the Passover with my disciples?"' 12 He will show you a large room upstairs, already furnished. Make preparations for us there." 13 So they went and found everything as he had told them; and they prepared the Passover meal.

14 When the hour came, he took his place at the table, and the apostles with him. 15 He said to them, "I have eagerly desired to eat this Passover with you before I suffer; 16 for I tell you, I will not eat it until it is fulfilled in the kingdom of God." 17 Then he took a cup, and after giving thanks he said, "Take this and divide it among yourselves; 18 for I tell you that from now on I will not drink of the fruit of the vine until the kingdom of God comes." 19 Then he took a loaf of bread, and when he had given thanks, he broke it and gave it to them, saying, "This is my body, which is given for you. Do this in remembrance of me." 20 And he did the same with the cup after supper, saying, "This cup that is poured out for you is the new covenant in my blood. 21 But see, the one who betrays me is with me, and his hand is on the table. 22 For the Son of Man is going as it has been determined, but woe

to that one by whom he is betrayed!" 23 Then they began to ask one another, which one of them it could be who would do this.

24 A dispute also arose among them as to which one of them was to be regarded as the greatest. 25 But he said to them, "The kings of the Gentiles lord it over them; and those in authority over them are called benefactors. 26 But not so with you; rather the greatest among you must become like the youngest, and the leader like one who serves. 27 For who is greater, the one who is at the table or the one who serves? Is it not the one at the table? But I am among you as one who serves.

28 "You are those who have stood by me in my trials; 29 and I confer on you, just as my Father has conferred on me, a kingdom, 30 so that you may eat and drink at my table in my kingdom, and you will sit on thrones judging the twelve tribes of Israel.

31 "Simon, Simon, listen! Satan has demanded to sift all of you like wheat, 32 but I have prayed for you that your own faith may not fail; and you, when once you have turned back, strengthen your brothers." 33 And he said to him, "Lord, I am ready to go with you to prison and to death!" 34 Jesus said, "I tell you, Peter, the cock will not crow this day, until you have denied three times that you know me."

35 He said to them, "When I sent you out without a purse, bag, or sandals, did you lack anything?" They said, "No, not a thing." 36 He said to them, "But now, the one who has a purse must take it, and likewise a bag. And the one who has no sword must sell his cloak and buy one. 37 For I tell you, this scripture must be fulfilled in me, 'And he was counted among the lawless'; and indeed what is written about me is being fulfilled." 38 They said, "Lord, look, here are two swords." He replied, "It is enough."

39 He came out and went, as was his custom, to the Mount of Olives; and the disciples followed him. 40 When he reached the place, he said to them, "Pray that you may not come into the time of trial." 41 Then he withdrew from them about a stone's throw, knelt down, and prayed, 42 "Father, if you are willing, remove this cup from me; yet, not my will but yours be done." 43 Then an angel from heaven appeared to him and gave him strength. 44 In his anguish he prayed more earnestly, and his sweat became like great drops of blood falling down on the ground. 45 When he got up from prayer, he came to the disciples and found them sleeping because of grief, 46 and he said to them, "Why are you sleeping? Get up and pray that you may not come into the time of trial."

47 While he was still speaking, suddenly a crowd came, and the one called Judas, one of the twelve, was leading them. He approached Jesus to kiss him; 48 but Jesus said to him, "Judas, is it with a kiss that you are betraying the Son of Man?" 49 When those who were around him saw what was coming, they asked, "Lord, should we strike with the sword?" 50 Then one of them struck the slave of the high priest and cut off his right ear. 51 But Jesus said, "No more of this!" And he touched his ear and healed him. 52 Then Jesus said to the chief priests, the officers of the temple police, and the elders who had come for him, "Have you come out with swords and clubs as if I were a bandit? 53 When I was with you day after day in the temple, you did not lay hands on me. But this is your hour, and the power of darkness!"

54 Then they seized him and led him away, bringing him into the high priest's house. But Peter was following at a distance. 55 When they had kindled a fire in the middle of the courtyard and sat down together, Peter sat among them. 56 Then a servant-girl, seeing him in the firelight, stared at him and said, "This man also was with him." 57 But he denied it, saying, "Woman, I do not know him." 58 A little later someone else, on seeing him, said, "You also are one of them." But Peter said, "Man, I am not!" 59 Then about an hour later still another kept insisting, "Surely this man also was with him; for he is a Galilean." 60 But Peter said, "Man, I do not know what you are talking about!" At that moment, while he was still speaking, the cock crowed. 61 The Lord turned and looked at Peter. Then Peter remembered the word of the Lord, how he had said to him, "Before the cock crows today, you will deny me three times." 62 And he went out and wept bitterly.

63 Now the men who were holding Jesus began to mock him and beat him; 64 they also blindfolded him and kept asking him, "Prophesy! Who is it that struck you?" 65 They kept heaping many other insults on him.

66 When day came, the assembly of the elders of the people, both chief priests and scribes, gathered together, and they brought him to their council. They said, 67 "If you are the Messiah, tell us." He replied, "If I tell you, you will not believe; 68 and if I question you, you will not answer. 69 But from now on the Son of Man will be seated at the right hand of the power of God." 70 All of them asked, "Are you, then, the Son of God?" He said to them, "You say that I am." 71 Then they said, "What further testimony do we need? We have heard it ourselves from his own lips!"

CHAPTER 23

Then the assembly rose as a body and brought Jesus before Pilate.

2 They began to accuse him, saying, "We found this man perverting our nation, forbidding us to pay taxes to the emperor, and saying that he himself is the Messiah, a king." 3 Then Pilate asked him, "Are you the king of the Jews?" He answered, "You say so." 4 Then Pilate said to the chief priests and the crowds, "I find no basis for an accusation against this man." 5 But they were insistent and said, "He stirs up the people by teaching throughout all Judea, from Galilee where he began even to this place."

6 When Pilate heard this, he asked whether the man was a Galilean. 7 And when he learned that he was under Herod's jurisdiction, he sent him off to Herod, who was himself in Jerusalem at that time. 8 When Herod saw Jesus, he was very glad, for he had been wanting to see him for a long time, because he had heard about him and was hoping to see him perform some sign. 9 He questioned him at some length, but Jesus gave him no answer. 10 The chief priests and the scribes stood by, vehemently accusing him. 11 Even Herod with his soldiers treated him with contempt and mocked him; then he put an elegant robe on him, and sent him back to Pilate. 12 That same day Herod and Pilate became friends with each other; before this they had been enemies.

13 Pilate then called together the chief priests, the leaders, and the people, 14 and said to them, "You brought me this man as one who was perverting the people; and here I have examined him in your presence and have not found this man guilty of any of your charges against him. 15 Neither has Herod, for he sent him back to us. Indeed, he has done nothing to deserve death. 16 I will therefore have him flogged and release him."

18 Then they all shouted out together, "Away with this fellow! Release Barabbas for us!" 19 (This was a man who had been put in prison for an insurrection that had taken place in the city, and for murder.) 20 Pilate, wanting to release Jesus, addressed them again; 21 but they kept shouting, "Crucify, crucify him!" 22 A third time he said to them, "Why, what evil has he done? I have found in him no ground for the sentence of death; I will therefore have him flogged and then release him." 23 But they kept urgently demanding with loud shouts that he should be crucified; and their voices prevailed. 24 So Pilate gave his verdict that their demand should be granted. 25 He released the man they asked for, the one who had been put in prison for insurrection and murder, and he handed Jesus over as they wished.

26 As they led him away, they seized a man, Simon of Cyrene, who was coming from the country, and they laid the cross on him, and made him carry it behind Jesus. 27 A great number of the people followed him, and among them were women who were beating their breasts and wailing for him. 28 But Jesus turned to them and said, "Daughters of Jerusalem, do not weep for me, but weep for yourselves

and for your children. 29 For the days are surely coming when they will say, 'Blessed are the barren, and the wombs that never bore, and the breasts that never nursed.' 30 Then they will begin to say to the mountains, 'Fall on us'; and to the hills, 'Cover us.' 31 For if they do this when the wood is green, what will happen when it is dry?"

32 Two others also, who were criminals, were led away to be put to death with him. 33 When they came to the place that is called The Skull, they crucified Jesus there with the criminals, one on his right and one on his left. 34 Then Jesus said, "Father, forgive them; for they do not know what they are doing." And they cast lots to divide his clothing. 35 And the people stood by, watching; but the leaders scoffed at him, saying, "He saved others; let him save himself if he is the Messiah of God, his chosen one!" 36 The soldiers also mocked him, coming up and offering him sour wine, 37 and saying, "If you are the King of the Jews, save yourself!" 38 There was also an inscription over him, "This is the King of the Jews."

39 One of the criminals who were hanged there kept deriding him and saying, "Are you not the Messiah? Save yourself and us!" 40 But the other rebuked him, saying, "Do you not fear God, since you are under the same sentence of condemna- tion? 41 And we indeed have been condemned justly, for we are getting what we deserve for our deeds, but this man has done nothing wrong." 42 Then he said, "Jesus, remember me when you come into your kingdom." 43 He replied, "Truly I tell you, today you will be with me in Paradise."

44 It was now about noon, and darkness came over the whole land until three in the afternoon, 45 while the sun's light failed; and the curtain of the temple was torn in two. 46 Then Jesus, crying with a loud voice, said, "Father , into your hands I commend my spirit." Having said this, he breathed his last. 47 When the centurion saw what had taken place, he praised God and said, "Certainly this man was innocent." 48 And when all the crowds who had gathered there for this spectacle saw what had taken place, they returned home, beating their breasts. 49 But all his acquaintances, including the women who had followed him from Galilee, stood at a distance, watching these things. 50 Now there was a good and righteous man named Joseph, who, though a member of the council, 51 had not agreed to their plan and action. He came from the Jewish town of Arimathea, and he was waiting expectantly for the kingdom of God. 52 This man went to Pilate and asked for the body of Jesus. 53 Then he took it down, wrapped it in a linen cloth, and laid it in a rock-hewn tomb where no one had ever been laid. 54 It was the day of Preparation, and the sabbath was beginning. 55 The women who had come with him from Galilee followed, and they saw the tomb and how his body was laid. 56 Then they returned, and prepared spices and ointments.

On the sabbath they rested according to the commandment.

CHAPTER 24

But on the first day of the week, at early dawn, they came to the tomb, taking the spices that they had prepared. 2 They found the stone rolled away from the tomb, 3 but when they went in, they did not find the body. 4 While they were perplexed about this, suddenly two men in dazzling clothes stood beside them. 5 The women were terrified and bowed their faces to the ground, but the men said to them, "Why do you look for the living among the dead? He is not here, but has risen. 6 Remember how he told you, while he was still in Galilee, 7 that the Son of Man must be handed over to sinners, and be crucified, and on the third day rise again." 8 Then they remembered his words, 9 and returning from the tomb, they told all this to the eleven and to all the rest. 10 Now it was Mary Magdalene, Joanna, Mary the mother of James, and the other women with them who told this to the apostles. 11 But these words seemed to them an idle tale, and they did not believe them. 12 But Peter got up and ran to the tomb; stooping and looking in, he saw the linen cloths by themselves; then he went home, amazed at what had happened.

13 Now on that same day two of them were going to a village called Emmaus, about seven miles from Jerusalem, 14 and talking with each other about all these things that had happened. 15 While they were talking and discussing, Jesus himself came near and went with them, 16 but their eyes were kept from recognizing him. 17 And he said to them, "What are you discussing with each other while you walk along?" They stood still, looking sad. 18 Then one of them, whose name was Cleopas, answered him, "Are you the only stranger in Jerusalem who does not know the things that have taken place there in these days?" 19 He asked them, "What things?" They replied, "The things about Jesus of Nazareth, who was a prophet mighty in deed and word before God and all the people, 20 and how our chief priests and leaders handed him over to be condemned to death and crucified him. 21 But we had hoped that he was the one to redeem Israel. Yes, and besides all this, it is now the third day since these things took place. 22 Moreover, some women of our group astounded us. They were at the tomb early this morning, 23 and when they did not find his body there, they came back and told us that they had indeed seen a vision of angels who said that he was alive. 24 Some of those who were with us went to the tomb and found it just as the women had said; but they did not see him." 25 Then he said to them, "Oh, how foolish you are, and how slow of heart to believe all that the prophets have declared!

26 Was it not necessary that the Messiah should suffer these things and then enter into his glory?" 27 Then beginning with Moses and all the prophets, he interpreted to them the things about himself in all the scriptures.

28 As they came near the village to which they were going, he walked ahead as if he were going on. 29 But they urged him strongly, saying, "Stay with us, because it is almost evening and the day is now nearly over." So he went in to stay with them. 30 When he was at the table with them, he took bread, blessed and broke it, and gave it to them. 31 Then their eyes were opened, and they recognized him; and he vanished from their sight. 32 They said to each other, "Were not our hearts burning within us while he was talking to us on the road, while he was opening the scriptures to us?" 33 That same hour they got up and returned to Jerusalem; and they found the eleven and their companions gathered together. 34 They were saying, "The Lord has risen indeed, and he has appeared to Simon!" 35 Then they told what had happened on the road, and how he had been made known to them in the breaking of the bread.

36 While they were talking about this, Jesus himself stood among them and said to them, "Peace be with you." 37 They were startled and terrified, and thought that they were seeing a ghost. 38 He said to them, "Why are you frightened, and why do doubts arise in your hearts? 39 Look at my hands and my feet; see that it is I myself. Touch me and see; for a ghost does not have flesh and bones as you see that I have." 40 And when he had said this, he showed them his hands and his feet. 41 While in their joy they were disbelieving and still wondering, he said to them, "Have you anything here to eat?" 42 They gave him a piece of broiled fish, 43 and he took it and ate in their presence.

44 Then he said to them, "These are my words that I spoke to you while I was still with you—that everything written about me in the law of Moses, the prophets, and the psalms must be fulfilled." 45 Then he opened their minds to understand the scriptures, 46 and he said to them, "Thus it is written, that the Messiah is to suffer and to rise from the dead on the third day, 47 and that repentance and forgiveness of sins is to be proclaimed in his name to all nations, beginning from Jerusalem. 48 You are witnesses of these things. 49 And see, I am sending upon you what my Father promised; so stay here in the city until you have been clothed with power from on high."

50 Then he led them out as far as Bethany, and, lifting up his hands, he blessed them. 51 While he was blessing them, he withdrew from them and was carried up into heaven. 52 And they worshiped him, and returned to Jerusalem with great joy; 53 and they were continually in the temple blessing God.

JOHN 18:1-21:25

CHAPTER 18

After Jesus had spoken these words, he went out with his disciples across the Kidron valley to a place where there was a garden, which he and his disciples entered. 2 Now Judas, who betrayed him, also knew the place, because Jesus often met there with his disciples. 3 So Judas brought a detachment of soldiers together with police from the chief priests and the Pharisees, and they came there with lanterns and torches and weapons. 4 Then Jesus, knowing all that was to happen to him, came forward and asked them, "Whom are you looking for?" 5 They answered, "Jesus of Nazareth." Jesus replied, "I am he." Judas, who betrayed him, was standing with them. 6 When Jesus said to them, "I am he," they stepped back and fell to the ground. 7 Again he asked them, "Whom are you looking for?" And they said, "Jesus of Nazareth." 8 Jesus answered, "I told you that I am he. So if you are looking for me, let these men go." 9 This was to fulfill the word that he had spoken, "I did not lose a single one of those whom you gave me." 10 Then Simon Peter, who had a sword, drew it, struck the high priest's slave, and cut off his right ear. The slave's name was Malchus. 11 Jesus said to Peter, "Put your sword back into its sheath. Am I not to drink the cup that the Father has given me?"

12 So the soldiers, their officer, and the Jewish police arrested Jesus and bound him. 13 First they took him to Annas, who was the father-in-law of Caiaphas, the high priest that year. 14 Caiaphas was the one who had advised the Jews that it was better to have one person die for the people.

15 Simon Peter and another disciple followed Jesus. Since that disciple was known to the high priest, he went with Jesus into the courtyard of the high priest, 16 but Peter was standing outside at the gate. So the other disciple, who was known to the high priest, went out, spoke to the woman who guarded the gate, and brought Peter in. 17 The woman said to Peter, "You are not also one of this man's disciples, are you?" He said, "I am not." 18 Now the slaves and the police had made a charcoal fire because it was cold, and they were standing around it and warming themselves. Peter also was standing with them and warming himself.

19 Then the high priest questioned Jesus about his disciples and about his teaching. 20 Jesus answered, "I have spoken openly to the world; I have always taught in synagogues and in the temple, where all the Jews come together. I have said nothing in secret. 21 Why do you ask me? Ask those who heard what I said to them; they know what I said." 22 When he had said this, one of the police standing nearby struck Jesus on the face, saying, "Is that how you answer the high priest?" 23 Jesus answered, "If I have spoken wrongly, testify to the wrong. But if I have spoken rightly, why do you strike me?" 24 Then Annas sent him bound to Caiaphas the high priest.

25 Now Simon Peter was standing and warming himself. They asked him, "You are not also one of his disciples, are you?" He denied it and said, "I am not." 26 One of the slaves of the high priest, a relative of the man whose ear Peter had cut off, asked, "Did I not see you in the garden with him?" 27 Again Peter denied it, and at that moment the cock crowed.

28 Then they took Jesus from Caiaphas to Pilate's headquarters. It was early in the morning. They themselves did not enter the headquarters, so as to avoid ritual defilement and to be able to eat the Passover. 29 So Pilate went out to them and said, "What accusation do you bring against this man?" 30 They answered, "If this man were not a criminal, we would not have handed him over to you." 31 Pilate said to them, "Take him yourselves and judge him according to your law." The Jews replied, "We are not permitted to put anyone to death." 32 (This was to fulfill what Jesus had said when he indicated the kind of death he was to die.)

33 Then Pilate entered the headquarters again, summoned Jesus, and asked him, "Are you the King of the Jews?" 34 Jesus answered, "Do you ask this on your own, or did others tell you about me?" 35 Pilate replied, "I am not a Jew, am I? Your own nation and the chief priests have handed you over to me. What have you done?" 36 Jesus answered, "My kingdom is not from this world. If my kingdom were from this world, my followers would be fighting to keep me from being handed over to the Jews. But as it is, my kingdom is not from here." 37 Pilate asked him, "So you are a king?" Jesus answered, "You say that I am a king. For this I was born, and for this I came into the world, to testify to the truth. Everyone who belongs to the truth listens to my voice." 38 Pilate asked him, "What is truth?"

After he had said this, he went out to the Jews again and told them, "I find no case against him. 39 But you have a custom that I release someone for you at the Passover. Do you want me to release for you the King of the Jews?" 40 They shouted in reply, "Not this man, but Barabbas!" Now Barabbas was a bandit.

CHAPTER 19

Then Pilate took Jesus and had him flogged. 2 And the soldiers wove a crown of thorns and put it on his head, and they dressed him in a purple robe. 3 They kept coming up to him, saying, "Hail, King of the Jews!" and striking him on the face. 4 Pilate went out again and said to them, "Look, I am bringing him out to you to let you know that I find no case against him." 5 So Jesus came out, wearing the crown of thorns and the purple robe. Pilate said to them, "Here is the man!" 6 When the chief priests and the police saw him, they shouted, "Crucify him! Crucify him!" Pilate said to them, "Take him yourselves and crucify him; I find no case against him." 7 The Jews answered him, "We have a law, and according to that law he ought to die because he has claimed to be the Son of God." 8 Now when Pilate heard this, he was more afraid than ever. 9 He entered his headquarters again and asked Jesus, "Where are you from?" But Jesus gave him no answer. 10 Pilate therefore said to him, "Do you refuse to speak to me? Do you not know that I have power to release you, and power to crucify you?" 11 Jesus answered him, "You would have no power over me unless it had been given you from above; therefore the one who handed me over to you is guilty of a greater sin."

12 From then on Pilate tried to release him, but the Jews cried out, "If you release this man, you are no friend of the emperor. Everyone who claims to be a king sets himself against the emperor." 13 When Pilate heard these words, he brought Jesus outside and sat on the judge's bench at a place called The Stone Pavement, or in Hebrew Gabbatha. 14 Now it was the day of Preparation for the Passover; and it was about noon. He said to the Jews, "Here is your King!" 15 They cried out, "Away with him! Away with him! Crucify him!" Pilate asked them, "Shall I crucify your King?" The chief priests answered, "We have no king but the emperor." 16 Then he handed him over to them to be crucified.

17 So they took Jesus; and carrying the cross by himself, he went out to what is called The Place of the Skull, which in Hebrew is called Golgotha. 18 There they crucified him, and with him two others, one on either side, with Jesus between them. 19 Pilate also had an inscription written and put on the cross. It read, "Jesus of Nazareth, the King of the Jews." 20 Many of the Jews read this inscription, because the place where Jesus was crucified was near the city; and it was written in Hebrew, in Latin, and in Greek. 21 Then the chief priests of the Jews said to Pilate, "Do not write, 'The King of the Jews,' but, 'This man said, I am King of the Jews.'" 22 Pilate answered, "What I have written I have written."

23 When the soldiers had crucified Jesus, they took his clothes and divided them into four parts, one for each soldier. They also took his tunic; now the tunic was seamless, woven in one piece from the top. 24 So they said to one another, "Let us not tear it, but cast lots for it to see who will get it." This was to fulfill what the scripture says,

> They divided my clothes among themselves,
> and for my clothing they cast lots."

25 And that is what the soldiers did. Meanwhile, standing near the cross of Jesus were his mother, and his mother's sister, Mary the wife of Clopas, and Mary Magdalene. 26 When Jesus saw his mother and the disciple whom he loved standing beside her, he said to his mother, "Woman, here is your son." 27 Then he said to the

disciple, "Here is your mother." And from that hour the disciple took her into his own home.

28 After this, when Jesus knew that all was now finished, he said (in order to fulfill the scripture), "I am thirsty." 29 A jar full of sour wine was standing there. So they put a sponge full of the wine on a branch of hyssop and held it to his mouth. 30 When Jesus had received the wine, he said, "It is finished." Then he bowed his head and gave up his spirit.

31 Since it was the day of Preparation, the Jews did not want the bodies left on the cross during the sabbath, especially because that sabbath was a day of great solemnity. So they asked Pilate to have the legs of the crucified men broken and the bodies removed. 32 Then the soldiers came and broke the legs of the first and of the other who had been crucified with him. 33 But when they came to Jesus and saw that he was already dead, they did not break his legs. 34 Instead, one of the soldiers pierced his side with a spear, and at once blood and water came out. 35 (He who saw this has testified so that you also may believe. His testimony is true, and he knows that he tells the truth.) 36 These things occurred so that the scripture might be fulfilled, "None of his bones shall be broken." 37 And again another passage of scripture says, "They will look on the one whom they have pierced."

38 After these things, Joseph of Arimathea, who was a disciple of Jesus, though a secret one because of his fear of the Jews, asked Pilate to let him take away the body of Jesus. Pilate gave him permission; so he came and removed his body. 39 Nicodemus, who had at first come to Jesus by night, also came, bringing a mixture of myrrh and aloes, weighing about a hundred pounds. 40 They took the body of Jesus and wrapped it with the spices in linen cloths, according to the burial custom of the Jews. 41 Now there was a garden in the place where he was crucified, and in the garden there was a new tomb in which no one had ever been laid. 42 And so, because it was the Jewish day of Preparation, and the tomb was nearby, they laid Jesus there.

CHAPTER 20

Early on the first day of the week, while it was still dark, Mary Magdalene came to the tomb and saw that the stone had been removed from the tomb. 2 So she ran and went to Simon Peter and the other disciple, the one whom Jesus loved, and said to them, "They have taken the Lord out of the tomb, and we do not know where they have laid him." 3 Then Peter and the other disciple set out and went toward the tomb. 4 The two were running together, but the other disciple outran Peter and reached the tomb first. 5 He bent down to look in and saw the linen wrappings lying there, but he did not go in. 6 Then Simon Peter came, following him, and went into the tomb. He saw the linen wrappings lying there, 7 and the cloth that had been on Jesus' head, not lying with the linen wrappings but rolled up in a place by itself. 8 Then the other disciple, who reached the tomb first, also went in, and he saw and believed; 9 for as yet they did not understand the scripture, that he must rise from the dead. 10 Then the disciples returned to their homes.

11 But Mary stood weeping outside the tomb. As she wept, she bent over to look into the tomb; 12 and she saw two angels in white, sitting where the body of Jesus had been lying, one at the head and the other at the feet. 13 They said to her, "Woman, why are you weeping?" She said to them, "They have taken away my Lord, and I do not know where they have laid him." 14 When she had said this, she turned around and saw Jesus standing there, but she did not know that it was Jesus. 15 Jesus said to her, "Woman, why are you weeping? Whom are you looking for?" Supposing him to be the gardener, she said to him, "Sir, if you have carried him away, tell me where you have laid him, and I will take him away." 16 Jesus said to her, "Mary!" She turned and said to him in Hebrew, "Rabbouni!" (which means Teacher). 17 Jesus said to her, "Do not hold on to me, because I have not yet ascended to the Father. But go to my brothers and say to them, 'I am ascending to my Father and your Father, to my God and your God.'" 18 Mary Magdalene went and announced to the disciples, "I have seen the Lord"; and she told them that he had said these things to her.

19 When it was evening on that day, the first day of the week, and the doors of the house where the disciples had met were locked for fear of the Jews, Jesus came and stood among them and said, "Peace be with you." 20 After he said this, he showed them his hands and his side. Then the disciples rejoiced when they saw the Lord. 21 Jesus said to them again, "Peace be with you. As the Father has sent me, so I send you." 22 When he had said this, he breathed on them and said to them, "Receive the Holy Spirit. 23 If you forgive the sins of any, they are forgiven them; if you retain the sins of any, they are retained."

24 But Thomas (who was called the Twin), one of the twelve, was not with them when Jesus came. 25 So the other disciples told him, "We have seen the Lord." But he said to them, "Unless I see the mark of the nails in his hands, and put my finger in the mark of the nails and my hand in his side, I will not believe."

26 A week later his disciples were again in the house, and Thomas was with them. Although the doors were shut, Jesus came and stood among them and said, "Peace be with you." 27 Then he said to Thomas, "Put your finger here and see my hands. Reach out your hand and put it in my side. Do not doubt but believe." 28 Thomas answered him, "My Lord and my God!" 29 Jesus said to him, "Have you

believed because you have seen me? Blessed are those who have not seen and yet have come to believe."

30 Now Jesus did many other signs in the presence of his disciples, which are not written in this book. 31 But these are written so that you may come to believe that Jesus is the Messiah, the Son of God, and that through believing you may have life in his name.

CHAPTER 21

After these things Jesus showed himself again to the disciples by the Sea of Tiberias; and he showed himself in this way. 2 Gathered there together were Simon Peter, Thomas called the Twin, Nathanael of Cana in Galilee, the sons of Zebedee, and two others of his disciples. 3 Simon Peter said to them, "I am going fishing." They said to him, "We will go with you." They went out and got into the boat, but that night they caught nothing.

4 Just after daybreak, Jesus stood on the beach; but the disciples did not know that it was Jesus. 5 Jesus said to them, "Children, you have no fish, have you?" They answered him, "No." 6 He said to them, "Cast the net to the right side of the boat, and you will find some." So they cast it, and now they were not able to haul it in because there were so many fish. 7 That disciple whom Jesus loved said to Peter, "It is the Lord!" When Simon Peter heard that it was the Lord, he put on some clothes, for he was naked, and jumped into the sea. 8 But the other disciples came in the boat, dragging the net full of fish, for they were not far from the land, only about a hundred yards off.

9 When they had gone ashore, they saw a charcoal fire there, with fish on it, and bread. 10 Jesus said to them, "Bring some of the fish that you have just caught." 11 So Simon Peter went aboard and hauled the net ashore, full of large fish, a hundred fifty-three of them; and though there were so many, the net was not torn. 12 Jesus said to them, "Come and have breakfast." Now none of the disciples dared to ask him, "Who are you?" because they knew it was the Lord. 13 Jesus came and took the bread and gave it to them, and did the same with the fish. 14 This was now the third time that Jesus appeared to the disciples after he was raised from the dead.

15 When they had finished breakfast, Jesus said to Simon Peter, "Simon son of John, do you love me more than these?" He said to him, "Yes, Lord; you know that I love you." Jesus said to him, "Feed my lambs." 16 A second time he said to him, "Simon son of John, do you love me?" He said to him, "Yes, Lord; you know that I love you." Jesus said to him, "Tend my sheep." 17 He said to him the third time, "Simon son of John, do you love me?" Peter felt hurt because he said to him

the third time, "Do you love me?" And he said to him, "Lord, you know everything; you know that I love you." Jesus said to him, "Feed my sheep. 18 Very truly, I tell you, when you were younger, you used to fasten your own belt and to go wherever you wished. But when you grow old, you will stretch out your hands, and someone else will fasten a belt around you and take you where you do not wish to go." 19 (He said this to indicate the kind of death by which he would glorify God.) After this he said to him, "Follow me."

20 Peter turned and saw the disciple whom Jesus loved following them; he was the one who had reclined next to Jesus at the supper and had said, "Lord, who is it that is going to betray you?" 21 When Peter saw him, he said to Jesus, "Lord, what about him?" 22 Jesus said to him, "If it is my will that he remain until I come, what is that to you? Follow me!" 23 So the rumor spread in the community that this disciple would not die. Yet Jesus did not say to him that he would not die, but, "If it is my will that he remain until I come, what is that to you?"

24 This is the disciple who is testifying to these things and has written them, and we know that his testimony is true.

25 But there are also many other things that Jesus did; if every one of them were written down, I suppose that the world itself could not contain the books that would be written.

SELECTED BIBLIOGRAPHY

Baeck, Leo. *The Essence of Judaism*. New York: Schocken Books, 1961.

Bauer, Yehuda, ed. *Remembering for the Future*. Oxford: Pergamon Press, 1991.

Berger, Alan, ed. *Bearing Witness to the Holocaust*. Lewiston, NY: Edwin Mellen Press, 1991.

Berger, Alan. *Crisis and Covenant*. Albany, NY: State University of New York Press, 1985.

Berkovits, Eliezer. *With God in Hell*. New York: Sanhedrin, 1979.

Braybrooke, Marcus. *Time to Meet*. Philadelphia: Trinity Press International, 1990.

Charlesworth, James. *Jews and Christians*. New York: Crossroad, 1990.

Cohn-Sherbok, Daniel. *On Earth As It Is In Heaven*. Maryknoll, NY: Orbis Books, 1987.

Colijn, G. Jan and Littell, Marcia, ed. *The Netherlands and Nazi Genocide.* Lewiston, NY: Edwin Mellen Press, 1992.

Davies, Alan, ed. *Anti-Semitism and the Foundations of Christianity. New York: Paulist Press, 1979.*

Eckhardt, Roy. *Elder and Younger Brothers.* New York: Charles Scribner's Sons, 1967.

Eckardt, Roy and Alice Eckardt. *Long Night's Journey Into Day.* Detroit, MI: Wayne State University Press, 1982.

Fackenheim, Emil. *God's Presence in History.* New York: Harper and Row, 1972.

Fackenheim, Emil. *The Jewish. Bible After the Holocaust.* Bloomington: Indiana University, 1990.

Fackenheim, Emil. *To Mend the World.* New York: Schocken Books, 1982.

Fleischner, Eva, ed. *Auschwitz: Beginning of a New Era?* New York: KTAV, 1974.

Garber, Zev, ed. *Methodology in the Academic Teaching of the Holocaust.* Lanham, MD: University Press of America, 1988.

Garber, Zev, ed. *Methodology in the Academic Teaching of Judaism.* Lanham, MD: University Press of America, 1986.

Herford, R. Travers. *Christianity in Talmud and Midrash.* New York: KTAV, 1903.

Isaac, Jules. *The Teaching of Contempt: Christian Roots of Anti-Semitism.* New York: Holt, Rinehart and Winston, 1964.

Jacob, Walter. *Christianity Through Jewish Eyes.* New York: Hebrew Union College Press, 1974.

Katz, Steven. *Post-Holocaust Dialogues*. New York: NYU, 1983.

Klein, Charlotte. *Anti-Judaism in Christian Theology*. Philadelphia: Fortress Press, 1978.

Klenicki, Leon, ed. *Issues in the Jewish-Christian Dialogue*. New York: Paulist Press, 1979.

Lang, Berel. *Act and Idea in the Nazi Genocide*. Chicago: University of Chicago Press, 1990.

Langmuir, Gavin. *History, Religion and Antisemitism*. Berkeley: University of California Press, 1990.

Langmuir, Gavin. *Toward a Definition of Antisemitism*. Berkeley: University of California Press, 1991.

Libowitz, Richard, ed. *Faith and Freedom*. New York: Pergamon Press, 1987.

Littell, Franklin. *The Crucifixion of the Jews*. Macon, Ga.: Mercer University Press, 1986.

Littell, Marcia, et.al., ed. *The Holocaust: Forty Years After*. Lewiston, NY: Edwin Mellen Press, 1989.

Miller, Judith. *One by One by One*. New York: Simon and Schuster, 1990.

Novak, David. *Jewish-Christian Dialogue*. New York: Oxford University Press, 1989.

Pawlikowski, John. *Christ in the Light of the Christian-Jewish Dialogue*. New York: Paulist Press, 1982.

Pawlikowski, John. *Jesus and the Theology of Israel*. Wilmington, DE: Michael Glazier, Inc., 1989.

Peck, Abraham. *Jews and Christians After the Holocaust.* Philadelphia: Fortress Press, 1982.

Petuchowski, Jacob, ed. *When Jews and Christians Meet.*

Albany, NY: State University of New York Press, 1988.

Ricoeur, Paul. *The Conflict of Interpretations.* Evanston: Northwestern University, 1974.

Ricoeur, Paul. *Interpretation Theory.* Fort Worth: Texas Christian University, 1976.

Rivkin, Ellis. *What Crucified Jesus?* Nashville: Abingdon Press, 1984.

Rivkin, Ellis. *A Hidden Revolution.* Nashville: Abingdon Press, 1978.

Rose, Paul Lawrence. *Revolutionary Antisemitism in Germany from Kant to Wagner.* Princeton: Princeton University Press, 1991.

Roskies, David. *Against the Apocalypse.* Cambridge: Harvard University, 1984.

Roth, John and Berenbaum, Michael, ed. *Holocaust.* New York: Paragon House, 1989.

Rubenstein, Richard. *After Auschwitz.* Indianapolis: Bobbs-Merrill, 1966.

Rubenstein, Richard and John Roth. *Approaches to Auschwitz.* Atlanta: John Knox Press, 1987.

Ruether, Rosemary. *Faith and Fratricide.* New York: Seabury Press, 1974.

Ryan, Michael. *Human Responses to the Holocaust.* Lewiston: Edwin Mellen Press, 1981.

Sandmel, Samuel. *Anti-Semitism in the New Testament.* Philadelphia: Fortress Press, 1978.

Saperstein, Marc. *Moments of Crisis in Jewish-Christian Relations.* Philadelphia: Trinity Press International, 1989.

Schuessler-Fiorenza, Elizabeth and David Tracy, ed. *The Holocaust as Interruption.* Edinburgh: T & T Clark, 1984.

Seeskin, Kenneth. *Jewish Philosophy in a Secular Age.* Albany: State University of New York Press, 1990.

Sherwin, Byron and Ament, Susan, ed. *Encountering the Holocaust.* Chicago: Impact Press, 1979.

Tec, Nechama. *When Light Pierced the Darkness.* New York: Oxford University Press, 1986.

Thoma, Clemens. *A Christian Theology of Judaism.* New York: Paulist Press, 1980.

Thoma, Clemens and Wyschograd, Michael, ed. *Das Reden vom einem Gott bei Juden und Christen.* Bern: Peter Lang, 1984.

Tracy, David. *Blessed Rage For Order.* New York: Crossroad, 1975.

Tracy, David. *The Analogical Imagination.* New York: Crossroad, 1981.

Tracy, David. *Plurality and Ambiguity.* New York: Harper and Row, 1987.

Tracy, David. *Dialogue With the Other.* Grand Rapids: Eerdmans, 1991.

Van Buren, Paul. *A Theology of the Jewish People:* Part I: *Discerning the Way.* 1980. Part II: *A Christian Theology of the People of Israel.* 1983. Part III: *Christ in Context.* 1988. New York: Harper and Row.

Weiss-Rosmarin, Trude. *Jewish Expressions on Jesus.* New York: KTAV, 1977.

Williamson, Clark. *Has God Rejected His People?* Nashville: Abingdon Press, 1982.

Williamson, Clark. *When Jews and Christians Meet.* St. Louis, MO: CBP Press, 1989.

Wyschograd, Edith. *Spirit in Ashes.* New Haven: Yale University, 1985.

Wiesel, Elie. *Messengers of God.* New York: Summit Books, 1976.

INDEX